DEDICATED
TO
MY REVERED PARENTS

Late Sri Satrughna Roy

&

Late Smt. Bharati Devi

"BETTER THAN TREASURES BROUGHT FROM ROME
ARE THE LIVING PICTURES I SEE AT HOME----
MY AGED FATHER WITH FROSTED HAIR,
AND MOTHER'S FACE LIKE A PAINTING RARE".

BUSINESS COMMUNICATION — THE BASICS

BY

DR. PARTHO PRATIM ROY

M.A.(English Honours), M.Com. (Business Administration), M.P.M. (Personnel Mgt.)
D.T.S. & D.O.T. (Trg. & Dev.), D.I.T. (C-DAC), D.T.L., Cer. P.M. & I.R.
LL.B. (Law), Ph.D. (Banking), Ex-WBCS (Executive)
Stephens Silver Medallist

FIRST EDITION: 2012

Himalaya Publishing House

MUMBAI ✩ DELHI ✩ NAGPUR ✩ BENGALURU ✩ HYDERABAD
✩ BHUBANESWAR ✩ CHENNAI ✩ PUNE ✩ INDORE ✩ AHMEDABAD
LUCKNOW ✩ ERNAKULAM ✩ KOLKATA ✩ GUWAHATI

Books by the same Author :

1. **ANATOMY OF TENSE** (An Exhaustive Treatise on Tense)
2. **KING'S ENGLISH** (A Text-book on English Grammar for schools)
3. **MANAGEMENT OF URBAN CO-OPERATIVE BANKS** (A Ph.D. Thesis in book form)
4. **BUSINESS COMMUNICATION – THE BASICS** (A Primer for management & other professional courses)
5. **EFFECTIVE BUSINESS COMMUNICATION —CONCEPTS & CONTEXTS** (A Comprehensive Text-book for Post-graduate management students) *[In the Press]*
6. **PRINCIPLES & PRACTICES OF INTERVIEWING** (A Practical Guide for Examinees of Central & State Civil Services, Bank, Railway, MNCs etc.) *[In the Press]*

FIRST EDITION : 2012

PUBLISHED BY : Mrs. Meena Pandey
for **HIMALAYA PUBLISHING HOUSE PVT. LTD.**
"Ramdoot", Dr. Bhalerao Marg, Girgaon, **Mumbai-400 004**
☎ 23860170 • 23863863 • Fax: 022-23877178
Email: himpub@vsnl.com
Website: www.himpub.com

BRANCH OFFICES

New Delhi : "Pooja Apartments", 4-B, Murari Lal Street, Ansari Road, Darya Ganj, **New Delhi-110 002.** ☎ 011-23270392 • 23278631 • Fax: 011-23256286

Nagpur : Kundanlal Chandak Industrial Estate, Ghat Road, **Nagpur-440 018** ☎ 0712-2738731 • 3296733 • Telefax: 0712-2721215

Bengaluru : No. 16/1 (Old 12/1), 1st Floor, Next to Hotel Highlands, Madhava Nagar, Race Course Road, **Bangalore-560 001.** ☎ 080-22281541 • 22385461 • Fax: 080-22286611

Hyderabad : No. 3-4-184, Lingampally, Beside Raghavendra Swamy Matham, Kachiguda, **Hyderabad-500 027.** ☎ 040-27560041•27550139 • 📱 09848130433

Chennai : No. 85/50, Bazullah Road, T-Nagar, **Chennai-600 017.** ☎ 044-28144004 • 28144005

Pune : No. 527, "Laksha Apartment", 1st Floor, Mehunpura, Shaniwarpeth, Near Prabhat Theatre, **Pune-411 030** ☎ 020-24496323 • 24496333

Lucknow : Jai Baba Bhavan, Near Manas Complex and Dr. Sanjiv Awasthi Clinic, Church Road, Aliganj, **Lucknow-226 024** ☎ 0522-2339329•4068914 📱 9305302158•9415349385 • 9389593752

Ahmedabad : 114, Shail, 1st Floor, Opp. Madhusudan House, C.G. Road, Navrangpura, **Ahmedabad-380 009.** ☎ 079-26560126 • 📱 09327324149• 09314679413

Ernakulam : No. 39/104A, Laxmi Apt., Karikkamuri Cross Road, Ernakulam, **Cochin-622 011.** ☎ 0484-2378012 • 2378016. 📱 09344199799

Bhubaneswar : 5, Station Square, Bhubaneshwar, Odisha - 751001. 📱 9861046007.

Indore : Kesardeep Avenue Extension, 73, Narayan Bagh, Flat No. 302, IIIrd Floor, Near Humpty Dumpty School, Narayan Bagh, **Indore (M.P.)** 📱 09301386468

Kolkata : 108/4, Beliaghata Main Road, Near ID Hospital, Opp. SBI Bank, **Kolkata-700 010,** 📱 09910440956

Guwahati : House No. 15, Behind Pragjyotish College, Near Sharma Printing Press, P.O. Bharalumukh, **Guwahati - 781 009, Assam.** 📱 09883055590, 09883055536

DTP by : Sudhakar Shetty (HPH Pvt. Ltd., Mumbai)

Printed at : M/s Atitya offset Printers (I) Pvt. Ltd. Hyderabad, On behalf of HPH, Mumbai.

FOREWORD

SYDENHAM INSTITUTE OF MANAGEMENT STUDIES,
RESEARCH AND ENTERPRENEURSHIP EDUCATION
(Government of Maharashtra)

DR. M. A. KHAN
DIRECTOR

FOREWORD

I am pleased to introduce the book ***"Business Communication - The Basics",*** authored by Dr. P. P.Roy. On minutely going through the final draft of the book, I find it provides an in-depth coverage of the cardinal principles of business communication throuth a reader-friendly approach. **Theo Haimann** once said, *"the sucess of all managerial functions depends on sucessful communication – whether oral or writen"*. That's why both industry and academic sectors have begun training employees and students on various principles and skills of business communication.

The present book is both a primer for the beginners as also a refresher for professionals, managers, students and teachers of hte subject. The thematic structure of the book is well-organized and the text is sequentially presented in clear, concise, manageable snippets with specific headings, studded with interesting boxes, illustrative diagrams and figures, innovative mnemonics and acronyms for easy navigation. Besides, each chapter at its end has main points summarized, key terms and concepts enlisted, review and discussion questions appended so that students can better relate theory to practice as also to their own experiences. Another unique feature included in the book is *"Laugh A Little, Think A Little"* theme interspersed with witty remarks at relevant places, which exuberates homogeneous foliage of laugh and thought at equal pace in all the chapters of the book.

There is a saying: ***"What is easy to read is difficult to write"***. And for both, Dr. Roy, the author of the book, deserves the readers' gratitude. The language used throughout the book is precise and simple to comprehend. Each chapter is developed with logical sequencing as also with aesthetic sense to imbibe in students the skill of analytical thinking and simultaneously make the learning process more entertaining. Thus the orientation of the book is student-friendly and possesses tremendous usage potential.

I congratulate the author, Shri Roy for his outstanding penmanship exhibited throughout this book on business communication, and wish him all sucess.

SOME OPINIONS ABOUT THE BOOK

(1)

Oriental Education Society's

ORIENTAL INSTITUTE OF MANAGEMENT

(Approved by AICTE, New Delhi, DTE Govt. of Maharashtra & Affiliated to University of Mumbai.)

DR. M. G. SHIRAHATTI

Director General

A number of books have been published on the subject of business communication. However, a book titled **"Business Communication – The Basics"** written by Dr. P. P. Roy has genuinely caught my imagination. The inherent intricacies wreathed around concepts and theories of business communication have found lucid, illustrative and comprehensive coverage in this book. It is a matter of great pleasure, joy and delight to go through this book, which unravels the magnificent mysteries and secrets of effective communication in a manner that simply astounds the reader. This book takes the reader on a journey that can only be experienced and not expressed.

With its unique style of presentation and a wealth of literature, this book provides simplistic explanation to complicated concepts of communication. Graphic illustrations, key highlights and informative snippets add to the beauty and quality of this book.

Also summary of main points, key terms, quotable quotes, objective and essay-type questions along with references and notes ignites the passion for learning and makes this book stand out.

I congratulate Dr. Roy for his painstaking, energetic and sustained efforts in bringing out a book that never ceases to amaze. I am sure that this book will add immense value to the existing body of knowledge and inspire any knowledge-seeker to challenge himself, broaden his horizons and conquer the pinnacle of sucess.

I wish Dr. P. P. Roy all the sucess in future.

(Dr. M. G. SHIRAHATTI)

Chairman,

BOARD OF STUDIES IN MANAGEMENT

UNIVERSITY OF MUMBAI.

SOME OPINIONS ABOUT THE BOOK

(2)

SVKM'S
Narsee Monjee Institute of Management Studies
(Declared as Deemed-to-be University under Section 3 of the UGC Act, 1956)

Dr. M. C. Agarwal **Date: 3rd September, 2011**
Associate Dean, Executive Education

Effective management is a function of effective communication. And effective comunication one can master only when he/she knows the essential concepts and basic behavioural approaches in communication.

This book *"Business Communication – The Basics"* authored by Dr. P. P. Roy addresses the fundamentals of effective communication through well-planed step-by-step user-friendly approach. Its coverage is comprehensive but at the same time lucid, simple and interesting. The topics are arranged from simpler to harder sequence. The text follows a unique systematic pattern – chapter contents followed by learning objectives, quotable quotes, main theme replete with diagrams, boxes, charts, tables, and then summary of major points, questions both objective and essay type, and finally references and notes.

I am confident this book will generate good response and interest in students, teachers, readers, professionals and all who wish to lern the basics of effective communication.

(Dr. M. C. Agarwal)

SOME OPINIONS ABOUT THE BOOK

(3)

Prof. V. H. Iyer
Dean

Management Development Center
WELINGKAR INSTITUTE OF MANAGEMENT
Matunge (East), Mumbai - 400 019.

Date: September 06, 2011

Dr. P. P. Roy's book on **"Business Communication – The Basics"** faithfully serves as a basic 'guide' during your maiden tour to the wonderland of communication skills. While reading the computer-print final draft of the book, the most important thing that **first** attracts my atteention is its style of presentation. It is so lucid, so simple, so comprehensive yet so fascinating that I have rarely come across in a book of this type. **Secondly,** the contents of hte book succeed to capture readers' interest through ample interesting examples which simultaneously help explaining rather complicated key concepts of communication. **Thirdly,** a plethora of boxes with entertaining snippets, juxtaposed to the theory just discussed, adds an enduring quality to the text. **Fourthly,** the book unfolds to you the myths and realities associated with communication. **Fifthly,** inclusion of summary, key terms and concepts quickly ruminates the bare essentials and stregthens the re-learning process. **Finally,** review and discussion questions appended at the end of each chapter fathom your depth of understanding the theoretical concepts.

Kudos to Dr. Roy for his energetic efforts put in to bring out such an excellent book which, I am sure, will be of immense use to any knowledge-seeker in the discipline of business communication.

SOME OPINIONS ABOUT THE BOOK

(4)

SMT K. G. MITTAL INSTITUTE OF MANAGEMENT, INFORMATION TECHNOLOGY & RESEARCH

(Approved by AICTE, New Delhi, Government of Maharashtra, DTE, Affiliated to University of Mumbai)

PROF. DR. BERNADETTE D'SILVA

Director

Communication effectiveness is a factor well-recognized in determining the effectiveness with which the organization performs as a whole. ***Gerald M. Goldhaber*** *rightly asserts, "Effective communication behaviours by members bolster an organization's total effectiveness". You can have the greatest ideas in the world, but they are of no use to your organization or your career if you can't express them clearly and persuasively in both witten or oral forms. Knowledge is indeed power, but communication skills are more powerful ingredients to convey that knowledge effectively to your clients so as to build a long-lasting professional relationships.*

I have gone through the draft copy of the book ***"Business Communication – The Basics"*** *and I find it systematically deals with the basic principles of communication skills. The form, contents and presentation of the book deserve praise from the readers' community for lucidity, logicality and coherence. The author has put in his best efforts to make the book interestingly readable by introducing a lot of unique features such as* ***"Laugh A Little, Think A Little"*** *boxes which are both humorous and thought-provoking,* ***"Acronyms & Mnemonics"*** *which are for better remembrance of the essentials,* ***multiple diagrams*** *which are exclusively desined by him to suit the thematic descriptions, as also* ***references & notes*** *for further readings.*

My hearty congratulations to Dr. Roy and I wish the book all sucess.

(Prof. Dr. Bernadette D'Silva)

PREFACE

"Always read the 'Preface' of a book. It enables you to survey more completely the book itself. You frequently also discover the character of the author from the Preface." — **B. W. Procter**

Winston S. Churchill once remarked, *'Writing a book was an adventure. To begin with, it was a toy and amusement; then it became a mistress, and then a master, and then a tyrant.'* Till now, writing a book — and that too, on Business Communication — is, to me, an amusement — an innocent pleasure. Emboldened by the encouraging response to my maiden publication, ***"Anatomy of Tense",*** followed by an increasing demand of my best-selling school text-book on English Grammar, ***"King's English",*** I feel immense pleasure in presenting this present volume, ***"Business Communication — The Basics" to*** you, — the thousands and millions of under-graduate college students and post-graduate management students as also to the students of other professional courses all over the world.

Today's competitive business environs are witnessing varied phenomenal transformations at a rapid pace. Heightened global competition, flattened management hierarchies, restructuring, downsizing, mergers, acquisitions, expanded team-based projects, innovative communication technologies, increasingly diverse workforce, emergence of knowledge-based economy have ushered in greater communication challenges. **G.A. Marken** has rightly said, *'Gone are the nine-to-five jobs, life-time security, predictable promotions, and even the conventional workplace as you have read and learnt earlier. Don't presume that your organization will provide you with a clearly defined career path or planned developmental experiences. And don't wait for someone to 'empower' you.'* To thrive in this new, dynamic and demanding work-world, in every organization, — be it big or small, national or global-, each personnel, — be it a manager, or a clerk, or a peon, — will have to *suo mottu* 'empower' himself or herself.

The most important step towards such empowerment you need is to acquire certain fundamental skills of which your ability to communicate effectively in writing and in speech stands out as the first and foremost. Your chances of climbing up the corporate ladder largely depend on how well you communicate in order to anticipate problems, make decisions, co-ordinate work-flow, supervise others, develop relationships, promote products and services. And the higher you climb, the more you will need brilliance in your communication skills. Improvement in your communication skills, therefore, improves your chances for success in whatever business you have.

Businesses want and need people with good communication skills but unfortunately business's need for employees with good communication skills is all too often not fulfilled. Most employees, even the college graduates, do not communicate well. **Dr. Julian McPhee** once said, *'the one consistent criticism made of business graduates of all colleges is that they don't know how to communicate their ideas effectively in speaking and writing'.* '**Peter F. Drucker** too echoed the same feeling that *very few college students have the ability to organize and express ideas in writing and speaking.* What they have stated is *mutatis mutandis* applicable in Indian context. However, it is heartening to note that **Business Communication** as a separate discipline of study has been receiving much-needed greater recognition in management schools and under-graduate colleges of Indian universities in recent years.

WHO WILL BENEFIT FROM THIS BOOK? :

The present book, as its title ***"Business Communication — The Basics"*** clearly indicates, is a modest attempt to deal with the basic theoretic introduction to business communication. This book is a ***primer,*** and, therefore, not at all intended to discuss at length the whole gamut of this vast subject in its entirety. The same has been exhaustively delineated in my forthcoming book ***"Effective Business Communication — Concepts & Contexts"*** which is now in the press. However, the primary objective of this present volume is to indoctrinate you, the young students of today – the business executives of tomorrow, with the rudimental but indispensable ***'must-know'*** ingredients of business communication in a lucid, simple, clear, concise, logical, systematic manner as also in a funny, enjoyable, interesting, lively, conversational style so much so that you will never feel bored to learn the apparently complex, seemingly ennuing, intelligibly uninteresting, principal principles of communication. This book will be of great interest and value *to those* who are already in a business or management position, and *to those* who simply like to learn ***'what, why and how'*** of business communication as also *to those* who are preparing for under-graduate, management, and professional examinations on the subject. To be more generic, this book is meant for you and also for everyone who aspires to better and boost their communication skills. I am sure this book will lead you all to progress from ***'I wish I could'*** mind-set syndrome and enable you all to join the ***'I can / I will'*** winning clubs.

ORGANIZATION OF THE BOOK :

The book is organized into sixteen chapters. The thematic presentation of the text is logical and it follows the following ***simpler to harder sequence*** :

Chapter I introduces you to the different means of communication and their roles in the communication process. **Chapter II** unearths both etymological and practical meanings of the term *'communication',* and attempts to define, articulate and and systematize the term *'communication'* in fifty different ways. **Chapter III** tells you fifteen major characteristic features of communication. **Chapter IV** familiarizes you with ten key elements of communication. **Chapter V** takes you to the management legend, Peter F. Drucker, to learn four fundamentals of communication. **Chapter VI** narrates seven broad categories of communication to you. **Chapter VII** accompanies you to the wonderland of seven postulates of communication. **Chapter VIII** drives you down to the four levels of communication.

Chapter IX divulges to you eleven salient natures of communication without any hiccup. **Chapter X** explores various scopes of communication and tells you *tete-a-tete* the tale of needs for communicating. **Chapter XI** acquaints you with the different objectives that communication processes serve within an organization. **Chapter XII** makes you aware of different views of different communication theorists as to diverse functions of communication. **Chapter XIII** presents you elaborative details of scholarly opinions / models advocated by various distinguished communication experts regarding multiple purposes of communication. **Chapter XIV** unlocks the golden gate to show you why communication is so important and significant in this constantly shifting kaleidoscope of competitive pressures and opportunities. **Chapter XV** serves you an oven-fresh delicious delicacy of fifteen principles of communication and the last **Chapter XVI** rescues you from falling into the black magic-trap of communication-myths and lays before you the sunny realities and concrete limitations of communication.

PEDAGOGICAL DEVICES :

In order to make this book more user-friendly, I have incorporated a number of pedagogical devices in a systematic manner throughout this book :

(A) At the beginning of each chapter, you will notice :

(i) **Chapter Contents** at a glance, providing you *an outline* of the respective chapter;

(ii) **Quotable Quotes**, both *thought-provoking* and *funny* as also *relevant* to the chapter concerned ;

(iii) **Learning Objectives** in each chapter, identifying specifically what should have been learnt after reading the chapter;

(iv) **Acronyms and Mnemonics** to help you master the prime points in an *'easy-to-remember'* mode.

(B) In the main text of each chapter, you will observe :

(i) **Introductory Quotation**, designed to kindle and capture your interest in the main theme;

(ii) **'Laugh A Little, Think A Little' Boxes,** a unique feature incorporated so as to mingle fun and *seriousness in one breath* to make the teaching and learning process more entertaining and enjoyable;

(iii) **Multiple Boxes,** presenting a series of high-interest, short readings culled from research articles, best-selling text-books on management, behavioural sciences, psychology, philosophy, religions, and also from different magazines, journals, newspapers etc.;

(iv) **Diagrams, Figures, Charts, Tables,** added as a highly effective learning tool to illustrate and analyze core concepts;

(v) **Copious examples** drawn from classroom experiences as also from various books and journals to explain dry precepts and thus make the text gainfully readable.

(C) At the end of each chapter, you will find :

(i) **Summary**, included to brief you the main points discussed in detail in the chapter;

(ii) **Key Terms & Concepts which have been** defined and explained in the chapter, enlisted once again at the end for your quick refresh and relearn;

(iii) **Review & Discussion Questions** comprising *objective-type questions, short answer-type questions, essay-type analytical questions* in order to assess your understanding of the theoretical concepts and thus reinforce learning;

(iv) **References & Notes** incorporated through *a simple numbering system* which is most favoured and preferred by students and researchers alike, in order to keep the main text uncluttered and easier to follow.

Further, towards the end of the book, I have added also **Appendices,** a separate chapter which contains additional ***Question Bank,*** new features such as ***Experiential Exercises*** and also ***Case Exercises.*** They are carefully designed to prompt you to learn and relate to your own experiences various concepts, models etc., discussed throughout the book. Experiential exercises are mainly classroom activities to be done under the guidance of class teachers. Many questions set in the Appendices will practically trigger self-insight and reflection. Further, another separate section styled ***'Suggested Readings'*** contains bibliography of some important books, journals & bulletins, which are primarily meant for those who may want to undertake a more detailed study of the subject or may like to go through them only for course projects.

I was a ***Member of Faculty for*** more than six years in a ***College of Banking*** of a premier banking institution and conducted ***more than 1500 executive training classes including seminars and workshops for executives of various banks from India as also other SAARC countries and the corporate world.*** Vast experiences gathered during the period have permeated in the text-design and articulated it through proper synthesis of matters collected from innumerable sources.

I myself have taken all the pains to edit, design numerous diagrams, and proof-read the entire book as many as four times at different stages of its preparation to make it error-free as far as practicable and to enhance its overall quality and get-up. Someone has said that the sun need not boast of his brightness nor the moon of her effulgence, because these are self-evident. ***The qualitative standard of this present volume will no doubt speak for itself. Nevertheless, the users are the best judge.*** I, therefore, earnestly solicit constructive feedbacks from all of you, — college teachers, business executives, and, of course, from under-graduate, graduate, post-graduate students, — bringing to my notice any error of omission or commission that might have crept in despite my best efforts to avoid them. Further, your comments, suggestions & observations for bringing about qualitative improvements in the book are most welcome.

I humbly believe the students of business communication in different universities and management institutions will find the text discussed in the book exhaustive, informative, instructive and interesting. Wishing you all to be a successful communicator.

GANESH CHATURTHI
September 01, 2011

DR. PARTHO PRATIM ROY

ACKNOWLEDGEMENTS

"Two heads are better than one, not because either is infallible, but because they are unlikely to go wrong in the same direction." — C. S. Lewis

No .one can write in vacuum. *Authors are all influenced by the thoughts and ideas of other distinguished authors in the same field.* During the preparation of this project, many wise minds have steered me in right direction. I bow my head in gratitude to all those reputed foreign and Indian authors on the subject, whose ideas I have freely and frankly drawn upon, adapted or built on. *I have acknowledged each and every source of work by those authors through references at appropriate places in the text of my book, but I apologize to any concerned if acknowledgement has inadvertently not been recorded owing to inability to trace the copyright owner and/or other requisite details.*

I don't claim originality of the book in the sense as **Montaigne** has said, "*I have made here merely a nosegay of other peoples' flowers, and have provided nothing of my own except the thread which holds them together*". But I most humbly claim such originality as is aptly said by **Carlyle,** "*The merit of originality is not novelty; it is sincerity*".

I extremely grateful to **Dr. M.A. Khan, Director, Sydenham Institute of Management Studies, Research and Entrepreneurship Education, Mumbai** for kindly writing the **Foreword** of this book. I am also grateful to **Dr. M.G. Shirahatti,** Vashi, Director General, **Oriental Institute of Management,** Navi Mumbai, **Prof. V.H. Iyer,** Dean, Management Development Centre, **Welingkar Institute of Management,** Matunga, Mumbai, **Dr. M.C. Agarwal,** Associate Dean, Executive Education, **NMIS University**, Vile Parle, Mumbai and **Dr (Mrs.) Bernadette D'Silva,** Director, **Smt. K.G. Mittal Institute of Management,** Malad, Mumbai for kindly reviewing my book despite their extremely busy schedules.

My special thanks are due to my greatest critic and my best friend, **Smt. Anjana Roy,** for her wonderful shepherding, loving support and unique patience, without which this project could not have virtually completed in time. I owe her everything and I am extremely grateful to her. I also express my deepest sense of love and affection to sweety **Priyanka**, master **Pritam**, and naughty **Poonam** for their unbridled enthusiasm, unstinted support and unquestioning encouragement.

Finally, I must acknowledge my gratitude to **Shri K.N.Pandey** and **Shri Anuj Pandey**, the Directors and driving forces of **Himalaya Publishing House** for taking keen interest in publishing this book. I am also grateful to **Shri Sudhakar Shetty** of Himalaya Publishing House for his tireless efforts for doing excellent DTP typeset and neatly bringing out this book within a short period of time.

DR. PARTHO PRATIM ROY

BUSINESS COMMUNICATION — THE BASICS

CONTENTS IN BRIEF

BUSINESS COMMUNICATION — THE BASICS

CONTENTS

[A] GENERAL : FORMAL TOPICS

[B] SPECIFIC : CHAPTERISATION IN DETAILS

LIST OF BOXES

LIST OF DIAGRAMS

LIST OF FIGURES

LAUGH A LITTLE THINK A LITTLE

CHAPTER

1

COMMUNICATION — ITS DIFFERENT MEANS & THEIR ROLES

CONTENTS

QUOTABLE QUOTES

1. "I will pay more for a man's ability to express himself than for any other quality he might possess."

CHARLES SCHWAB

2. "Andrew Carnegie, once the wealthiest man in the United States, at one point had 43 millionaires working for him. When asked what made these people so valuable to him, he replied that it wasn't their knowledge of steel but of people that made them so valuable. They were, it seems, excellent communicators who worked effectively with others.

ANON

3. "Meaning is in the receiver, and not in the symbols."

G.C. HEAVISIDE

4. "The first executive function is to develop and maintain a system of communication."

CHESTER I. BARNARD

LEARNING OBJECTIVES

After going through this chapter, you should be able to —

- Identify the role of sounds, signs, symbols in communication;
- Understand how old communication is;
- Explain why you cannot not communicate;
- Describe multiple meanings of words and the 'Abstraction Ladder';
- Understand the role of language in communication;
- State why people don't communicate well;
- Scan how men differ from women in communication styles;
- Outline the role of communication in physical well-being of human beings, financial well-being of business organizations, and in executing the functions of 'ears and eyes' of management.

1.1. INTRODUCTION

"The time has come", the Walrus said,
"To talk of many things;
Of shoes — and ships — and sealing wax —
Of cabbages — and kings — ."

➡ **Lewis Carroll,** ***Alice in Wonderland***

And, like **Lewis Carroll**'s *Walrus*, we talk daily of so many things. Communicating to people is our everyday activity. According to **Marion M. Wood,**[1] individuals spend nearly 70% of their waking hours in communicating — 9% in writing, 16% in reading, 30% in talking, and 45% in listening (*cf.* ***Diagram 1.1***).

DIAGRAM 1.1 : DISTRIBUTION OF TIME IN COMMUNICATION ACTIVITIES FOR INDIVIDUALS

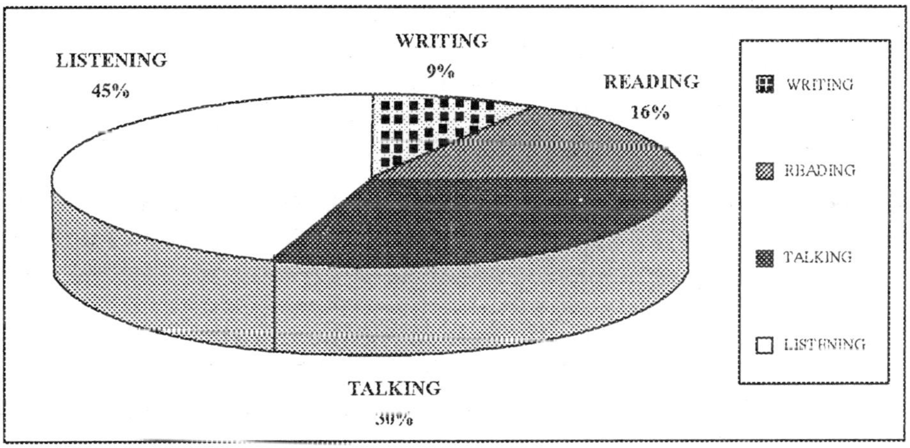

Source: Based on **Marion M. Wood**

Diagram: Exclusively designed by the Author (**Dr. Roy**).

From the time, we wake in the morning till night before we sleep, we communicate with a lot of people — wife, children, parents, friends, milkman, bus conductor, boss, secretary, salesman, and many others. Each day we are involved in conversations, discussions, giving and receiving orders, expressing concern, tenderness or even annoyance. Our daily contact with other people consists of communicating ideas and feelings.[2] These are at times communicated through **sounds, signs, symbols** and **gestures.**

For example, we communicate pleasure by a ***smile***, approval by a ***nod***, direction by a ***sketch*** and pain by a ***groan***. Babies don't need words, grammar or syntax. They yell at different frequencies depending on whether they are hungry, frustrated or have a full nappy. And their mother can get the message.

Nevertheless, **words** and, to speak more precisely, ***language*** remain by far the commonest and most important means of communication.

BOX 1.1 : HOW OLD IS HUMAN COMMUNICATION?

*For many years, it has been thought that the speech function was unique to modern Homo Sapiens. However, just within the past few years, evidence has been found that the first creatures to use spoken communication were Neanderthals, or more ancient Homo Sapiens dating back 60,000 years... **Mr. Terrence Deacon,** a neuroanatomist of Harvard University says that Neanderthals had a more restricted vocal range than we do. They had nasal voices, but could probably pronounce every consonant and vowel sound except "oo" and "ee". They are articulate, intelligent humans we would be able to understand and interact with.*

Source: **Dr. Stewart L. Tubbs & Ms. Sylvia Moss,** *Human Communication: Principles & Contexts*, McGraw-Hill, New York, 9th Edition, 2003, p. 4.

1.2. ROLE OF DIFFERENT MEANS OF COMMUNICATION

1.2.1 Sounds — Its Role in Communication

According to **Phonetics**, the ***Science of Sounds***, the world, both living and non-living, is full of sounds. Winds, clouds, animals, birds, fishes, bees, plants, flowers — all have particular sounds of their own.

For example, winds whistle, clouds rumble, lightning thunders, windows clatter, clocks tick, bees buzz, crickets sing, birds chirp, cattle low, cocks crow, snake hisses, horse neighs.

But in no other species among the living beings on the earth is the art of audible sound more fully developed than in man. And the more advanced the society of man, the richer the language he speaks, the greater the variety of sounds he employs.

1.2.2 Signs — Its Role In Communication

Signs are basic elements in communication. Signs are cues or signals to which we learn to respond because they stand for other stimuli.

Charles J. Margerison[3] has explained through the message matrix how we communicate (*cf. Box. 1.2*):

BOX 1.2 : THE MESSAGE MATRIX

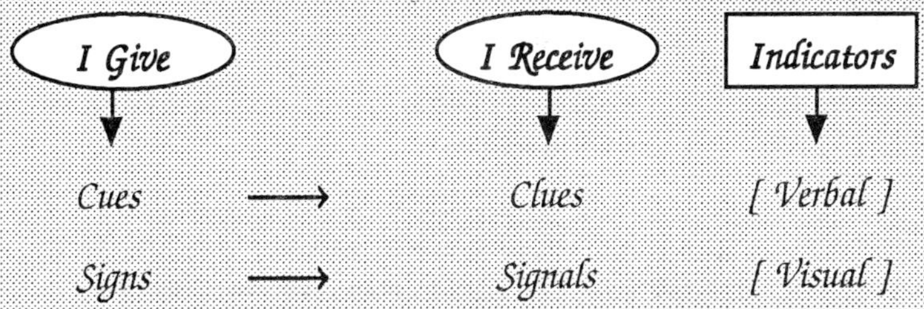

Analysis:

1. *Cues refer to the verbal indicators that you give to others.*
2. *Clues refer to the verbal indicators that others give to you.*
3. *Signs refer to the visual, behavioral indicators, such as smiles, groans or hand movements, that you give to others.*
4. *Signals refer to the visual, behavioral indicators others give to you.*

Source: Based on **Charles J. Margerison**

Although the words — signs and signals — derive from the same Latin origin **"signum"** meaning a mark or a token, they are not absolutely synonymous. A **sign** is always visual and static with elements of communication remaining unchanged (*e.g., a still photograph*) while a **signal** is audio-visual and dynamic with elements of communication always on the move (*e.g., a traffic signal*). Signs become meaningful through what **Psychologists** call the "conditioned" response — that is, a response which we learn through frequent association with a stimulus, even though that particular response would not normally be evoked by that stimulus.

For example, the sound of a dinner bell may cause our salivary glands to operate if we have learnt that the ringing of this bell is usually followed by the presence of food. The **'bell cue'** stands in place of the **'food cue'**, and, hence, is called a **sign**.

Signs too play an effective role in non-human communication. ***For example,*** bees perform a dance that signals other bees to go for nectar. A dog may show hunger by walking back and forth to the dog bowl. Even the elements of nature send signs to communicate. ***For example,*** dark clouds signal the prospect of rain or bad weather.

Stan Richards in his delightful book titled ***"Hobo Signs"*** describes the ingenious signs used by hobos to advise those who follow of the conditions ahead (*cf.* ***Diagram 1.2***).

DIAGRAM 1.2 : COMMUNICATION SIGNS FOR HOBOS

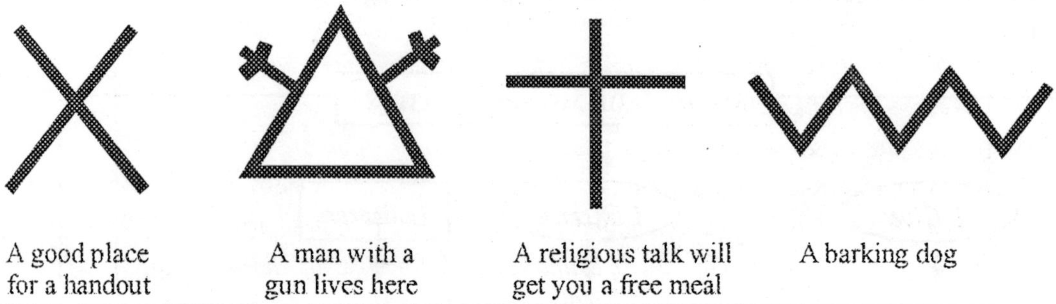

Source: Barlenmir House Publishers: Illustrations, "A Good Place For A Handout," "A Man with a Gun Lives Here," "A Religious Talk Will Get You A Free Meal," and A Barking Dog," from the book *Hobo Signs* by **Stan Richards**, © by Stan Richards & Associates. Published by Barlenmir House Publishers, New York, N.Y.

These messages create understanding, and the communication among these "travellers of the road" is effective.

Placed below are some common, familiar examples of signs you frequently come across in your daily life (*cf.* ***Diagram 1.3***) :

DIAGRAM 1.3 : SOME COMMON, FAMILIAR EXAMPLES OF SIGNS

•	→	Full stop / Period	=	→	Equal to	+	→	Addition	Σ	→	Summation
,	→	Comma	≠	→	Not equal to	−	→	Subtraction / Dash	Δ	→	Triangle
?	→	Question Mark	>	→	Greater than	×	→	Multiplication	□	→	Square
!	→	Exclamation Mark	<	→	Less than	÷	→	Division	▭	→	Rectangle

1.2.3 Symbols — Its Role in Communication

All of us have been using symbols throughout our entire life. In fact, our life style, our behavior, and the meaning of our lives are all symbol-controlled, symbol-motivated, and symbol-evaluated. Therefore, in a study of communication, it is necessary to understand the meaning of symbols. **Prof. S. I. Hayakawa** defines symbols as *"things-that-stand-for-other-things"* and says that *"the process by means of which human beings can arbitrarily make certain things stand for other things may be called the symbolic process."*[4]

BOX 1.3 : YOU CANNOT NOT COMMUNICATE

Communication is so intrinsic to our lives it can be argued that it is impossible to not communicate. Say, for instance, that you are in line next to someone in the grocery store. You may choose to overtly communicate with that person, perhaps by smiling or saying hello. However, if you avoid eye contact or turn away from that person, you are telling them that you are closed to them, which tells much. Every move we make, every facial expression, even the clothing we wear communicates messages about ourselves. Not only is communication inevitable, it is also irreversible. Once a message is sent out, it cannot be called back. Not that many of us try to avoid communication. The urge and the ability to communicate are innate.

Source: **Brent C. Oberg,** *Interpersonal Communication — An Introduction to Human Interaction,* Jaico Publishing House, Mumbai, Second Impression, 2006, p. 4.

Nearly all communication is symbolic — that is, it is achieved using symbols to suggest certain meanings. Symbols are special, complex kinds of signs. The meaning of a symbol is arbitrary and is less closely associated with its cues. **Symbols are merely a map that describes a territory, but they are not the real territory itself.** Hence, they must be interpretated.

For example, the word "dog" does not look like a dog, sound like a dog, or smell like a dog, but it means a dog because we have made it a symbol for a dog. The Indian flag in a history book is an example of a non-verbal symbol. Words or mathematical notations are examples of verbal and numerical symbols. Certain symbols are standardized too, e.g. traffic symbols, symbols for family planning, no smoking, toilets, telephone, hospital, eye bank etc., (*cf.* ***Diagram 1.4(i)***) and they convey clear, definite meaning to anybody at any place. Some symbols refer to manners of representation of some particular ideas e.g. **Lion** for strength or supremacy, a **balance** for justice, certain **colours** for certain virtues as symbolised in our national flag etc. (*cf.* ***Diagram 1.4(ii)***)

DIAGRAM 1.4 : EXAMPLES OF SOME STANDARDIZED SYMBOLS

(i)

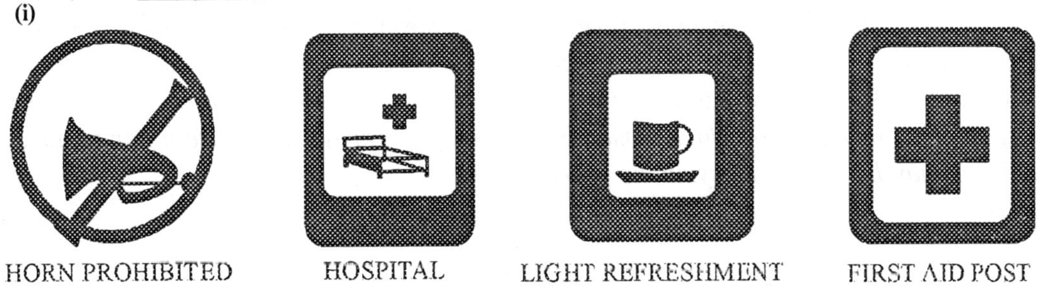

(ii)

Symbol for **STRENGTH**

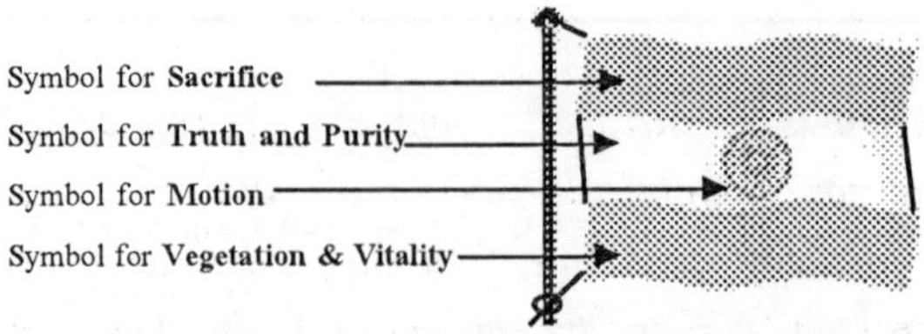

Symbol for **SACRIFICE, PEACE & VITALITY**

Symbol for **JUSTICE**

BOX 1.4 : A UNIQUE WAY OF COMMUNICATING

Julia Butterfly Hill, a 23 year-old woman, decided to send a message. She felt passionate about the environment and decided that in order to save one giant redwood tree from being cut down, she would live 180 feet up in the tree. She stayed in the tree for 738 days! Think about it. She spent over two years of her life to send a message. However, through her dedication and passive methods, she was able to reach an agreement with the logging companies to develop better methods for preserving the rights and interest of both the parties. Later she was featured in ***People Magazine****'s "25 Most Intriguing People of the Year."*

Source: Adapted from **Dr. Stewart L. Tubbs & Ms. Sylvia Moss,** *Human Communication, Principles & Contexts,* McGraw-Hill, New York, 9th Edition, 2003, p. 4.

1.2.4 Words — Its Role in Communication

We live in an ocean of words, but like a fish in water we are not aware of it. There are close to 2½ billion of us on the planet today, and practically everyone of us, except very young children, is constantly talking, listening to talk, learning to talk.[5]

Just as ***air*** is the ***medium of sound,*** so ***words*** are the ***vehicle of communication.*** Just as ***air*** is a ***mixture of different gases***, so a ***word*** is a ***combination of different letters***. Letters are ***symbolized sounds*** and ***words*** are units of ***symbolized ideas and feelings.*** Words are considered as the smallest components of a language (*cf.* ***Box 1.5***).

BOX 1.5 : LANGUAGE — DIFFERENT COMPONENTS

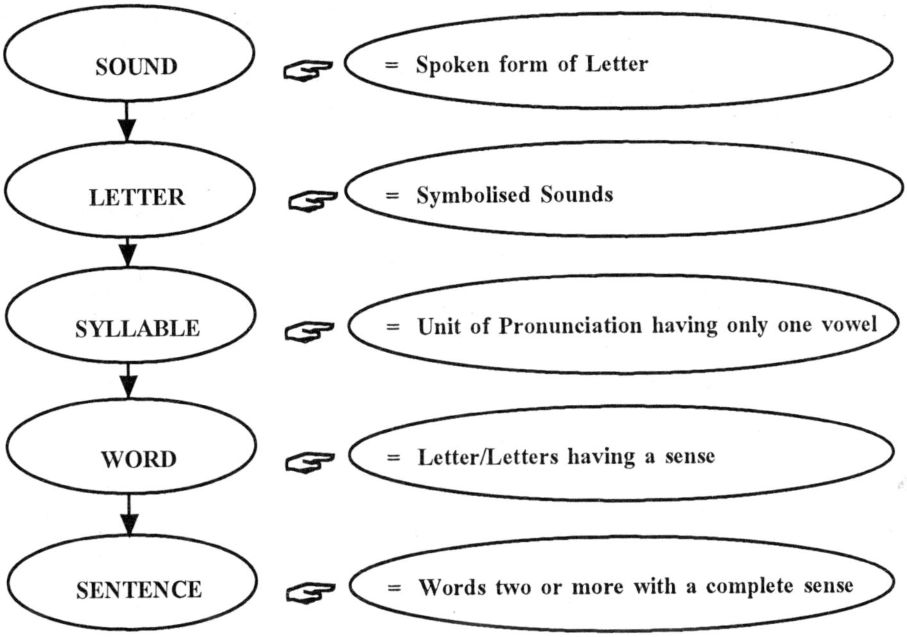

Source: Based on *Anatomy of Tense* by **Dr. P.P. Roy,**[6] p. 1.

[a] Words *Often Confused* :

Communication becomes effective only when the words communicated convey precisely the same meaning for the listener as they do for the speaker. Only then there can be true ***"meeting of minds"*** between the speaker and the listener. **Mark Twain** once said that ***the difference between the right word and the almost right word is the difference between 'lightning' and the 'lightning bug'.*** The speaker must, therefore, carefully select words that convey exactly what he wants them to convey and use them in sentences framed so as to leave no room for misunderstanding.

For example, the speaker must not confuse the words in Group 'A' with those shown thereagainst in Group 'B' (*cf.* ***Figure 1.1***).

FIGURE 1.1 : WORDS OFTEN CONFUSED — AN ILLUSTRATION

GROUP - A		GROUP - B
Avocation (= sub-ordinate occupation usually for pleasure)	with	**Vocation** (= occupation/trade or profession)
Continuous (= without a gap or break)	with	**Continual** (= with occasional breaks)
Disinterested (= unselfish/objective/ free from prejudice)	with	**Uninterested** (= indifferent/the state of not being interested)
Economic (= concerning material needs of man)	with	**Economical** (= thrifty/not wasteful)
Official (= As a noun → officer, As an adjective → connected with an office)	with	**Officious** (= meddlesome/interfering/too ready to offer help that is not wanted)
Silly (= deficiency of intellect)	with	**Foolish** (= abuse of intellect)
Stupid (= a cloudy perception of everything)	with	**Simple** (= want of experiential quick-sightedness)
Virtual (= de facto/not actual but in effect)	with	Virtuous (= righteous/chaste)
Zealous (= full of enthusiasm)	with	**Jealous** (= envious)
Reward (= something that is given in return for good or evil done)	with	**Award** (= something that is conferred or bestowed)

[b] *Multiple Meanings* of Words :

Almost every word has multiple meanings. The variety of word meanings is often surprising. A standard desk dictionary reports **79 (seventy-nine) different meanings** for the popular word **"ROUND"** of which

18 (eighteen) are used as an ***Adjective***,
19 (nineteen) are used as a ***Noun***,
26 (twenty-six) are used as a ***Verb***,
9 (nine) are used as a ***Preposition***, and
7 (seven) convey ***special meanings.***

Many of the meanings are entirely different, as shown through six examples in the following diagram (*cf.* ***Diagram 1.5***).

DIAGRAM 1.5 : MULTIPLE MEANINGS OF WORDS

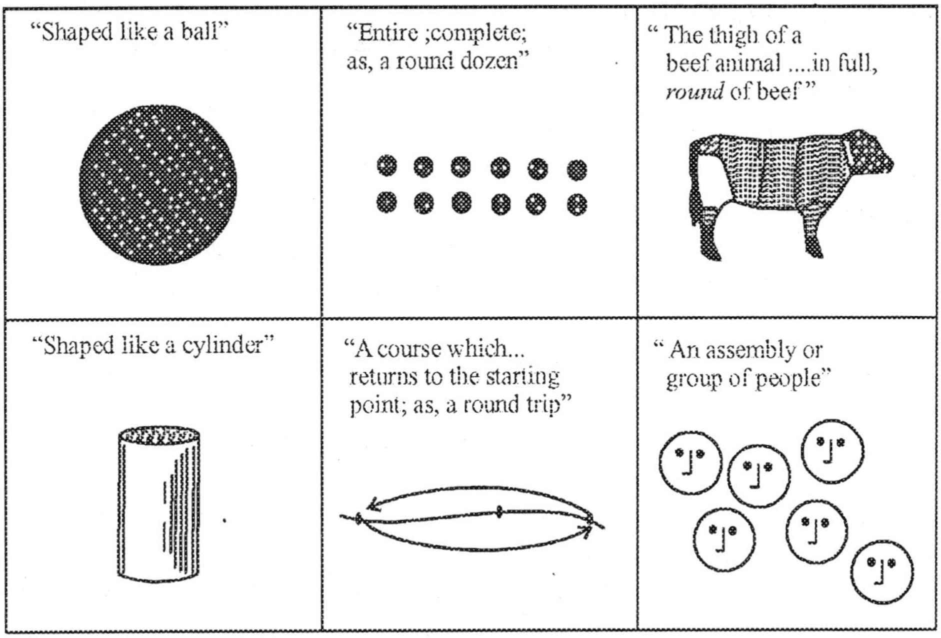

Source: **Webster's New World Dictionary,** College Edition, 1964 & Quoted by **Dr. Keith Davis.**

Similarly, the word **"RUN"** can be used in **110 different ways**. It has **71 meanings** as a ***verb***, another **35** as a ***noun***, and **4** more as an ***adjective***. Some of the examples showing different shades of meaning in word **'RUN'** are cited below:[7]

Babe Ruth scored a ***run***.
I have a ***run*** in my stocking.
Did you ever see him ***run***?
What headline do you want to ***run*** today?
There was a ***run*** on the bank today.
Who will ***run*** for President this year?
Please ***run*** my bath water etc. etc.

A study of a larger dictionary, the **Oxford Dictionary**, reports there are about 6,00,000 (six lakhs) words in the English language. An educated adult in daily conversation uses about 2,000 words of which the most commonly used words are 500. And an average of *28 (twenty eight) separate meanings* we have for each of the 500 most used words in the English Language.[8] A study by **Lydia Strong**[9] largely substantiates this view. **Strong** concluded that for the 500 most common words in English language, there are 4070 dictionary definitions. Is it really possible then that we can guess the right meaning every time?

Ossie Davis in ***Roget's Thesaurus*** counted *120 synonyms* for **'blackness'** and noted that most of them had unpleasant connotations. In the same book are cited *134 synonyms* for the word **'white'** with positive connotations.[10]

According to **Alison Theaker,**[11] words have as many as *four types of meanings* which can be described as follows:

1. **Denotative** i.e. *what the word means in the dictionary sense i.e. literal meaning of a word.* It just informs and names objects without suggesting any positive or negative qualities. ***For example,*** the word 'CHAIR' simply means a piece of furniture for sitting on.
2. **Connotative.** i.e.*what the subjective, emotional meaning you attach to a word.* Such meaning derives from qualitative judgements, personal reactions, images or associations created in the mind of the receiver. Some words like 'competent', 'honest', 'sincere' etc. have positive connotations, while some others like 'incompetent', 'coward', 'selfish' etc. have negative connotations. Besides, certain words have both favourable and unfavourable connotations in different contexts. ***For example,*** one such word is **CHEAP**:

Use of words	Implication(s)	Nature of connotations
1. This shop sells cheap things	Refers to quality	Negative, unfavourable
2. This shop sells things cheap	Refers to prices	Positive, favourable

3. **Ambiguous.** i.e. *where the same word means different things* in a given language. *For example,* the word **'BEAR'** can be a noun describing a woolly beast or a verb meaning to carry. Similar examples:

Word	As a noun	As a verb
1. DEAL	A business agreement	To distribute / behave
2. RUN	A unit of scoring in cricket	To move swiftly / flee

Puns and poems depend on ambiguity for their effect.

4. **Polysemic.** i.e. *where readers/viewers can derive different meanings from the same set of information — pictures or text.* This builds on the different connotations people bring to a message, but reflects the wider social context of a message, not just the subjective response. ***For example,*** an image of a woman in a swimming costume may represent different meanings to people of different cultures or different political and ideological views.

If words have really no certain meaning, how, then, can we make sense with them while communicating with others? The obvious answer to this question is the *'context'* in which it is used. ***For example,*** the term **"dummy"** in an argument *at the office* may be derogatory/ uncomplimentary, when we use the said term to refer to the person serving as dummy *in a game of bridge* is acceptable and meaningful. **So, individual words, despite having so many meanings, become meaningless until they are put into *context.*** Consequently, effective communicators are idea-centered, rather than word-centered. They know that **words do not mean — people mean**[12] (*cf.* ***Box. 1.6***). That is, the meaning of words are not in words, but in people's mind. Words have, therefore, meaning only in terms of people's experience. **G.C. Heaviside** is, therefore, right when, after summarising much research on communication, concluded : **'Meaning is in the receiver and not in the symbols'.**

BOX 1.6 : A YOUNG BEAUTIFUL WOMAN AND A FAMOUS ARTIST

MEANING IS IN THE RECEIVER

A young, beautiful woman contacted a famous artist and offered him Rs. 5,000/- to paint her in nude. He refused saying that it was against his principle. A week later she called the artist again and offered him Rs. 10,000/-. Again the artist refused. When the lady called the artist the third time and offered him Rs. 25,000/-, he said that he will consider it. The next day, the artist telephoned, "I can do it, madam, but I have to wear at least socks, because I need a place for my brushes."

Source: Unknown

[c] Abstraction of Words

Everyone abstracts. It occurs when anything is deleted or left out. The abstracting process, by leaving out details, permits classification. **Professor S. I. Hayakawa** provided a classic example by abstractly classifying a cow on an **"Abstraction Ladder"** [*cf.* ***Diagram 1.6***] .

The cow, 'BESSIE', is uniquely herself, and differs from all other objects in the same classifications. This uniqueness is an important point. With his ***'ladder of abstraction',*** **Mr. Hayakawa** endeavours to make the point that objects begin at the perception and microscopic levels (=**II** & **I** respectively) while symbols begin at the **III** (= third) level. Levels **III**rd to **VIII**th on the abstraction ladder illustrate how many degrees of specification we have in our complex symbol system.

The object we see is an abstraction of the lowest level. As we ascend the ladder, the verbal categories become more general as 'BESSIE' is placed into broader categories in which we conceive some similarity."[13]

DIAGRAM 1.6 : THE ABSTRACTION LADDER

(Start reading from the bottom up)

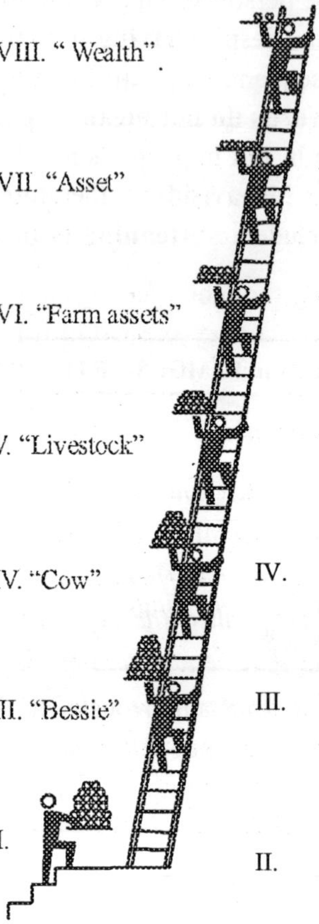

VIII. The word "wealth" is at an extremely high level of abstraction, omitting *almost* all reference to the characteristics of Bessie.

VII. When Bessie is referred to as an "asset", still more of her characteristics are left out.

VI. When Bessie is included among "farm assets," reference is made only to what she has in common with all other saleable items on the farm.

V. When Bessie is referred to as "livestock," only those characteristics she has in common with pigs, chickens, goats, etc. are referred to.

IV. The word "cow" stands for the characteristics we have abstracted as common to cow_1, cow_2, cow_3, ... cow_n. Characteristics peculiar to specific cows are left out.

III. The word "Bessie" (cow_1): This is the *name* we give to the object of perception of level II. The name *is not* the object; it merely *stands for* the object and omits reference to many of the characteristics of the object.

II. The cow we perceive, not the word, but the object of experience; that which our nervous system abstracts (selects) from the totality that constitutes the process-cow. Many of the characteristics of the process-cow are left out.

I. The cow known to science: ultimately consisting of atoms, electrons, etc., according to present-day scientific inference. Characteristics (represented by circles) are infinite at this level and ever changing. This is the *process level.*

Source: **Prof. S.I. Hayakawa,** *Language in Thought and Action,* Harcourt, Brace & World Inc., New York, 2nd Edition, 1964.

By giving an object a name, we have in a sense *'created'* that object. The symbols, we have chosen to represent the *'things'* of the world actually structure our perception of that world whether we use our eye or a microscope. We cannot *'see'* what we cannot symbolize. Because of our cultural heritage we have chosen to symbolize some parts of the environment and not others.[14]

1.2.5 Language — Its Role in Communication

"Language is the dress of thought." — **Samuel Johnson**

When many words with generally accepted meanings are used by a group of persons, they have a language. Languages are main vehicles for expressing thoughts, feelings and knowledge. To communicate perfectly, a language would have to exactly convey the world it represents. **If we want to discover the meaning of a speaker's words, the only way to be certain is to ask the speaker what they mean when we are in doubt.** Instead of wondering what the words in a message mean, a better approach is to wonder what the speaker means.[15]

For example, there is a famous story of a carpenter and his assistant. The carpenter picked up a nail of a huge size and said to his assistant,

> ***"When I hold this nail in position and nod my head, hit it hard with the hammer."***

And the tragedy we all know that the poor carpenter died instantaneously. It all happened because by the word ***'it'***, the assistant understood ***"my head"*** and not ***"the nail"***.

There is another popular anecdote about a business owner charging his manager with the responsibility for the concern before going off on a lengthy vacation.

> ***"Treat this company as though it were your own,"***

said the boss. Within two weeks, the manager sold the place. The receiver's attitude had dramatically conditioned his interpretation of the message, and hence his response.

Don Fabun[16] has prescribed the following two golden rules to lessen the chance of communication failures:

> **Firstly,** don't assume that everyone knows what you are talking about;
> **Secondly,** don't assume that you know what others are talking about without asking them questions to make certain what they are talking about.

The 'hapless' carpenter erroneously made the first assumption, and his 'imperceptive' assistant made the second!

> So, never **"ASSUME".** Because when yŏu **ass u me**, you often make an **ass** out of **u** and an **ass** out of **me**! i.e. it makes an **ass** (of) ***u*** (&) **me**!

Stan Kosen[17] has cautioned us that the following **five important factors** should be remembered about meanings of words:

(*a*) Words have many meanings;
(*b*) Words sometimes have regional meanings;
(*c*) Words develop new meanings;
(*d*) New words are continually added; and
(*e*) A difference in tone can change the meaning of a word.

Sometimes, words in the message, the emphasis given in communicating the message and sometimes faulty interpretation of the message convey wrong meaning to a communication. ***For example,*** examine the following message:

Love him not hate him.

The messages due to lack of precision and emphasis may be interpreted in any of the following two ways:

(*a*) **Love him, not hate him.**
or
(*b*) **Love him not, hate him.**

In order, therefore, to have a correct response from the communicatee, the communicator must communicate correctly the emphasis contained in the message.

Sometimes, punctuation may determine the meaning of words used. ***For example,*** look at the following sentence having no appropriate punctuation mark:

Woman without her man is nothing.

Most ***men*** will punctuate the above sentence to mean :

Woman, without her man, is nothing.

While most ***women*** will punctuate the sentence to read :

Woman! without her, man is nothing.

Social Psychologist **Joost A. M. Meerloo**[18] has cited some of the potential meanings that is conveyed by the statement, ***"I LOVE YOU'*** *(cf.* ***Box 1.7****).*

BOX 1.7 : SHADES OF MEANING IN "I LOVE YOU"

"... It may be a stage song, repeated daily without any meaning, or a barely audible murmur, full of surrender. ***Sometimes it means:*** *I desire you or I want you sexually.* ***It may mean:*** *I hope you love me or I hope that I will be able to love you.* ***Often it means:*** *It may be that a love relationship can develop between us or even I hate you.* ***Often it is a wish for emotional exchange:*** *I want your admiration in exchange for mine or I give my love in exchange for some passion or I want to feel cozy and at home with you or I admire some of your qualities.* ***A declaration of love is mostly a request:*** *I desire you or I want you to gratify me, or I want your protection or I want to be intimate with you or I want to exploit your loveliness.* ***Sometimes it is the need for security and tenderness, for parental treatment. It may mean:*** *My self-love goes out to you. But it* ***may also express submissiveness:*** *Please take me as I am, or I feel guilty about you, I want through you to correct the mistakes I have made in human relations.* ***It may be self-sacrifice or a masochistic wish*** *for dependency. However,* ***it may also be a full affirmation of the other,*** *taking the responsibility for mutual exchange of feelings.* ***It may be a week feeling of friendliness, it may be*** *the scarcely even* ***whispered expression of ecstacy.*** *"I love you" — wish, desire, submission, conquest; it is never the word itself that tells the real meaning here."*

Source: **J.A.M. Meerloo,** *Conversation & Communication,* p. 83.

In any language short sentences do not always guarantee the elimination of misunderstanding. Wayne Sanders[19], the president of Sanders Associates, Missourie, USA, has cited an interesting example of a short, simple sentence and showed how many different meanings the sentence can convey if each word of the sentence is emphasized in turn (*cf. **Fig. 1.2***).

FIGURE 1.2 : CHANGE IN MEANING WITH SHIFTING OF EMPHASIS ON EACH WORD IN A SENTENCE

The sentence with the emphasized word shown in bold & italics	*The consequential change in meaning*
I never said he stole money.	Possibly someone else said it, not I.
I ***never*** said he stole money.	Now I am denying I ever said it.
I never ***said*** he stole money.	I may have thought he did, though.
I never said ***he*** stole money.	Someone did, but not him.
I never said he ***stole*** money.	He borrowed it, embezzled it, got it as a gift.
I never said he stole ***money.***	May be not money, but a car, savings bond, and so on.

Let's take another example of **intonation** (i.e. *voice modulation*) and see how it can change the meaning of a message (*cf. **Figure 1.3***) :

FIGURE 1.3 : INTONATIONS — IT'S THE WAY YOU SAY IT

Change your tone and you change your meaning :

Placement of the Emphasis [ ]	**What it means**
Why don't I take [**you**] to dinner to-night ?	I was going to take someone else.
Why don't [**I**] take you to dinner to-night ?	Instead of the guy you were going with.
Why [**don't**] I take you to dinner to-night ?	I'm trying to find a reason why I shouldn't take you.
[**Why**] don't I take you to dinner to-night ?	Do you have a problem with me ?
Why don't I [**take**] you to dinner to-night ?	Instead of going on your own.
Why don't I take you to [**dinner**] to-night ?	Instead of lunch tomorrow.
Why don't I take you to dinner [**to-night**] ?	Not tomorrow night.

Source : Based on **M. Kiely,** "When 'No' Means 'Yes' ", *Marketing,* October 1993, pp. 7-9. Reproduced in **A. Huczynski & D. Buchanan,** *Organizational Behaviour,* Pearson Education, Essex, UK, 4th Edition, 2001, p. 194.

Sometimes wrong expressions, faulty sentence structures distort the meaning and vitiate the purpose of communication (*cf. **Fig. 1.4***) :

FIGURE 1.4 : SAY WHAT YOU MEAN

The communicator must not say	*When he means*
1. Wanted for a baby a nurse three months old.	1. Wanted a nurse for a baby three months old.
2. I saw a dead cow walking across the field.	2. Walking across the field, I saw a dead cow.
3. George enjoys having breakfast in his pajamas.	3. In his pajamas, George enjoys having breakfast.

DIAGRAM 1.7 : DESTRUCTION OF SENTENCE CONSTRUCTION

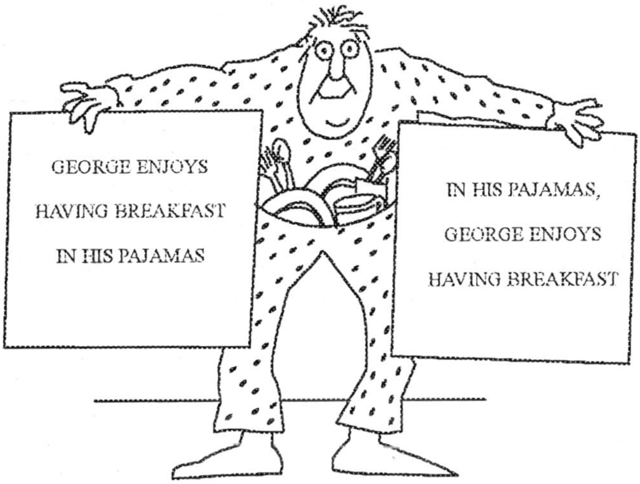

Source : **Sy Lazarus,** *Loud and Clear,* AMACOM, New York, 1975, p. 53.

Let us take for example the following dialogue between a doctor and a patient which is humorous per se due to misinterpretation of the message:

LAUGH A LITTLE THINK A LITTLE

IS YOUR COLD ANY BETTER ?

Here is a humorous illustration of misinterpretated message :

Doctor : Is your cold any better?

Patient : No!

Doctor : Did you follow my instructions and drink some orange juice after the hot bath?

Patient : No! After drinking the hot bath, I couldn't get any orange juice down.

Source: Based on **Sy Lazarus,** *op. cit.*, p. 27.

1.3. MULTIFARIOUS ROLES OF COMMUNICATION

"People don't get along,
Because they fear each other.
They fear each other,
Because they don't know each other.
They don't know each other,
Because they haven't communicated with each other."

Martin Luther King

1.3.1 Role of Communication in Our Lives

Communication arises out of the need to reduce uncertainty, to act effectively, to defend or strengthen the ego. On some occasions, words are used to ward off anxiety. On other occasions, they are means of evolving more deeply satisfying ways of expressing ourselves. Research studies indicate that communication has been linked to physical well-being of human beings (*cf.* ***Box. 1.8***)

BOX 1.8 : ROLE OF COMMUNICATION IN PHYSICAL WELL-BEING OF HUMAN BEINGS

***Stewart** (1986) indicates that socially isolated people are more likely to die prematurely; divorced men die at double the normal rate from cancer, heart disease, and strokes, five times the normal rate from hypertension, five times the normal rate from suicide, seven times the normal rate from cirrhosis of the liver, and ten times the normal rate from tuberculosis. Also, poor communication skills have been found to contribute to coronary heart disease, and the likelihood of death increases when a marriage partner dies.*

Source: Quoted by **Dr. Stewart & Ms. Sylvia Moss:** *Human Communication — Principles & Contexts*, The McGraw-Hill Cos., Inc., New York, 9th Edition, 2003, p. 6.

The aim of communication is to increase the number and consistency of our meanings within the limits set by patterns of evaluation that have proven successful in the past, our emerging needs and drives, and the demands of the physical and social setting of the moment. Communication ceases when meanings are adequate; it is initiated as soon as new meanings are required. However, since man is a homeostatic, rather than static organism, it is impossible for him to discover any permanently satisfying way of relating all his needs; each temporary adjustment is both relieving and disturbing, leading to successively novel ways of relating to himself and his environment.[20]

Communication does more than enable us to survive. It is the way — indeed, the only way — we learn who we are. **Our sense of identity comes from the way we interact with other people.** Are we smart or stupid, attractive or ugly, skillful or inept? The answers to these questions don't come from looking in the mirror. We decide who we are based on how others react to us. (*cf.* ***Box. 1.9***).

BOX 1.9 : COMMUNICATION MAKES US LEARN 'WHO WE ARE'. *i.e.,* SENSE OF IDENTITY

Deprived of communication with others, we would have no sense of identity. In his book ***'Bridges, Not Walls', John Stewart***[21] *dramatically illustrates this fact by citing the case of the famous* ***"Wild Boy of Aveyron"****, who spent his early childhood without any apparent human contact. The boy was discovered in January 1800 while digging for vegetables in a French village garden. He showed no behaviors one would expect in a social human. The boy could not speak but uttered only weird cries. More significant than this absence of social skills was his lack of any identity as a human being. As author* ***Roger Shattuck***[22] *put it, "The boy had no human sense of being in the world. He had no sense of himself as a person related to other persons." Only after the influence of a loving* ***'mother'*** *did the boy begin to behave — and, we can imagine, think of himself as a human.*

Contemporary stories support the essential role that communication plays in shaping identity. In 1970, authorities discovered a twelve-year-old girl (whom they called ***"Genie"****) who had spent virtually all her life in an otherwise empty, darkened bedroom with almost no human contact. The child could not speak and had no sense of herself as a person until she was removed from her family and 'nourished' by a team of care-givers.*[23]

Like ***Genie*** *and the* ***Boy of Aveyron****, each of us enters the world with little or no sense of identity. We gain an idea of* ***'who we are'*** *from the ways others define us.*

Source: Quoted by **Ronald B. Adler & George Rodman,** *Understanding Human Communication*, Oxford University Press, New York, 9th Edition, 2006, p. 10.

Besides helping to define **"identity needs"**, communication provides a vital link with others. **Researchers and theorists**[24] have identified a range of ***"social needs"**** we satisfy by communicating:

(*i*) **pleasure** e.g. 'because it's fun,' 'to have a good time';
(*ii*) **affection** e.g. 'to help others', 'to let others know I care';
(*iii*) **inclusion** e.g. 'because I need someone to talk, to or be with', 'because it makes me less lonely';
(*iv*) **escape** e.g. 'put off doing something I should be doing';
(*v*) **relaxation** e.g. 'because it allows me to unwind'; and
(*vi*) **control** e.g. 'because I want someone to do something for me', 'to get something I don't have'.

*		
	Acronym :	**PAI — ERCo**
	Mnemonic :	**P**akistan, **A**ustralia & **I**ndia **E**qually **R**eputed in the game of **C**ricket.

As you look at this list of social needs for communicating, imagine how empty your life would be if these needs were not satisfied, and remember that it would be impossible to fulfill them without communicating with others.

BOX 1.10 : MAN DIFFERS FROM WOMAN IN COMMUNICATION STYLES

Deborah Tannen, *a prominent researcher in the differences in communication styles of men and women, suggests that the two sexes use language in entirely different ways, creating miscommunication on a regular basis. For women, language is the glue that holds relationships together, for men, activities hold relationships together; and language is used to negotiate their position. According to* ***Tannen's research,*** *women suggest and men command. Women react to commands with feelings of being bullied; men perceive women's indirect requests as manipulative. An additional finding is that American men in business settings like to discuss business and not waste time on personal talk. Women, like business people in certain other cultures, feel that personal talk establishes a comfortable relationship that can provide the basis for working together. These differences in style cause confusion and resentment in many cases.*

Source: **D. Tannen,** *You Just Don't Understand: Women & Men in Conversation,* Ballentine Books, New York, 1991 and also **D. Tannen,** *Talking from 9 to 5,* William Morrow, New York, 1995.

1.3.2 Role of Communication in Business Organization

Business organizations are human associations constituted for achieving certain specified objectives. How well organizations achieve those objectives depends largely upon how well they communicate with their human resources. *Communication is the life-blood of every organization.* Communication is the means by which organized activity is unified, by which behavior is modified, change is effected, information is made productive and goals are achieved.[25]

BOX 1.11 : WHY PEOPLE DON'T COMMUNICATE WELL ?

There are many number of reasons why people do not communicate well, out of which the following four are the major problem areas:

First, people do not communicate well because they often have emotional blocks. *They are more concerned with things like, "Does this person like me?" "Does this person think I know what I'm doing?" "Do I appear qualified to do the job I am doing? etc. etc. than they are about getting their message across. Emotional blocks come from all kinds of sources: anger, fear, nervousness, defensiveness, uncertainty, and so on. They may be due to the fact that the individual has had unsatisfactory experiences in previous interaction encounters or that he/she got up on the wrong side of the bed that morning or that he/she is just a normally oversensitive person. Regardless of the source of the emotional block or its type, it must be removed before good communication can take place. When we are emotionally aroused, we are neither a good communicator nor a good receptor. Like a football quarterback, we must keep our cool if we are to do our best.*

Second, people do not communicate well if they come from different environments or have different frames of reference. *This means, for example, that an agent and an underwriting person do not have on the surface a common purpose and a common goal. Just as in hockey, some people are trying to drive the puck into the cage and the goalkeeper is trying to keep them from so doing; however, in this instance they are not on the same team. Actions and symbols mean different things to different individuals. For any two individuals to communicate well, they must find some common ground in order to get acceptance and agreement.*

Third, some people cannot communicate well because they are incapable of expressing themselves *through the use of the spoken and/or written word. In order to communicate, one must have the capacity to use words, since words are the medium through which we express thoughts, ideas, and feelings. Some people have a limited inventory of words with* *which to express themselves, or their recall in a given situation is limited. An individual might think that he or she is saying the right thing, but it always seems to come out wrong. Words are building blocks, and the correct use of the building blocks creates the structure — or the ideas, feelings, and attitudes toward which we are driving. Other people have the basic words necessary to express their ideas, but they have one of the many different types of speech impediments. In either case the individual must work very hard to overcome these handicaps through education and training, development, and experience.*

Finally, some people cannot communicate effectively because they are unable to use their personality effectively. *Communication depends in a large measure on the vibrations one sends out in the process of communicating. One's outward appearance, gestures, smile, animation, eyes, bodily posture, vitality, and voice quality all express one's personality. These factors are particularly important in face-to-face communication where individuals are constantly looking for the "meaning of meaning" and are aware of the goodness of intent or the soundness of what the individual is attempting to communicate.*

Source: Adapted from **Arnold E. Schneider, William C. Donaghy & Pamela Jane Newman,** *Organizational Communication,* McGraw-Hill Kogakusha Ltd., Tokyo, 1975, pp. 69-70.

1.3.3 Role of Communication in Management

[a] Communication — *No. 1 Management Problem* :

Alvin Dodd, the former President of American Management Association described *communication as the No. 1 management problem* today. In the words of **Dr. Raymond L. Hilgart,** Professor of Management and Industrial Relations, Washington University, Missouri, 'in every organization that I have come into contact with, *communicating is usually the number one problem,* or it is at least associated with virtually every major problem which the organization faces.' This ranges from basic problems of human understanding, all the way to major financial, marketing, and production problems associated with the inability of people to properly communicate with one another.[26]

Fred Luthans[27] opines, there seems little doubt that communication plays an important role in managerial and organizational effectiveness. Yet, on the other side of the same coin, ***communication is commonly cited as being at the root of practically all the problems of the world. It is given as the explanation for lovers' quarrels, ethnic prejudice, war between nations, the generation gap, industrial disputes, and organizational conflict.*** These are only representatives of numerous problems attributed to ineffective communication. Obviously, this thinking can go too far — communication can become a convenient scapegoat or crutch. Not all organization and interpersonal difficulties are the result of communication breakdown. Other matters such as motivation, decision-making and control, stress, organization structure, to name but a few — can also contribute to problems. Yet it is also true that the *communication process is a central problem* in most human and organizational activities.

[b] Communication — *Eyes and Ears of Management* :

Communication is the focal point of executive actions, is central to the control and survival of organizations and is a requisite to effective management. **Chester I. Barnard** has rightly said that ***the first executive function is to develop and maintain a system of communication.***[28] All great management ideas are strictly *armchair thoughts* until a manager puts them into effect through communication.[29] Communication can be described as the *eyes and ears* of management. Since management is getting things done through and with the efforts of others, all management functions — styled as **PODSCORB*** (*i.e. **P**lanning, **O**rganizing, **D**irecting, **S**taffing, **C**o-ordinating, **R**eporting, **B**udgeting*) — pass through the bottleneck of communication.

*		
Acronym	:	**PODSCORB**
Mnemonic	:	Prince **O**f **D**enmark **S**aved **C**hildren **O**f **R**oyal **B**hutan.

All these major seven management functions have been diagrammatically illustrated in ***Diagram 1.8*** as under :

DIAGRAM 1.8: MANAGEMENT FUNCTIONS & COMMUNICATION BOTTLENECK

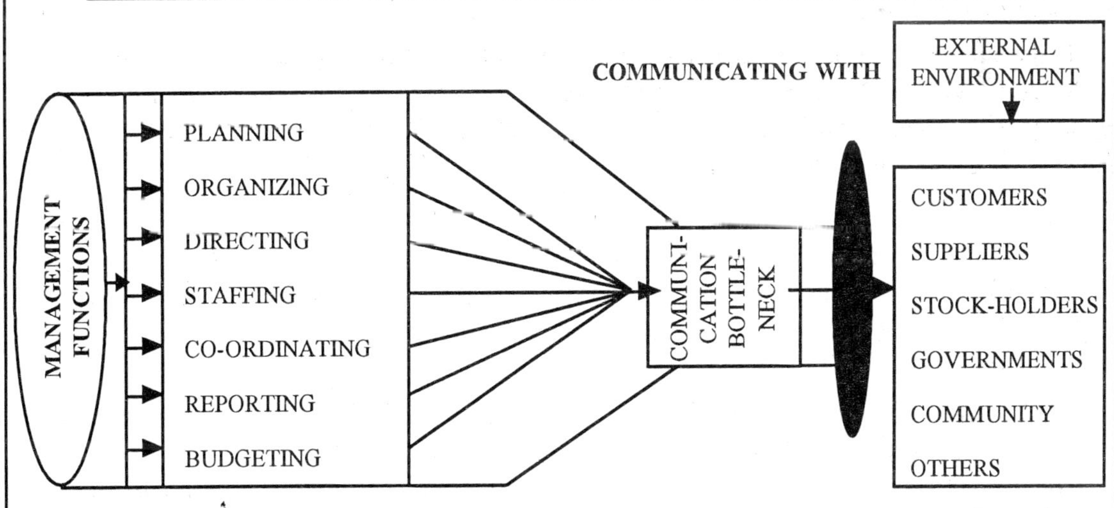

Source: Based on **Keith Davis** and also **Koontz & Weihrich.**

Out of the aforesaid broad management functions, managers at all levels engage in at least four main types of activity which can be acronymed as **POLE** (i.e., **P**lanning, **O**rganizing, **L**eading, **E**valuating):

- **Planning** : deciding priorities, setting time-objectives and targets, and devising action plans to meet organizational goals.
- **Organizing** : directing and co-ordinating the work of staff, making decisions about their actual duties, monitoring expenditure, and allocating tasks to individuals and teams.
- **Leading** : motivating staff to work to their optimum level, directing and appraising as they carry out tasks, maintaining good working relationships, and allocating rewards and sanctions to ensure compliance.
- **Evaluating** : assessing whether organizational goals have been met, measuring outputs and work performance compared to the set targets, implementing corrective actions to meet shortfalls, and to devise new plans, if necessary.

And communication is involved in all the aforesaid four stages.

According to **W.D. Johnson,** the-then Vice President of Personnel, Baxter Travenol Labs Inc., communication with employees is a critical requirement of good managers. In the words of **Peter F. Drucker,** ***good communication is the foundation for sound management.***[30] Communication is important for managers for two reasons. ***Firstly,*** it is the process by which the management functions are accomplished. ***Secondly,*** it is the activity to which managers devote an overwhelming proportion of their time.[31] Managers, in general, spend as much as 37.5 hours communicating per week.[32]

In the late 1960s, **Henry Mintzberg,** a graduate student at MIT, after systematic observations of chief executives' work, concluded that ***verbal interaction accounts for 78 per cent of managers' time and 67 per cent of their activities.***[33] A great deal of this time is spent in meetings and on telephone calls (*cf.* ***Diagrams 1.9 and 1.10***).

DIAGRAM 1.9: DISTRIBUTION OF HOURS IN MANAGERIAL COMMUNICATION

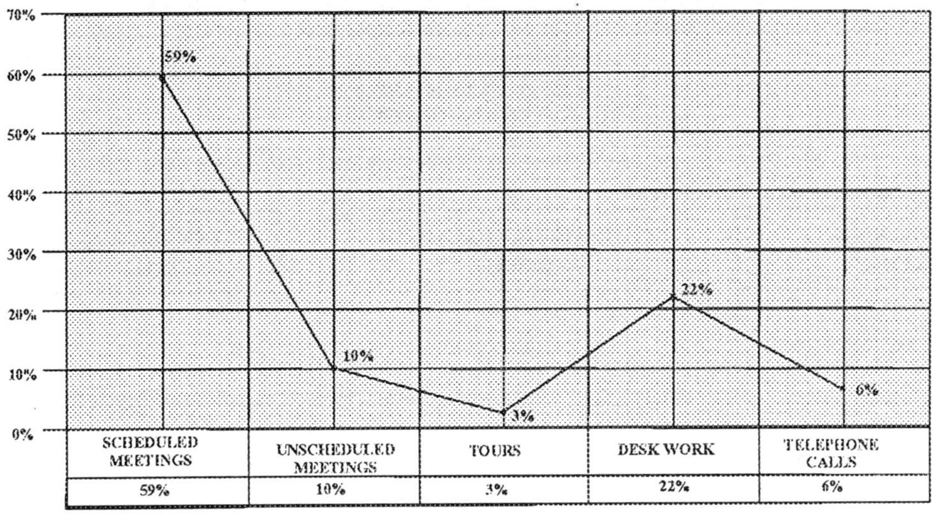

Source : Based on **Henry Mintzberg**
Diagram : Exclusively designed by the Author **(Dr. Roy)**

DIAGRAM 1.10 :DISTRIBUTION OF NUMBER OF ACTIVITIES IN MANAGERIAL COMMUNICATION

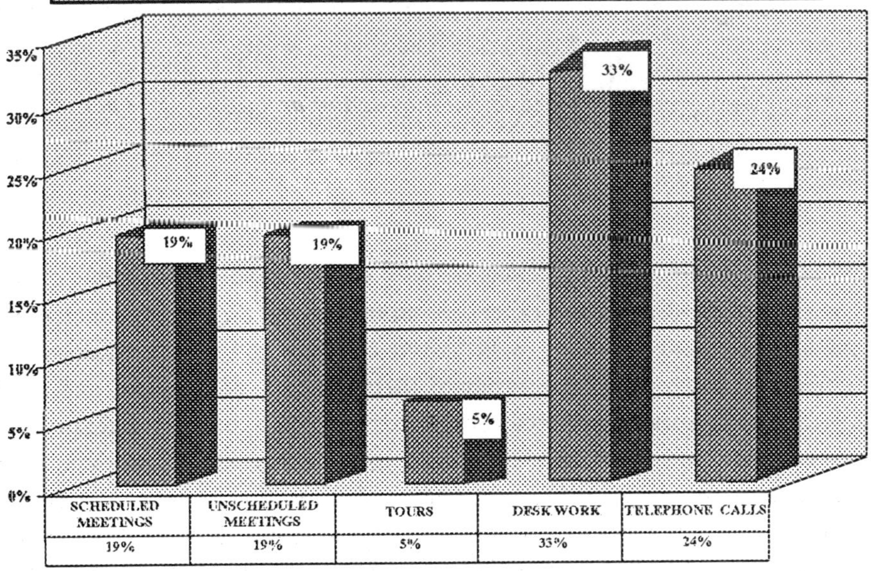

Source: Based on **Henry Mintzberg.**
Diagram : Exclusively designed by the Author **(Dr. Roy).**

According to **Mintzberg**, a manager has to perform ten types of roles under three broad categories in the organization, and communication plays a vital role in each[34] (*cf. Fig. 1.5*).

FIGURE 1.5 : MINTZBERG'S CATEGORIZATION OF MANAGER'S ROLES

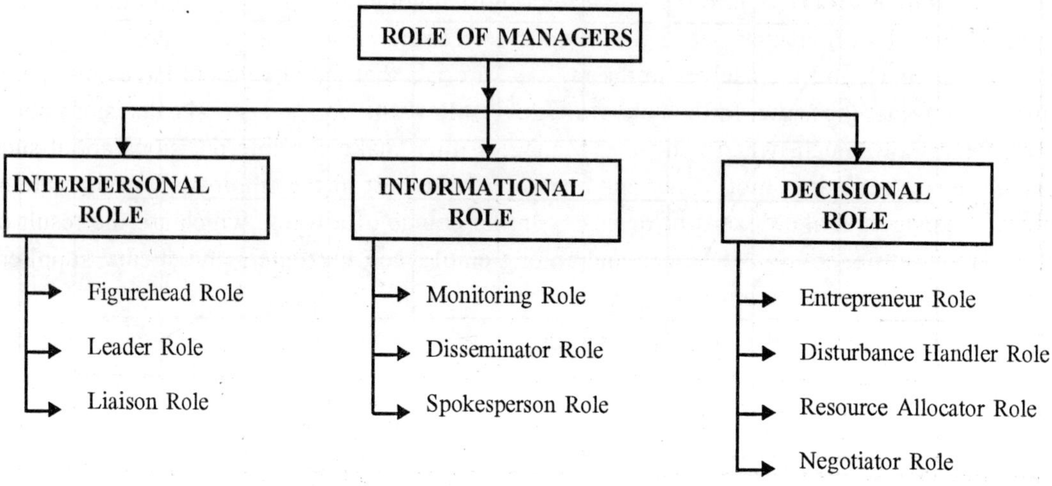

Source: Based on **Mintzberg**

In the ***interpersonal role,*** a manager acts as the figurehead and leader of the organization unit interacting with subordinates, customers, suppliers and peers in the organization. According to Mintzberg, the influence of managers is most clearly seen in the **leader role**. Formal authority vests them with great potential power. Leadership determines, in large part, how much power they will realise.[35] In **liaison role**, managers establish and maintain contacts outside of the vertical chain of command. In **Rosemary Stewart's** study, 160 British middle and top managers spent 47 per cent of their time with peers, 41 per cent of their time with people inside their time with peers, 41 per cent of their time with people inside their unit, and only 12 per cent of their time with superiors.[36]

In the ***informational role,*** a manager acts as both receiver and disseminator of information from and for his peers, subordinates and others. As **monitors,** managers are constantly scanning the environment for information, talking with liaison contacts and subordinates, and receiving unsolicited information, much of it as a result of their network of personal contacts. A good portion of this information arrives in verbal form, often as gossip, hearsay and speculation.[37] In the **role of disseminator**, managers pass privileged information directly to subordinates, who might otherwise have no access to it. Managers must also decide not only who should receive such information, but how much of it, how often and in what form. In the role of **spokesperson,** managers send information to people outside of their organizations. They are also asked to deal with representatives of the news media, providing both factual and opinion-based responses that will be printed or broadcast to vast unseen audiences, often directly or with very little editing.

And in the ***decisional role,*** a manager has to take some of the decisions based on information that has been communicated to him and such decisions are communicated downward to subordinates to achieve organizational goals. As **entrepreneurs,** managers seek to improve their businesses, adapt to changing market conditions, and react to opportunities as they present themselves. In the **role of disturbance or crisis handler**, managers must involuntarily react to conditions. Crises can arise because bad managers let circumstances deteriorate or spin out of control, but just as often good managers find themselves in the midst of a crisis that they could not have anticipated but must react to just the same. In the **role of resource allocator**, managers make decisions about who gets what, how much, when and why. Managers must make sensible decisions about such matters while still retaining, motivating and developing the best of the employees. In the **role of negotiator,** managers make dozens of decisions in the course of a week, which are the result of brief but important negotiations between and among employees, customers and clients, suppliers and others with whom managers must deal.[38]

Therefore, the more effective and purposeful the communication system is within the organization, the better the performance, the greater the job satisfaction, the optimum the productivity of personnel in that organization.

[c] *Importance* of Communication in Management :

Importance of communication in management has been widely recognized in recent years. Effective system of communications helps management in the following ways:

(i) Smooth Running of the Organization

In every organization, big or small, all personnel — be it a manager, or a clerk, or a peon, — are busy with the disposal of some sort of communication. ***The more complex the organization the more difficult it becomes to establish that the correct information is passed on to the right person at the right time through the right medium.*** Through communication, **"skill to work"** is brought in touch with **"will to work"** and both combined together lead to successful teamwork. In any organization, the communication from the superior is the basis on which the work of his subordinate depends. This is the medium through which the subordinate knows his limitations, regulates his work and expects reward or punishment for his approved or disapproved behavior. Without a rich flow of communication from his boss, the subordinate cannot judge which direction he should be going or how well he is doing and the like. Similarly, the communication from the subordinate to his superior is a necessity for a successful organizer to plan his work.[39] ***Communication thus lubricates the entire organization and helps in running the organization smoothly and uninterruptedly.***

(ii) Proper Planning and Co-ordination

Good planning is a pre-condition for getting the task done, and this can be effectively secured only through communication. According to **Browne & Neitzel,** the longer the chain of communications and the greater the number of supervisory levels, the more opportunities there are for misinterpretation and misunderstandings.[40] ***Co-ordination is, therefore, required to be achieved,***

as in almost every human relationship, largely through communications. According to **Mary Cushing Niles,**[41] good communications are essential to co-ordination. They are necessary — upward, downward and sideways — through all the levels of authority and advice for the transmission, interpretation and adoption of policies, for the sharing of knowledge and information, and for the more subtle needs of good morale and mutual understanding.

(iii) Prompt and Proper Decision-Making

Effective communication is the *'sine qua non'* for prompt and proper decision making and its systematic implementation. ***Just as without soul human body is but a corpse, similarly howsoever intelligent and painstaking the personnel of management may be, it would be of no avail unless the top management can effectively communicate*** either the policy or the decision to those who can translate it into action.

LAUGH A LITTLE
THINK A LITTLE

PROMPT & PROPER DECISION MAKING

Here is a story regarding prompt and proper decision-making. Three men — a project manager, a software engineer and a hardware engineer — are helping out on a project. About midweek they decide to walk up and down the beach during their lunch hour. Half-way up the beach, they stumbled upon a lamp. As they rub the lamp, a genie appears and says in a soft voice, "Normally I would grant three wishes, but since there are three of you, I'll grant each of you only one wish."

The hardware engineer went first. "I would like to spend the rest of my life living in a huge house in California with no money worries." The genie granted him his wish and sent him off to California.

The software engineer went next. "I would like to spend the rest of my life living on a huge yacht cruising the Mediterranean with no money worries." The genie granted him his wish and sent him off to the Mediterranean.

Now it was the project manager's turn. "And what would your wish be?" asked the genie. "I want them both back after lunch", replied promptly the project manager.

Source : Not Known

(iv) Maximum Productivity with Minimum of Cost

All prudent managements aim at greater, better and cheaper production. ***Merely a heap of A-grade men, machines, materials, methods, market, money cannot accelerate productivity. For this, management has to sell ideas, motivate the workers to work with a will, and build up high morale in the company. Communication, as an influence process, plays a vital role here.*** It becomes, thus, a part of education, propaganda, leadership and guidance function of the management.[42]

(v) Conflict Resolutions and Morale Building

Most of the conflicts in business are not basic but are caused by misunderstood motives and ignorance of the facts. ***Proper communications between the interested parties reduce the points of friction and minimize those that inevitably arise.*** Management at every work level is primarily charged with the responsibility of seeing that proper procedures are established for sympathetic interchange of information between all parties concerned.[43] ***A group which knows what to do but lacks the will to do it, finds it hard to go in a competitive economy. Similarly, a group which has the will to do but does not know what to do, wastes its energy.*** Hence, by effective communication, a group having *'skill'* and *'will'* to do is to be built up. **Morale-boosting through effective communication creates in all personnel of the organization a strong sense of belongingness to the organization and eventually results in greater productivity and better management.**

But there is a word of caution too. As **Shobhana Khandwala** has aptly put it, communication is not a substitute for good management, but it requires good management to operate it effectively and efficiently.

William R. Kelly,[44] General Sales Manager, Sinclair Refining Company, Chicago, points out that *management relates to communication in five ways.* i.e. Delegating Authority, Control, Set Goals, Measure Results, Motivation*:

First is **Delegating Authority.** A manager succeeds in the degree that he can get things done through his people. ***And delegation is not possible without communication.***

Next comes **Control**. In any workable system of delegation there also must be a measure of control. ***But proper control depends upon speed and accuracy in getting decisions down the line and in getting vital information up the line through communication.***

Third, we must **Set Goals** that are understandable and obviously fair to those who will aim for them, ***and we must, of course, communicate the workers about such goals.***

Fourth, we must **Measure Results** ***and it won't be possible without reasonably prompt information from reliable sources.***

Lastly, the most important and the most difficult function of management is **Motivation**. ***Motivation depends not only on close and continuous communication but upon the kind of communication, the kind that makes people want to participate and produce.***

* ***Acronym :*** **DCSM²**
Mnemonic : Delhi Chalo, Shakuni Mama.

Communication is thus a vital and intrinsic part of management. In a variation on *Peters'* and *Waterman's* concept of *"Managing by Walking Around (MbWA)"*, we might say that management is also a complex practice of ***"Managing by Talking Around (MbTA)"*** the organization.[45] **K. Luderman** is of the view that communication by way of upward feedback helps managers **"Walk the Talk"** in an effective way (*see **Box 1.12***).

BOX 1.12 : UPWARD FEEDBACK HELPS MANAGERS "WALK THE TALK"

Many companies are installing programs designed to increase employee commitment to the organization through various empowerment practices. Such programs create employee expectations that managers will change their behaviors toward them. If such behavior changes do not occur, employee dissatisfactions rise, and employees will become discouraged. However, executives or managers may not be aware that their behaviors are not modelling those required by the new change programs their company is trying to implement.

Executives may inadvertently derail the very programs that they verbally support through the way they delegate tasks, make decisions, and provide feedback to others. Using an empowerment rhetoric is not enough, they must "walk the talk" or recognise that the new company attitudes must permeate their own behavior.

Actual studies show that employees in companies do perceive that there is a gap between a company's quality talk and the actual actions of managers. In addition, the,e have been some decreases in recent years in the degree to which employees feel that their managers really seek their suggestions or even act on those they receive. In fact, one survey indicated that only 18 per cent of hourly employees felt that their suggestions were not ignored.

One aid in getting managers to "walk the talk" is to use assessments of their behavior by others, since they may be blind to their own attitudes. Such assessments can be gathered from peers, subordinates, customers or superiors. Such assessments will not only help change managerial behaviors by providing managers with feedback about their behavior, but will also create pressure to change behavior by the very fact that managers know that their behaviors are going to be monitored.

Source: From **Luderman, K.** (1993) "Upward Feedback Helps Managers Walk the Talk" *HR Magazine*, 38(5), 85-93 [40]. Cited by **H.L. Tosi, J.R. Rizzo & S.J. Carrol,** *Handbook of Organizational Behavior*, Infinity Books, New Delhi, 2008, pp. 373-74.

SUMMARY

'Brevity is the soul of wit.'

➡ WILLIAM SHAKESPEARE

Human beings spend nearly 70% of their waking hours in communicating — 9% in writing, 16% in reading, 30% in talking and 45% in listening. Sounds, signs and symbols are basic elements in communication. Letters are symbolised sounds and words are units of symbolised ideas and feelings. Words have as many as four types of meaning viz., denotative, connotative, ambiguous and polysemic. Despite having so many meanings, individual words become meaningless until they are put into context. Words do not mean, people mean. When many words with generally accepted meanings are used by a group of persons, they have a language. Languages are main vehicles for communication. Communication does more than enable us to survive. It makes us learn 'who we are' i.e. our sense of identity comes from the way we interact with other people. Man differs from woman in communication styles. A range of social needs viz., pleasure, affection, inclusion, escape, relaxation, control etc., we satisfy through communication. How well business organizations achieve their specified objectives depends largely upon how well they communicate with their human resources. Communication is the focal point of executive actions, is central to the control and survival of organizations and is the 'ears & eyes' of management.

KEY TERMS & CONCEPTS

'Most of the disputes in the world arise from words.'

➡ WILLIAM MURRAY

- Communication
- Listening
- Cues
- Clues
- Signs
- Signals
- Vowel sounds
- Hobo Signs
- Denotative
- Connotative
- Ambiguous
- Polysemic
- Abstraction Ladder
- Language
- Sense of Identity
- Emotional Blocks
- PODSCORB
- POLE
- Productivity
- Motivation
- Morale
- Interpersonal Role of Managers
- Informational Role of Managers
- Decisional Role of Managers
- Management by Walking Around (MbWA)
- Management By Talking Around (MbTA)

REVIEW & DISCUSSION QUESTIONS

'Questions clarify the concepts.'

→ **ANON**

Group A : OBJECTIVE TYPE QUESTIONS :

1. Fill in the blanks:

(a) Human beings spend nearly _____% of their waking hours in communicating.

(b) A sign is always _______ and ______ with elements of communication of ______ ______ while a signal is _______ and _______ with elements of communication always _____ ______ ______.

(c) Denotative is the _______ meaning of a word, whereas connotative is the _______ meaning that you attach to a word.

(d) PODSCORB is the acronym of ______, ______, ______, ______, ______, ______, ______, ______.

(e) According to Henry Mintzberg, a manager has to perform ______ types of roles under ______ broad categories, namely ______, ______, and ______.

(2) State whether the following statements are True (T) or False (F) and JUSTIFY your answer :

(i) Cues refer to the verbal indicators that others give to you, whereas clues refer to the verbal indicators that you give to others.

(ii) Dark clouds signal the prospect of sunny weather.

(iii) Under polysemic meaning, the same word means different things in a given language.

(iv) Good communication is the foundation for sound management.

(v) Communication is not a substitute for good management, but it requires good management to operate it effectively and efficiently.

Group B : SHORT ANSWER TYPE QUESTIONS :

1. How does an individual spend his waking hours in communicating?
2. "Our daily contact with other people consists of communicating ideas and feelings." Explain.
3. "Signs become meaningful through 'conditioned' response." How?
4. 'Symbols are merely a map that describes a territory, but they are not the real territory itself'. Bring out the significance of this statement.
5. Find out the consequential change in meaning with shifting of position of the word 'ONLY' each time in the following sentence:

THE MISCHIEVIOUS "ONLY"

- **ONLY** HE SAID THAT HE LOVED HER.
- HE **ONLY** SAID THAT HE LOVED HER.
- HE SAID **ONLY** THAT HE LOVED HER.
- HE SAID THAT **ONLY** HE LOVED HER.
- HE SAID THAT HE **ONLY** LOVED HER.
- HE SAID THAT HE LOVED **ONLY** HER.
- HE SAID THAT HE LOVED HER **ONLY**.

Group C : ESSAY TYPE QUESTIONS :

1. What are the different means of communication? Analyse the role of sounds, signs and symbols in communication.
2. According to Alison Theaker, words have as many as four types of meanings. Describe each of them with appropriate examples.
3. Enumerate the reasons why people don't communicate well.
4. Discuss the role of communication in physical well-being of human beings.
5. How, according to Deborah Tannen, does a man differ from a woman in communication styles?
6. Explain the role of communication in managing business organizations.
7. Fred Luthans opines that communication is at the root of practically all the problems of the world. Explain.
8. Describe, after Henry Mintzberg, how communication helps a manager perform ten types of roles in an organization.
9. Can you exemplify how communication makes you learn a sense of identity?
10. Discuss in brief the importance of communication in management.

REFERENCES & NOTES

1. Marion M. Wood, *"The Give and Take of Communication"* in *Effective Communication on the Job* edited by William K. Fallon, American Management Association, New York, 3rd Edition, 1981, p. 2. Incidentally, such estimate was made by P. Rankin as early as 1926 in his Ph.D. dissertation entitled *'The Measurement of the Ability to Understand Spoken Language'* (p. 43) submitted at the University of Michigan, USA.
2. Beryl Williams, *Communicating Effectively,* Sterling Publishers Pvt. Ltd., New Delhi, 1977, p.7.

3. Charles J. Margerison, *The Art of Effective Communication,* Excel Books, New Delhi. 1st Edition, 1996, p. 17.
4. Prof. S.I. Hayakawa, *Language in Thought and Action,* Harcourt, Brace Jovanovich, New York, 1964, 2nd Edition, pp. 24-25.
5. Stuart Chase, *Power of Words,* Harcourt, Brace Jovanovich, New York, 1954, p. 3.
6. Dr. Partho Pratim Roy, *Anatomy of Tense,* PPR Prakashan, Calcutta, 1985, p. 1.
7. Lydia Strong, 'Do You Know How to Listen?' in *Effective Communication on the Job,* ed. M. Joseph Dooher & Vivienne Marquis, American Management Association, New York, 1956, p. 28.
8. William M. Sattler, *Talking Ourselves into Communication Crises*, Michigan Business Review, July 1957, p. 30.
9. Lydia Strong, *op. cit.,* p. 28.
10. This study of the effect of language was conducted at Pro Deo University in Rome. It is reported and evaluated by N. Cousins, *The Environment of Language.* Saturday Review, April 8, 1967, p. 36.
11. Alison Theaker, *The Public Relations Handbook,* Routledge, London, 1st Edition, 2001, p. 19.
12. Dr. Keith Davis, *Human Behavior At Work,* Tata McGraw-Hill, New Delhi, 5th Edition, 1979, pp. 380-381.
13. Prof. S.I. Hayakawa, *Language in Thought and Action,* Harcourt, Brace Jovanovich, Inc., New York, 2nd Edition, 1964, pp. 173-180.
14. Dr. Arnold E. Schneider, Dr. William C. Donaghy & Dr. P.J. Newman, *Organizational Communication,* McGraw Hill Kogakusha Ltd., Tokyo, 1975, p. 17.
15. Stan Kossen, *The Human Side of Organizations,* Harper Collins Publishers Inc., New York, 5th Edition, 1991, p. 61.
16. Don Fabun, *Three Roads to Awareness — Motivation, Creativity, Communication,* Glencoe Press, Beverly Hills, 1970, p. 109.
17. Stan Kosen, *The Human Side of Organizations,* Canfield Press, Sanfrancisco, 1978, p. 50.
18. J.A.M. Meerloo, *Conversation & Communication,* International Universities, New York, p. 83.
19. Wayne Sanders, *Chances are You're not Communicating*. Supervisory Management, October, 1979.
20. Dean C. Barnlund, *'Toward a Meaning-Centered Philosophy of Communication'* in *Journal of Communication,* New York, 1962.
21. J. Stewart, *Bridges, Not Walls: A Book about Interpersonal Communication,* McGraw-Hill, New York, 9th Edition, 2004, p. 11.
22. R. Shattuck, *The Forbidden Experiment: The Story of the Wild Boy of Aveyron,* Farrar, Straus & Giroux, New York, 1980, p. 37.
23. For a fascinating account of Genie's story, see. R. Rymer, *Genie: An Abused Child's Flight from Silence*, Harper Collins, New York, 1993. Linguist *Susan Curtiss* provides a more specialised account of the case in her book, *Genie: A Psycholinguistic Study of a Modern-Day 'Wild Child',* Academic Press, San Diego, 1977.
24. R.B. Rubin, E.M. Perse & C.A. Barbato, 'Conceptualisation & Measurement of Interpersonal Communication Motives', *Human Communication Research* 14, 1988, pp. 602-628.

25. Koontz & Weihrich, *Essentials of Management,* Tata McGraw Hill, New Delhi, 5th Edition, 1990, p. 366.
26. Cited in Paul R. Limm, *Managerial Communication,* Englewood Cliffs, N.J.: Prentice-Hall, 2nd Edition, 1986, p. 21.
27. Fred Luthans, *Organizational Behavior,* McGraw-Hill, New York, 1989.
28. Chester I. Barnard, *The Functions of the Executive,* Harvard University Press, Cambridge, 1938, p. 226.
29. Keith Davis, *Human Behavior At Work,* Tata McGraw Hill, New Delhi, 1979, p. 374.
30. Peter F. Drucker, *The Practice of Management,* Harper & Brothers, New York, 1954.
31. James A.F. Stoner, *Management,* Prentice-Hall, Englewood Cliffs, 1982.
32. Klemmer & Snyder, "Measurement of Time Spent on Communication", *Journal of Communication,* June 1972, pp. 142-152.
33. Henry Mintzberg, *The Nature of Managerial Work,* Harper & Rowe, New York, 1943, pp. 38-39.
34. Henry Mintzberg, "A New Look at the Chief Executives' Job", *Organization Dynamics,* Winter, 1973.
35. Henry Mintzberg, "The Manager's Job : Folklore and Fact," p. 168.
36. Rosemary Stewart, *Managers & Their Jobs,* Macmillan, London, U.K., 1967.
37. Henry Mintzberg, "The Manager's Job : Folklore and Fact" pp. 168-170.
38. *Ibid.,* pp. 167-171.
39. K.C. Batra, *Concept of Communication in Production Management,* published in The Economic Times.
40. C.G. Browne & B.J. Neitzel, *Communication, Supervision and Morale,* in the Journal of Applied Psychology, Vol. 35, No. 2, April 1962, pp. 86-91.
41. Mary Cushing Niles, *The Essence of Management,* pp. 390-91.
42. Shobhana Khandwala, *Communication in Industry* in The Industrial Times, August 1, 1964, p. 11.
43. *Ibid.,* p. 12.
44. William R. Kelly, *Blueprint for Employee Communication* in Effective Communication on the Job ed. by E. Marting, R.E. Finley & A. Ward, American Management Association., Inc., USA, 1977, pp. 109-110.
45. Fred Luthans & Janet K. Larsen, *"How Managers Really Communicate,"* Human Relations, Vol. 39, 1986, pp. 161-78.

❐ ❐ ❐

CHAPTER

2

COMMUNICATION — ITS MEANINGS & DEFINITIONS

CONTENTS

QUOTABLE QUOTES

1. "Communication function is the means by which organized activity is unified, ... social inputs are fed into social systems, ... behaviour is modified, change is effected, information is made productive, and goals are achieved."

   ➡ **Dr. KOONTZ & Dr. WEIHRICH**

2. "Think like a wise man, but communicate in the language of the people."

   ➡ **W.B. YEATS**

3. "Watch your thoughts; they become words.
   Watch your words; they become actions.
   Watch your actions; they become habits.
   Watch your habits; they become character.
   Watch your character; it becomes your destiny,"

   ➡ **FRANK OUTLAW**

4. "Communication has many definitions — more than one hundred, according to one study. One reason for this plurality is that we cannot always readily distinguish communication from other forms of behaviour. *For example,* is walking through an office carrying a large stack of file folders a form of communication? Is working through the lunch hour a type of communication? The best answer is '**Yes** and **No**.' Though neither action may have represented an intent to communicate (though they easily could have), each may have sent meaningful signals to one or more other people."

   ➡ **DALMAR FISHER**

LEARNING OBJECTIVES

After going through this chapter, you should be able to —

- Decipher the etymological meaning of the term 'Communication';
- Understand the practical meaning of the term 'Communication';
- Distinguish between 'Communication (ending without 's') & 'Communications' (ending with s);
- Examine important definitions of communication advanced by different communication theorists.

2.1. COMMUNICATION — ITS MEANINGS

Communication is a ***'chameleon'*** of a word, changing the colour of its meaning with the speaker or the listener more than most. By the word ***'Communication',*** the ***historian*** thinks of an army's 'lines of communication', the ***civil engineer*** thinks of roads and railway lines, the ***electronic engineer*** thinks of telegrams and telephone lines, the ***sociologist*** thinks of newspapers and broadcasting.[1]

2.1.1 Etymological Meaning

However, **etymologically** the English word ***'Communication'*** has been derived from the Latin word ***'Communicare'*** which has its origin in the Latin term ***'Communis'***, meaning something ***'common'*** or ***'to make common'*** (*cf.* ***Box 2.1).*** Now, when something is made *'common',* it implies *'sharing'*. When we communicate, we share our point of view, the meaning we have assigned to a situation with another person. We want that person to understand in the same way as we have understood it. In communication, it is, therefore, essential that the generation of meaning by one person and attribution of meaning by the other person should be **'common'**. Essence of communication, therefore, lies in the establishment of **'commonness'** by the communicator with the communicatee i.e. the receiver.

BOX 2.1 : COMMUNICATION — ETYMOLOGICAL MEANING

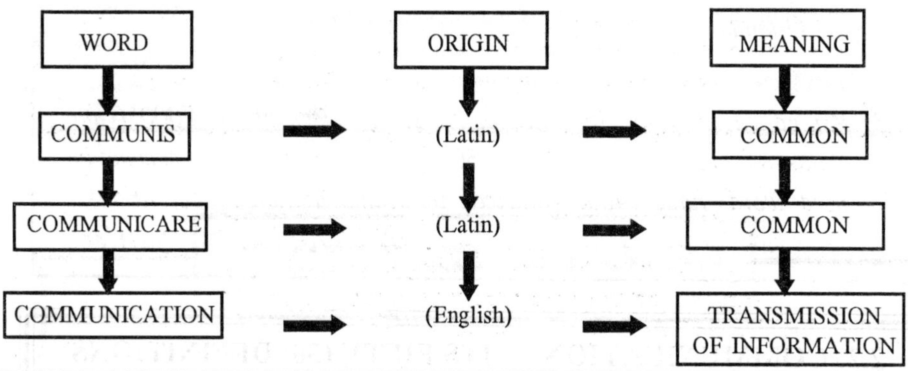

Source: **Great Illustrated Dictionary,** Reader's Digest Association Ltd., New York, 1984, p. 357.

2.1.2 Practical Meaning

Practically, communication is the act of conveying information and ideas. It involves telling, listening and understanding. It is the transfer of information and understanding from individuals and/or organizations to another. Communication encompasses all human behavior that results in sharing or exchange of facts, ideas, opinions or emotions. However sound your ideas or well-reasoned your decisions, they become effective only when they are transmitted to others and achieve the desired response. Communication involves transmission and reception of messages. **Just as an artist uses a brush and paint to depict a beautiful sunset or landscape, so too, do communicators use messages to represent their perceptions, thoughts, and feelings.**[2]

2.1.3 Communication vs. Communications

According to **Brent Rubin**,[3] traditioinally, the term **'communications'** (with an 's' at the end) has been used *when referring to activities involving technology and the mass media.* And the term **'Communication'** (without an 's' at the end) is typically used *to describe face-to-face and written messages, as well as the field as a whole.* **With the growth of communication technology, the two terms are being used interchangeably more often.**

BOX 2.2 : SOME INTERESTING FACTS ABOUT COMMUNICATION

1. *Most people think at a rate of 400 to 500 words a minute but most people speak at only about 125 words a minute. And while writing, the pace is even slower — only at 25 to 30 words a minute.*

   ➡ ***George R. Terry & Stephen G. Franklin***

2. *Animals live without knowing how they live, and they communicate without knowing how they communicate. By and large, so do we. Unlike animals, however, we speculate about how we live and how we communicate. Our better brain and our unique means of communication — language — make such speculation possible.*

   ➡ ***John R Pierce***

3. *An educated adult in daily conversation uses about 2000 (two thousand) words, of which the 500 (five hundred) most commonly used words have 14000 (fourteen thousand) dictionary definitions.*

   ➡ ***William M. Sattler***

2.2. COMMUNICATION — ITS FIFTY (50) DEFINITIONS

The term 'communication' has been defined differently by different communication theorists. Some important definitions of communication (arranged alphabetically) are quoted below:

1. **ALLEN, LOUIS A. :**

   Communication is the sum of all the things one person does when he wants to create understanding in the mind of another. It is a bridge of meaning. It involves a systematic and continuous process of telling, listening and understanding.

2. **AMERICAN MANAGEMENT ASSOCIATION (AMA) :**
   Communication is any behavior that results in an exchange of meaning.
3. **AMERICAN SOCIETY FOR TRAINING & DEVELOPMENT (ASTD) :**
   Communication is the interchange of thought or information to bring about mutual understanding and confidence or good human relations.
4. **BAIRD JR., JOHN E. :**
   Communication is the process involving the transmission and reception of symbols eliciting meaning in the minds of the participants by making common their life-experiences.
5. **BIRVENU :**
   Communication is the process of transmitting feelings, attitudes, beliefs and ideas between living beings.
6. **BITTEL, LESTER R. :**
   Communication is the process in human relations of passing information and understanding from one person to another.
7. **BRILHART & GALANES :**
   Communication is the perception, interpretation and response of people to signals produced by other people.
8. **BROWN, C.A. :**
   Communication is the process of transmitting ideas or thoughts from one person to another person for the purpose of creating understanding in the thinking of the person receiving the communication.
9. **BROWN, LELAND :**
   Communication is the transmission and interchange of facts, ideas, feelings, or course of action.
10. **CARTIER, F.A. & HARWOOD, K.A. :**
    Communication is a process for conducting the attention of another person for the purpose of replicating memories.
11. **CHAPPELL & READ :**
    Communication is any means by which thought is transferred from one person to another.
12. **CUNNING, M.W. :**
    Communication is the process of conveying messages (facts, ideas, attitudes and opinion) from one person to another so that they are understood.
13. **DANCE, F.E.X. :**
    Communication to the process by which people seek to share meaning via the transmission of symbolic messages.

BOX 2.3 : COMMUNICATION DEFINED

'Communication is the process of transferring thoughts and ideas from one person to another.' On the surface this definition sounds good. However, the words 'transferring'

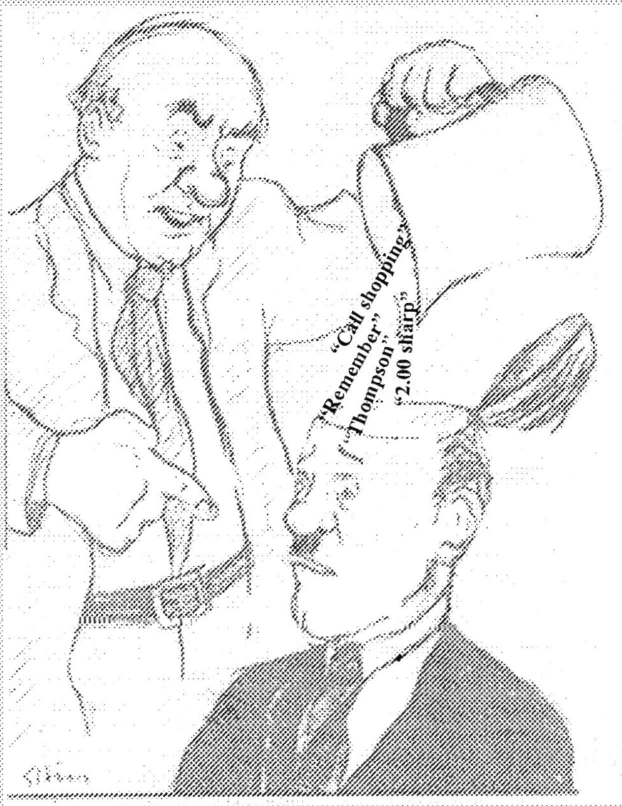

Figure 1.1 : "I'm only going to tell you this one time, Thompson. And you'd better get it right"

and 'from one person to another' inaccurately imply that communication is like pouring liquid from a pitcher. In other words, the definition implies a simple, one-way action where person 'A' takes knowledge from his or her head and simply pours (transfers) it into the head of person 'B' (see Figure 1.1). Obviously, communication is not so simple. Person B may refuse to accept A's ideas and may, instead, wish to present his or her own ideas (give feedback). Or person B may completely misinterpret A's message. According to ***David Berlo****, 'Communication does not consist of the transmission of meaning. Meanings are not transferable. Only messages are transmittable, and meanings are not in the message, they are in the message-user'.*

A more accurate definition of communication would, therefore be : communication is the process of people sharing thoughts, ideas, and feelings with each other in commonly understandable ways.'

Source: **Cheryl Hamilton & Cordell Parker**, *Communicating for Results*, Wadsworth Publishing Co., California, 2nd Edition, 1987, pp. 3-4.

14. DAVIS, KEITH :

Communication is the process of passing information and understanding from one person to another. It is essentially a bridge of meaning between people. By using this bridge of meaning, a person can safely cross the river of misunderstanding that separates all people.

15. DAWSON, TONY :

Communication is a two-way process, involving the sending and the receipt of a message and that one major criterion in the judgement of the success of a communication exercise is whether the receiver actually receives what the transmitter thinks he or she has transmitted.

16. DUNCAN, W. JACK :

Communication is the process of transferring information meaningfully from one person to another.

17. FLIPPO, EDWIN B. & MUNSINGER, GARRY M. :

Communication is the act of intercourse by words, letters, symbols or messages and is a way that one organization member shares meaning and understanding with another.

18. GIBSON, IVANCEVICH & DONNELLY :

Communication is the transmission of information and understanding through the use of common symbols.

19. HAIMANN, THEO :

Communication is the process of passing information and understanding from one person to another. It is the process of imparting ideas and making oneself understood by others.

20. HEDGE, BILLY J. :

Communication can be thought of as an attempt to achieve as complete and as accurate an understanding as possible between two or more people. It is an act characterized by a desire in one or more individuals to exchange information, ideas or feelings.

21. HITT, MIDDLEMIST & MATHIS :

Communication is the exchange of information between two or more people in a way that creates understanding.

22. HUDSON, CYRIL L. :

Communication in its simplest form is conveying of information from one person to another.

23. JAQUES :

Communication is the sum-total of directly and indirectly, consciously and unconsciously transmitted feelings, attitudes and wishes.

24. KATZ & KAHN :

Communication — the exchange of information and the transmission of meaning — is the very essence of a social system or an organization.

25. KELLY, JOE :

Communication is a field of knowledge dealing with systematic application of symbols to acquire common information regarding an object or event.

26. KOONTZ & O'DONNELL :

Communication is a way in which one organization member shares meaning and understanding with another.

27. LEAVITT :

To communicate is to shoot information and to hit a target with it. Shooting alone is not communication. ... To have more than chance probability of hitting a target requires that the sender gets feedback from the target about the accuracy of his shots.

28. LITTLE, PETER :

Communication is the process by which information is transmitted between individuals and / or organizations so that an understanding response results.

29. LUTHANS, FRED :

Communication is the transmission of commonly meaningful information. It is a personal process that involves the exchange of behaviours.

30. McFARLAND, Dr. E. :

Communication may be broadly defined as the process of meaningful interaction among human beings. More specifically, it is the process by which meanings are perceived and understandings are reached among human beings.

31. MEGGINSON, LEON C. :

Communication is the chain of understanding that integrates the members of an organization from top to bottom, from bottom to top and laterally.

32. MERRIHUE, WILLIARD V. :

Communication is any initiated behavior on the part of the sender which conveys the desired meaning to the receiver and causes desired responsive behavior from the receiver.

33. MOONMAN, ERIC :

Communication is the capacity of an individual or a group to carry ideas and feelings to another individual or a group, and where necessary, to evoke a discriminating response.

34. MYERS, M.T. & MYERS, G.E. :

Communication refers to a special kind of patterning : patterning which is expressed in symbolic form. For communication to take place between or among people, two requirements must be met: (i) a symbolic system must be shared by the people involved (*we need to speak the same language or jargon or dialects*), and (ii) the associations between the symbols and their referents must be shared.

35. NATIONAL SOCIETY FOR THE STUDY OF COMMUNICATION (NSSC), U.S.A. :

Communication is a mutual exchange of facts, thoughts, opinions or emotions. This requires presentation and reception, resulting in common understanding among all parties.

36. NEWMAN, W.H. & SUMMER, C.F. :

Communication is an exchange of facts, ideas, opinions or emotions by two or more persons.

37. O'REILLY, CHARLES A. & PONDY, LOUIS R. :

The process that two or more parties use to share information and meaning is called communication.

LAUGH A LITTLE
THINK A LITTLE

A STORY WITH THREE MORALS

Here is a story with three morals :

A little bird freezes on a cold day and falls to the ground. A passing cow drops a lot of dung on it. The bird, revived by the warmth, begins to chirp gaily. A fox appears, hears the chirping, cleans the bird and eats it up.

Moral : *(1) Not everyone who covers you with shit is your enemy.*

(2) Not everyone who cleans you up is your friend.

(3) More importantly, if you are in deep shit, don't make a sound.

Source : Unknown

38. ORDWAY TEAD :

Communicating is a composite of information given and received, of a learning experience in which certain attitudes, knowledge and skills change, carving with them alterations of behavior, of listening effort by all involved, of a sympathetic fresh examination of issues by the communicator himself, of a sensitive interacting points of view, leading to a higher level of shared understanding and common intention.

39. REDFIELD, CHARLES E. :

Communication is the broad field of human interchange of facts and opinions and not the technologies of telephone, telegraph, radio and the like.

40. REILLY, BERNARD & DIANGELO, JOSEPH Jr. :

Communication inivolves one individual projecting a message to one or more others that results in all people arriving at a common meaning of a message.

41. RICHARDS, I.A. :

Communication is the exchange of meanings between individuals through a common system of symbols.

42. ROBBINS, STEPHEN P. :

Communication includes both the transference and the understanding of meaning.

43. SANSFORD, AUBREY C. :

Communication is the process of transferring information and understanding to another person.

44. SCOTT & SPRIGEL :

Communication is the process involving the transmission and accurate replication of ideas reinforced by feedback purporting to stimulate actions to accomplish organizational goals.

45. SIGBAND, NORMAN B. :

Communication is the transmission and reception of ideas, feelings and attitudes both verbally and non-verbally eliciting a response. It is a dynamic concept underlying all kinds of living systems.

46. SIMON, HERBERT A. :

Communication may be formally defined as any process whereby decisional premises are transmitted from one member of an organization to another.

47. TERRY, GEORGE R. :

Communication is a continuing and thinking process dealing with the transmission and interchange with understanding of ideas, facts and courses of action.

48. THAYER, LEE :

Communication is the process of effecting an interchange of understanding between two or more people.

49. VARDAMAN, GEORGE T. & HALTERMAN, CARNOLL C. :

By communication we mean the flow of material, information, perception and understanding between various parts and members of an organization, ... all the methods, means, and media of communication (*communication technology*), all the chennels, networks and systems of communication (*organizational structure*), all the person-to-person interchange (*interpersonal communication*).

Summing Up :

A simple but concise definition of the term 'communication', according to me, can be framed as follows:

DR. PARTHO PRATIM ROY :

Communication is a dynamic, social and continuous process of transmitting, by means of a common system of signs, symbols and words, any meaningful information from one person to another person or a group of persons so as to cause a desired effect in or to elicit an understanding response-behavior from the communicatee.

LAUGH A LITTLE
THINK A LITTLE

WHY DO YOU FEEL TIRED ?

Do you feel really tired of working too much ? Please then listen carefully to what George Bernard Shaw says :

Sayings	*Calculation*
"The year is made up of 365 days, each having 24 hours, 12 of which are night-time hours, which add upto a total of 182 days. This leaves you with 183 days to work minus 52 Sundays, which leaves you with 79 days to work. But there are four hours each day set aside for eating, which adds upto 60 days, which leaves you 19 days for working. But you are entitled to 15 days of your vacation, which means you have 4 days left for work minus 3 days, which you usually take off due to illness or other emergencies, which leaves you only 1 day to work which happens to be Labour day, which is a holiday."	***Total :** **365 days** in a year (Less) 182 days i.e., **night-time hours** @ 12 hrs./day*
	***Balance : 183 days** left for working*
	*(Less) 104 days i.e., 52 days each for **Saturdays & Sundays***
	***Balance : 79 days** left for working*
	*(Less) 60 days i.e. earmarked for **eating** annually @ 4 hrs/day*
	***Balance : 19 days** left for working*
	*(Less) 15 days meant for **vacation***
	***Balance : 4 days** left for working*
	*(Less) 3 days earmarked for **illness/ emergencies***
	***Balance : 1 day** left for working*
	*(Less) 1 day meant for **Labour Day** i.e., Holiday*
	***Balance : 0 (Zero)** day left for working*
	So, why do you feel tired ?

Source : George Bernard Shaw

SUMMARY

'Brevity is the soul of wit.'

➡ **WILLIAM SHAKESPEARE**

Etymologically, the English word 'communication' is derived from Latin words 'communis' and 'communicare' which mean *'common'/'to share'*. Essence of communication lies in the establishment of a *'common'* ground of understanding. It involves imparting the common meaning in another person. In every communicaiton situation, there are two parties viz. a sender and a receiver, who interact within a *'common'* frame of reference. Without a *'common'* background, objective and interest, there can be no effective communication. Communication, thus stands for *commonness* or *sharing* of information and ideas among individuals or groups to create a mutual understanding.

Practically, communication is the process of exchange of facts and feelings, thoughts and ideas, attitudes or opinions between individuals and/or organizations. It refers to the transmission and reception of messages between two parties to evoke an understanding response. Communications (with an 's' at the end) differs from communication (without an 's' at the end) in that the former, unlike the later, refers particularly to activities involving technology and the mass media.

The term 'communication' has been defined variously by various communication theorists. A simple but concise definition of the term has been framed by the author, which is as follows: Communication is a dynamic, social and continuous process of transmitting, by means of a common system of signs, symbols and words, any meaningful information from one person to another person or a group of persons so as to cause a desired effect in or to elicit an understanding response-behaviour from the communicatee.

KEY-TERMS & CONCEPTS

'Most of the disputes in the world arise from words.'

➡ **WILLIAM MURRAY** ***(1st Earl of Mansfield)***

- Etymology
- Generation of Meaning
- Attribution of Meaning
- Theorists
- Organization
- Response-behaviour
- Transmission
- Reception
- Information
- Understanding
- Replication of Ideas
- Feedback

REVIEW & DISCUSSION QUESTIONS

'Questions clarify the concepts.'

➡ ANON

Group A : OBJECTIVE TYPE QUESTIONS :

1. Fill in the blanks :

(a) By the word 'Communication., the historian thinks of an army's ________, the civil engineer thinks of ________, the electronic engineer thinks of ________, the sociologist thinks of ________.

(b) Essence of Communication lies in the establishment of ________ by the ________ with the ________.

(c) Most people think at a rate of ________ to ________ words a minute but most people speak at only about ________ words a minute and while writing, the pace is only ________ to ________ words a minute.

(d) An educated adult in daily conversation uses about ________ words of which ________ most commonly used words have ________ dictionary definitions.

(e) Communication is the process of passing ________ and ________ from one person to another. It is essentially a ________ of meaning between people. By using this ________ of meaning, a person can safely cross the river of ________ that separates all people.

2. State whether the following statements are True (T) or False (F), and JUSTIFY your answer:

(i) Communication is a 'chameleon' of a word, changing the colour of its meaning with the speaker or the listener more than most.

(ii) In communication, it is essential that the generation of meaning by one person and attribution of meaning by the other person should be different.

(iii) However sound your ideas or well-reasoned your decisions, they become defective only when they are transmitted to others and achieve the desired response.

(iv) Like animals, human beings live without knowing how they live, and they communicate without knowing how they communicate.

(v) The two terms viz., Communication (without an 's' at the end) and communications (with an 's' at the end) despite their difference in meaning are being used interchangeably more often.

Group B : SHORT ANSWER TYPE QUESTIONS :

1. Why is communication compared to a chameleon?
2. How do different professions perceive communication?
3. What is the etymological meaning of the word 'communication'?
4. What does the word 'communicaton' practically mean?
5. Is there any difference between the terms 'communication' and 'communications'?

Group C : ESSAY TYPE QUESTIONS :

1. Compare and contrast the definition of communication advanced by Mr. Louis A. Allen and by Dr. Keith Davis. Which one do you prefer and why?
2. Analyse the characteristics of communication defined by Myers & Myers. Examine whether Stephen P. Robbins' definition of communication is the improvement upon it.
3. Bring out the salient features of communication as suggested by Ordway Tead while defining communication.
4. American Management Association (AMA), American Society for Training and Development (ASTD), and National Society for the study of Communication (NSSC), USA have defined the word 'communication' in their own ways. Justify your preference for one over the rest.
5. Analyse the definition of communication advanced by the author of this book and enumerate the essential points embodied in it.

REFERENCES & NOTES

1. Peter Little, *Communication in Business,* 2nd Edition, p. 3.
2. Donald D. White & David A. Bednar, *Organizational Behaviour,* Boston, Allyn & Bacon Inc., 1986, p. 405.
3. Brent Rubin, *Communication & Human Behaviour,* quoted by Ronald B. Adler & George Rodman, *Understanding Human Communication,* Oxford University Press, New York, 9th Edition, 2006, p. 5.

❐ ❐ ❐

CHAPTER

3

COMMUNICATION — ITS CHARACTERISTICS

CONTENTS

QUOTABLE QUOTES

1. "A tongue, five inch long, can dig a grave five feet deep."

   ➡ **JAPANESE PROVERB**

2. "Communication is a process involving the sorting, selecting, and sending of symbols in such a way as to help a listener perceive and recreate in his own mind the meaning contained in the mind of the communicator.

   ➡ **RAYMOND ROSS**

3. "If a wise man were granted a life of abundance of everything material so that he had leisure to contemplate everything worth knowing, still if he could not communicate with another human being, he would abandon life."

   ➡ **CICERO**

4. "You can never not communicate."

   ➡ **R. BIRDWHISTELL**

LEARNING OBJECTIVES

After going through this chapter, you should be able to —

- ❖ Identify three significant connotations in the word 'communication';
- ❖ Understand fifteen important characteristics of communication.

A close study of the aforesaid definitions of communication learnt in the previous chapter (i.e. Chapter 2), both in their individual and collective aspects as also in their true and wider perspectives, transpires one cardinal issue that *communication means all things to all persons.* **Seymour H. Fersh** has rightly observed that dictionaries carry definitions but people carry connotations, and the latter rules thinking and influences behavior.[1]

A simple analysis of the definitions of communication advanced by different experts calls attention to three essential points,[2] viz.

(*a*) That communication involves **people**, and that understanding communication, therefore, involves trying to understand how people relate to each other;

(*b*) That communication involves **shared meaning**, which suggests that in order for people to communicate, they must agree on the definitions of the terms they are using; and

(*c*) That communication involves **symbols** — gestures, sound, letters, numbers and words — can only represent or approximate the ideas that they are meant to communicate.

However, a detailed analysis of those definitions reveals the following important characteristics* of communication (*cf. Diagram 3.1*):

* *Acronym :*	**ND–SOS–MMCI–PTM–AUI–C**
Mnemonic :	**N**ew **D**elhi **S**ent **O**ne **S**MS to **M**umbai-**M**angalore **C**ricket **I**nstitute to **P**lay **T**$_{20}$ **M**atches **A**t **U**ttarakhand **I**ntercity **C**lub.

(*i*) ***Necessity of two persons :***

Communication in order to take place requires at least two persons viz. *a sender* (i.e. a communicator) and *a receiver* (i.e. a communicatee). The sender is the person who has a thought or an idea, which is encoded into a message and sent to the person for whom it is meant i.e. to the receiver. Accurate communication can occur only when both the sender and the receiver attach the same or at least similar meanings to the symbols used for the message. So, communication is not complete unless it is understood.

(*ii*) ***Dynamic process :***

Communication is a dynamic process. It changes with changes in the moods and thinking of both the receiver and the sender of the message. **R. Birdwhistell,**[3] a famous communication theorist, therefore, rightly said, ***'You can never not communicate.'*** Although the statement contains too many negatives to accommodate the English Grammarian, it is indeed true that you can't keep mum when you are receiving communication stimuli almost constantly from a wide variety of sources.

BOX 3.1 : "BITS" OF INFORMATION

1. *Whilst we receive an estimated* ***2.4 million 'bits'*** *of information every minute through our various senses, we can consciously handle about* ***300 to 500 'bits'*** *of information per minute. The remaining* ***2.35 million 'bits'*** *of information are filtered and dealt with at the unconscious level.*

➡ *Adapted*

2. *Half the world is composed of people* ***who have something to say and can't,*** *and the other half* ***who have nothing to say and keep on saying it.***

➡ *Robert Frost*

(*iii*) Social *process* :

Communication is a social process. It is through interaction we reach others and enable others to reach us. Communication becomes the vehicle through which we test out our perceptions and ideas with others. Since man is a social animal and no man is an island, all of us need others and this need is satisfied through communication.

(iv) On-going process :

Communication is an on-going process. It never stops. It is taking place constantly all around us. Information from thousands of events and combination of events, both past and present, is processed constantly by our cognitive structure.

(v) Short-lived process :

Communication is a short-lived process. It only lasts till it is understood and responded by the receiver.

(vi) Mutual exchange of information :

Communication involves mutual exchange of information i.e. facts, figures, feelings, ideas, attitudes, beliefs, behaviours, etc.

LAUGH A LITTLE
THINK A LITTLE

"DECODING" BREAK-DOWN

Here's an excellent example of 'decoding' break-down caused by differences in frame of reference :

A college professor was a member of a particular credit bank. Needing a quick loan one day, she filled out all the necessary application forms and waited while the employee typed the request into the computer terminal. When the answer was received, the employee told the professor, "I'm very sorry, but we can't give you a loan."

"Why not ?" asked the professor, who knew her creditworthiness was good.

"I don't know why, but the computer says we can't."

"What does the computer say ?" asked the professor.

"The computer has typed the words — 'NO LOAN THIS MEMBER'."

The professor then urged the employee to refer the matter to his higher-up. The employee immediately referred the matter to the manager and discovered that ***'No loan this member'*** *meant that the professor did not have a loan. If the professor had already had a loan with the credit bank, the computer would have responded with 'ONE LOAN THIS MEMBER.'*

Source : Unknown

(vii) *Media :*

Communication necessitates use of several means or media viz. signs, symbols, words, actions, body languages etc. Some authorities ascribe '*silence*' too as an effective means of communication.

(viii) *Creation of meaning in the listener :*

Since meaning cannot be transferred, the sender attempts to create a meaning in the mind of the listener similar to the meaning in his own mind.

(ix) *Involvement of potential stimuli :*

Communication involves thousands of potential stimuli. A stimulus becomes a message when the individual assigns it a meaning.

(*x*) ***Purposeful/Goal-oriented :***

Behind every communication, there is usually a purpose or a goal. People may not be consciously aware of their goals as they communicate, but these nevertheless guide actions.

(*xi*) ***Two-way process :***

Communication is essentially a two-way process. The process starts with the passing of information and is completed when feedback is received from the receiver. Of course, it can be one-way too, when the sender expects no feedback from the receiver.

DIAGRAM 3.1 : CHARACTERISTICS OF COMMUNICATION

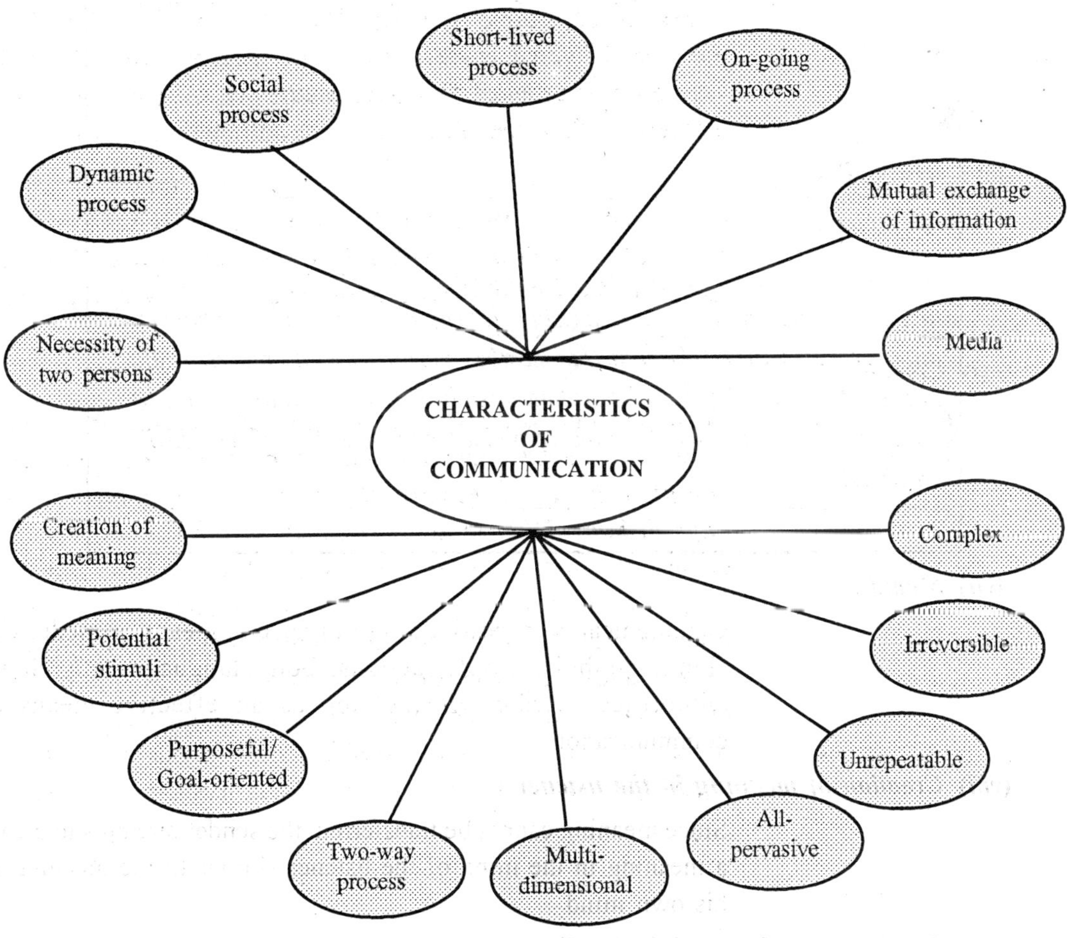

Source : Based on different Communication Theorists
Diagram : Exclusively designed by the Author (**Dr. Roy**).

(*xii*) ***Multi-dimensional :***

Communication occurs simultaneously at many directions and dimensions viz. downward, upward or horizontal, formal or informal, verbal or non-verbal, etc.

(*xiii*) ***All-pervasive :***

Communication pervades all types of organizations and at all levels of management.

(*xiv*) ***Unrepeatable :***

HERACLITUS, a Greek philosopher-mathematician, once wrote that ***"no man can step in the same river twice."*** What he meant was that if you attempt to repeat an experience, the experience will be different — circumstances change and so will you. This is exactly applicable in respect of communication. The same message delivered twice to the same listeners won't have the same experience. Even the same message delivered to two different listeners won't be the same, but will be definitely slightly different.

(*xv*) ***Irreversible :***

Communication is irreversible. The Roman poet **HORACE** rightly remarked, ***"Words once spoken can never be recalled."*** We can apologise for what we have said or done, but in a very real sense, the damage remains.

(*xvi*) ***Complex :***

Communication is far from simple, primarily because it is human beings who do the communicating. ***People make communication complex because people themselves are complex and unpredictable.*** Their attitudes, orientations, perceptions, and ideas get involved in the process of sending and receiving information. People will hear not what was said, but what they think was said. Rarely will an individual transmit completely objective information without adding some element of the subjective.[4] And that makes the communication complex. Various communication theorists, therefore, rightly said, ***nothing is simple or entirely straightforward*** about the ways in which people communicate.[5]

BOX 3.2 : THE ROYAL ROAD TO REACH THE TOP

The one consistent criticism made of business graduates of all colleges is that they do not know how to communicate their ideas effectively in speaking and writing. I have heard this criticism from every executive I have talked with the past five years. The road to the top in any business or profession requires technical know-how, but it also requires the ability to communicate with others.

➡ ***Dr. JULIAN A. McPHEE, Associated Press, June 2, 1957***

SUMMARY

'Brevity is the soul of wit.'

➡ **WILLIAM SHAKESPEARE**

Communication cannot take place till there are at least two persons, a medium, a purpose, and a stimulus in the form of a message. It is a dynamic, social, on-going, short-lived, two way process. It is multi-dimensional, all pervasive and irreversible.

KEY TERMS & CONCEPTS

'Most of the disputes in the world arise from words.'

➡ **WILLIAM MURRAY**

- Dynamic process
- Social process
- On-going process
- Media
- Two-way process
- Multi-dimensional
- All-pervasive
- Irreversible

REVIEW & DISCUSSION QUESTIONS

'Questions clarify the concepts.'

➡ **ANON**

Group A : OBJECTIVE TYPE QUESTIONS :

1. Fill in the blanks :

(a) Communication in order to take place requires two persons, viz. _______ and _______.

(b) Communication is a social process because man is a _______ animal.

(c) Communication is a _______ process because it only lasts till it is understood and responded by the receiver.

(d) Silence also is an effective _______ of communication.

(e) Words once _______ can never be _______.

2. State whether the following statements are True (T) or False (F) and JUSTIFY your answer:

(i) Communication cannot essentially be a dialogue.

(ii) Communication is static.

(iii) Communication can take place without a medium.

(v) Gossip is not a communication.

(v) Communication is reversible.

Group B : SHORT ANSWER TYPE QUESTIONS :

1. Explain whether monologue can be termed as communication.
2. Why is Communication a social process? Illustrate with reasons.
3. Communication is a short-lived process. It ends with feedback. Do you agree? If yes, why? If not, why not?
4. Can silence be one of the means of communication? If so, how?
5. Communication is goal-oriented. Do you then think gossip is a communication?

Group C : ESSAY TYPE QUESTIONS :

1. Enumerate, citing appropriate examples, the various characteristics of communication .
2. "Dictionaries carry definitions but people carry connotations."
   — In the light of the above statement, enlist three connotations you can derive from an analysis of varied definitions of communication learnt in the previous chapter.
3. "You cannot not communicate." Bring ou the significance of the statement.
4. "No man can step in the same river twice." Who said this and why ? Do you agree with the above statement ? Cite examples in support thereof.
5. "Communication is complex." Explaiin the reasons therefor.

REFERENCES & NOTES

1. Cited in the article *"Semantics and the Study of Ways of Life etc."* written by Seymour H. Fersh and published in *A Review of General Semantics,* Vol. 21, No. 2 (June 1964), pp. 133-140.
2. Layman W. Porter & Karlene H. Roberts, "Communication in Organizations" in Marvin D. Dunnett, ed. *Handbook of Industrial & Occupational Psychology,* 2nd Edition, New York, Wiley, 1983, pp. 1553-1589.
3. R. Birdwhistell, *Kinesics & Context*, University of Pennsylvania, Philadelphia, 1970, p. 16.
4. Gray T. Hunt, *Communication Skills in the Organization,* Prentice Hall, Inc., Englewood Cliffs, New Jersey, USA, pp. 32-33.
5. J.A. DeVito, *The Interpersonal Communication Book,* Harper Collins, New York, 5th Edition, 1989, pp. 23-36. Also see P. Watzlawick, J.H. Beavin & J.D. Jackson, *Pragmatics of Human Communication : A Study of Interactional Patterns, Pathologies and Paradoxes*, Norton, New York, 1967.

❒ ❒ ❒

CHAPTER

4

COMMUNICATION — ITS ELEMENTS

CONTENTS

QUOTABLE QUOTES

1. "If language is not clear, then what is said is not what is meant; if what is said is not what is meant, then what ought to be done remains undone."

   ➨ **CONFUCIUS**

2. "Some hear with their ears,
   Some with their stomachs,
   Some with their pockets,
   And some hear not at all."

   ➨ **KHALIL GIBRAN**

3. "There seems to be *six key aspects* to communication. **First,** there is the *communicator* — who has something to share. **Secondly**, there is the *intention or aim* which lies behind the communication. **Thirdly,** there is the other person or persons, the *receivers or communicants*. The *content* or *matter* of the communication forms the **fourth** ingredient. **Fifthly**, the *means* or *methods* of the communication constitutes an independent element in its own right. **Lastly**, the *context* or *situation* in which it all takes place influences the nature and outcome of all communication."

   ➨ **JOHN ADAIR**

4. "The message to be communicated is carried by the three 'v' elements — **verbal, vocal** and **visual**. The words we use make up the **verbal** element. The **vocal** element includes the tone and intensity of our voice and other vocal qualities that are often referred to as the *'music we play with our voice.'* The **visual** element incorporates everything that the listener can see."

   ➨ **Dr. ALESSANDRA & Dr. HUNSAKER**

LEARNING OBJECTIVES

After going through this chapter, you should be able to —

- Identify and define the communicator (sender) & communicatee (receiver);
- Understand and illustrate the concepts of encoding, decoding, message, medium, purpose, response or action;
- Diagnose and explain feedback and noise.

4.1 ELEMENTS OF COMMUNICATION

As our gaze sweeps across the wider vistas of communication, writes **Owen Hargie**[1] **et. al.**, we can observe a number of peaks which define the terrain. These peaks are literally ten in number. They are termed as ten key aspects or elements* to any communication.

* ***Acronym***	:	**CEM–ACC–DAFeN**
Mnemonic	:	**Children Eat Mangoes, Adults Collect Cash; Dogs Ate Flemingos with Nectars.**

All the ten elements are as follows:

First, a *communicator,* in his mind, forms an idea. **Secondly,** the formed idea is *encoded* by the communicator. **Thirdly,** the encoded idea takes the shape of a *message*. **Fourthly,** the message has always an *aim or purpose* to convey. **Fifthly,** the message is transmitted through a proper *channel* or *medium*. **Sixthly,** the message is received by the *communicatee/receiver*. **Seventhly,** the receiver *decodes,* interprets and analyses the message. **Eighthly,** the receiver takes *action*/gives *response* as per his understanding of the message. **Ninthly,** the receiver sends back his reaction to the sender's message in the form of *feedback*, and **finally,** there is the *noise*, the interferring element (*cf.* ***Diagram 4.1***).

DIAGRAM 4.1 : THE TEN ELEMENTS OF COMMUNICATION

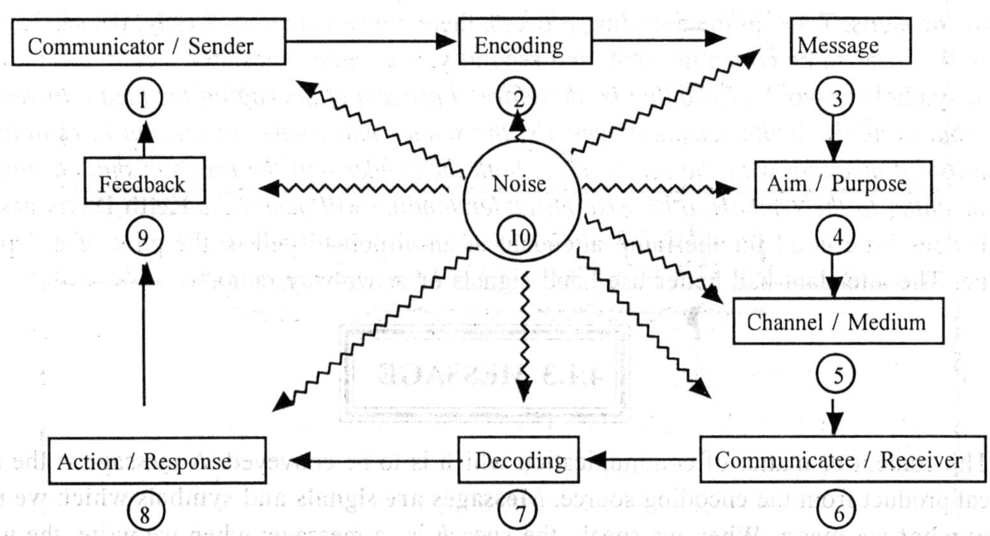

Source **:** Based on **Owen Hargie,** et. al. & also others.
Diagram **:** Exclusively designed by the Author (**Dr. Roy**).

Let us now briefly explain each of these elements in the succeeding paragraphs:

4.1.1 COMMUNICATOR / SENDER / TRANSMITTER

A person who is speaking, sending or transmitting a message. **He is the originator of the message.** He receives a **"stimulus"** i.e. an event that creates within the individual the need to communicate. This stimulus can be **internal** or **external**. An **internal stimulus** is simply an idea that forms within your mind. **External stimulus** comes to you through your sensory organs — your eyes, ears, nose, mouth and skin. You respond to the stimulus by formulating a message — a **verbal message** (written or spoken words), a **non-verbal message** (non-written and non-spoken signals) or some combination of the two.[2] *The efficacy of any communication will depend in part on the quality of the communicator,* **just as music varies with its performer.** *We are not only the musicians, we are also the musical instruments. The quality and tone of our instrument is made up partly from such more-or-less fixed attributes as our personality, character, intelligence, experience, age and sex.*[3] A communicator is the source which may be an individual, a group or an entire organization.

4.1.2 ENCODING

Translating an idea into a code (e.g. written or spoken words or symbols). **Encoding is the process inside the human mind or brain in the form of motor skills, muscle system or sensory skills that translates ideas, facts, feelings, opinions to be transmitted into a series of symbols or signs.** Thus, in the encoding process, there are two steps — **firstly**, the sender thinks through the ideas to be communicated; and **secondly,** the sender translates these ideas into some code or symbols or words. *Encoding is, therefore, a process of packaging the idea into verbal or non-verbal symbols. While selecting symbols, the sender must make an attempt to establish the 'mutuality' of meaning with the receiver i.e. both the sender and the receiver should attach the same meaning to the symbols, otherwise misunderstanding will occur.* As **Keith Davis** has aptly said, it does little good for the ramp attendant at an airport to yell to the pilot of a departing airplane. The attendant had better use hand signals or a two-way radio.[4]

4.1.3 MESSAGE

The content or matter of communication which is to be conveyed. A message is the actual physical product from the encoding source. **Messages are signals and symbols which we use to convey what we mean.** When we speak, the *speech* is a message; when we write, the *writing* is the message. When we paint, the *picture* is the message. When we gesture, the *movements of our arms and the expression on our face* are the message.[5]

BOX 4.1 : PITFALLS OF BAD MESSAGE

While communicating any message, skilled communicators always choose familiar words with concrete meanings on which both senders and receivers agree. In selecting proper words, symbols etc., senders must be alert to the receiver's communication skills, attitudes, background, experiences and culture. How will the selected words affect the receiver? Here is an example:

A Dr. Pepper Cola promotion failed miserably in Great Britain because American managers had not done their homework. They had to change their "I'm a Pepper" slogan after learning that 'pepper' is British slang for "prostitute."

Source : Cited by **Dr. Mary Ellen Guffey**, *Business Communication*, Thomson Asia Pvt. Ltd., Singapore, 2005, p. 12.

Communication messages are usually delivered in the following format*:

(*i*) **Visual** [*written* or *non-verbal*]

(*ii*) **Auditory** [*oral, i.e. face to face* or *telephone*]

(*iii*) **Tactile** [*i.e. relating to use of touch and bodily contact e.g. handshakes, hugs, kisses, etc.*]

(*iv*) **Olfactory** [*i.e. relating to use of perfumes, aftershaves, deodorants, and other types of scent to disguise our natural body odours and project a certain image*].

* ***Acronym*** : **VATO**
Mnemonic : **V**iswanathan **A**nand, the **T**opper in chess **O**lympics.

The message should be clearly worded in order to be easily understood by the communicatee. However, success at communicating depends not only on the purpose and content of the message but also, just as important, on how skillful you are communicating, how well you know your audience i.e. the person or persons with whom you're communicating, and how much you hold in common with your audience.[6]

BOX 4.2 : WINSTON CHURCHILL ON THE IMPORTANCE OF CAREFUL MESSAGE PREPARATION IN PUBLIC SPEAKING

On being approached by the authorities of London School of Business to speak on graduating ceremony of their alumni, Winston Churchill said :

> *"If you want me to speak for an hour, you could approach me one day before the ceremony; if for half an hour, you could approach a couple of months before; but if for ten minutes, I require a year's notice."*

Churchill's remarks insightfully suggest the importance of careful message preparation, especially where time is of the essence — as it is in most business organizations.

Source : Anon

4.1.4. AIM / INTENTION / PURPOSE

The aim / intention / purpose which lies in the sender's mind in initiating the communication. **The sender must know "why" to communicate, what is the basic purpose?** Is it to inform, advise, order, appraise, persuade, propose, suggest, praise, consult, counsel, explain, influence, encourage, motivate, apologise, thank, reprimand, warn and so on. As **Keith Davis** has said, ***'Don't start talking until you begin thinking. Be sure that your brain is engaged before putting your mouth in gear.*** The ultimate purpose of all human communication may be three-fold:[7]

(*a*) To further the common enterprise of humanity,

(*b*) To create and express unity, and

(*c*) To build up the personal lives of individuals.

The overlap between these three areas, ever changing as the centrifugal and centripetal forces press it with tensions, may be what we recognise as true peace, the legitimate end of all good communication.

4.1.5. CHANNEL / MEDIUM / MEANS

The vehicle/medium/means through which the message is transmitted from the sender to the receiver. **A channel is the link between the source's message and the receiver.** Channel describes both the medium and the means used to deliver messages.

BOX 4.3 : MEANS OR METHODS OF COMMUNICATION

The fifth element in communication is the means or methods employed. Mistress of all intercourse is language, followed closely by pictures. These are all marks or signs upon paper or in the shape of noises which we use to convey a concept from one mind to another, to share our apprehension of reality. Within the family of language there is a variety of 'ready-made' constructs to hand, the forms made available by our history: conversations, speeches, essays, books, lectures, presentations and letters. Technology has lengthened their arms in the 'tele-' cluster of inventions, just as printing has vastly extended the range of the written word.

These methods or forms — the earthernware jars which carry the action of our communications — also have a life of their own. They are like beasts of burden — horse, oxen, mules, camels — which are pressed into service yet retain their own strengths and weaknesses. Sometimes, like fractious animals, they attempt 'to put the cart before the horse' and take over. Once, when riding in the Jordanian desert, I found myself on a semi-wild camel, who periodically insisted on bending his swan-like neck to bite me. Methods of communication are like that, always trying to buck you off their backs. The means is always potentially in a state of tension with the end; the form declares war on the content.

Methods or means of communication should not dazzle us by their variety or win us by novelty alone. Like old clothes, some of the ancient forms of communication are still the most comfortable, practical and serviceable. We cannot avoid using some method or other, and they usually involve language in either the written or spoken versions. But there is an area of choice here. We may not be able to choose what to say, but we can select from several possible ways of saying it.

Source **: John Adair,** *Training for Communication*, Macdonald & Co., London, 1973, p. 33.

A channel can be **audio-visual, print-media, mechanical** or **personal** :

(*i*) **Audio-visual** [*television, radio, cinema etc.*]

(*ii*) **Print media** [*newspaper, magazine etc.*]

(*iii*) **Mechanical** [*telephone, fax, e-mail, computer etc.*]

(*iv*) **Personal** [*face to face contacts*]

A skilled communicator will select and maximize the use of the channel most appropriate to the achievement of the goals. **Oral messages** might be transmitted through a staff meeting, personal conference, telephone conversion, press conference, voice mail, or even such informal means as the company grapevine. **Written messages** might be transmitted through a memorandum, a report, a letter, a contract, a brochure, a bulletin-board notice, e-mail, a company newsletter, a press release, or an addition to the policies and procedures manual. And **non-verbal messages** might be transmitted through facial expressions, gestures, or body movement.[8] In general, communication is most effective when it uses multiple channels, such as both oral and written messages.[9] **Marshall McLuhan** popularized the phrase — **"the medium is the message."** Though this may exaggerate the importance of the medium to the total communication process, but many writers agree that it is clearly no overstatement to say the right medium for the right message improves the chances of gaining a desired response from a receiver.[10]

4.1.6. COMMUNICATEE / RECEIVER / ADDRESSEE

Another person or persons to whom the message is conveyed. ***He is the target of the message.*** Like the source, (*i.e.* communicator), the receivers symbolise response and they can be an individual, a group or an entire organization. As receivers, we do not, however, receive the same messages in the same way because each one of us has a unique perception of reality, based on our individual experiences, culture, emotions at the moment, personality, knowledge, socio-economic status, and a host of other variables. These variables act as a *"Filter"* in shaping everyone's unique impressions of reality.[11] ***Our receiving apparatus is like a computer*** in that we bring a store of patterns and readymade interpretations to the work of listening, watching or reading. **Nevertheless, the way in which we interpret information depends upon the *contents of our mental filing-system, our 'stock of labels' or concepts.*[12]** Two people can receive a similar signal and yet interpret it differently. The same people can receive a similar signal later in life and yet interpret it differently again. If the sender and the receiver do not share a common stock of labels, then communication must go astray.[13]

4.1.7. DECODING

Converting the message back to the sender's original ideas. Once a message is received, the recipient begins the process of decoding. **Decoding is the process of re-translation of an encoded message back to the sender's original ideas.** This can involve two steps: **firstly,** the receiver must perceive the message and **secondly,** he must comprehend and interpret it in the way as intended by the sender. **Of course, the ability to comprehend and to interpret information received from the sender is restricted by the receiver's past experience, personal assessment of the symbols used, expectations, language skills, subject knowledge, and mutuality of meaning with the sender.** In general, the more the receiver's decoding matches the sender's intended message, the more effective is the communication.

BOX 4.4 : WHAT IS EFFECTIVE COMMUNICATION ?

Communication is effective when the message i.e the stimulus as it was initiated and intended by the sender or source [S] corresponds closely to the feedback i.e. the stimulus as it is perceived and responded to by the receiver [R]. Communication is whole and complete, when the response intends [S] and the response provides [R] are identical :

$$\frac{R}{S} = \frac{\text{Receiver's Meaning}}{\text{Sender's Meaning}} = 1$$

We rarely reach 1 i.e. perfect sharing of meaning. As a matter of fact, we never reach 1. We approximate it.

Source : **Dr. Stewart L. Tubbs & Ms. Sylvia Moss,** *Human Communication — Principles & Contexts*, McGraw-Hill, New York, 9th Edition, 2003, pp. 21-22.

4.1.8. ACTION / RESPONSE

To put into action the intention of the message i.e., acting according to the message. **It is the initiation of response given by the receiver to the sender's message. Under this step, the receiver acts or reacts to the message he has interpreted.** The action on his part may be to ignore it, to perform the task assigned, or to store and file the message for future reference. According to **Dale Yoder**, the process of responding is recognised as an important condition of the whole process. Modern theory holds that listening may be as important as transmitting (*listening in broader sense responding*). Reception is a process involving positive action.[14]

4.1.9. FEEDBACK

Sending back to the sender necessary information about the action or non-action. **Feedback ensures that the flow of information is actually having a reciprocating effect on behaviour.**[15] *Feedback is what makes the difference between* **one-way communication** (where the sender has no knowledge — or possibly interest — in the receiver's response) and **two-way communication** (where the receiver can comment or even alter events by responding to a message). **David K. Berlo**, while writing about feedback, said, *"How can anyone know that a communication has taken place unless there is a response from the receiver?"*[16] The errors and flaws that abound in business situations are basically the result of a lack of feedback.

BOX 4.5 : SOLICITING FEEDBACKS FROM DISSATISFIED CUSTOMERS GAINFULLY PAY YOU BACK

Organizations are now learning that it pays to solicit feedback from customers particularly the dissatisfied ones. The dissatisfied customer who feels someone is listening to his or her complaints, is more likely to remain a customer than the person who doesn't communicate his or her dissatisfaction. As a result, an increasing number of companies, such as Coca-Cola, American Express, and Procter and Gamble, maintain 800 telephone numbers to encourage customers to voice their complaints.

***Source* : Patricia Sellers,** *"How to Handle Customer's Gripes"*, FORTUNE, October, 24, 1988, pp. 88-100.

To be effective, feedback needs to be skillfully given and the receiver must hear, understand, accept and act upon the feedback. However accurate the feedback if the receiver rejects it, its purpose gets defected. Therefore, always consider the ***'human element"*** during feedback :

H	➡	Hear
U	➡	Understand
M	➡	Motivate
A	➡	Accept
N	➡	Negotiate

The giving and receiving of feedback are skills which require very careful handling. They require courage, tact, honesty, understanding and respect — both for yourself and for others. Typically, most individuals have no difficulty receiving **positive feedback**. But receiving feedback that is negative is generally more problematic. Yet, when you are receiving a **negative feedback**, it is often helpful to paraphrase what is being said so that you can check your perceptions, ask for clarifications and examples regarding any points that are unclear or with which you disagree, and avoid reacting defensively.[17]

LAUGH A LITTLE
THINK A LITTLE

FEEDBACK THROUGH HUMOUR

In the old cathedral at Chester, there is a prayer which captures the spirit of useful feedback. It says simply:

"Give me a sense of humour, Lord.
Give me the grace to see a joke,
To get some happiness from life and to pass it on to other folk.

***Source* : Not Known**

4.1.10. NOISE

The most interfering element that hinders effective communication. **Noise is an element in the process of communication that distorts the clarity of a message.** It can occur at any point in the communication process. *For example,* noise can occur in the form of interruptions while the sender is encoding, too full of static on telephone lines as a message is being transmitted, and fatigue on the part of the receiver while he or she is decoding.[18]

There are three different types of noise:

(*i*) **Psychological Noise :** Perhaps you are distracted as you read this. You may be tired or have your mind on something else. Such thoughts and feelings are called *psychological noise.* It consists of forces within the receiver, that interfere with understanding. Egotism, defensiveness, hostility, preoccupation, fear — all these constitute psychological noise.

(*ii*) **Physical Noise :** *Physical noise* consists of external distractions that occur when communication takes place in a noisy restaurant, or over blaring music or on a loud and crowded street.

(*iii*) **Semantic Noise :** Finally, when individuals have different meanings for symbols, like when a speaker uses a word not understood by the listener, *semantic noise* occurs.[19] According to **Owen Hargie et. al.,** semantic noise occurs when the actual meaning of what is being communicated becomes distroted due to language or cultural differences between the communication.[20]

DIAGRAM 4.2 : BASIC ELEMENTS OF COMMUNICATION

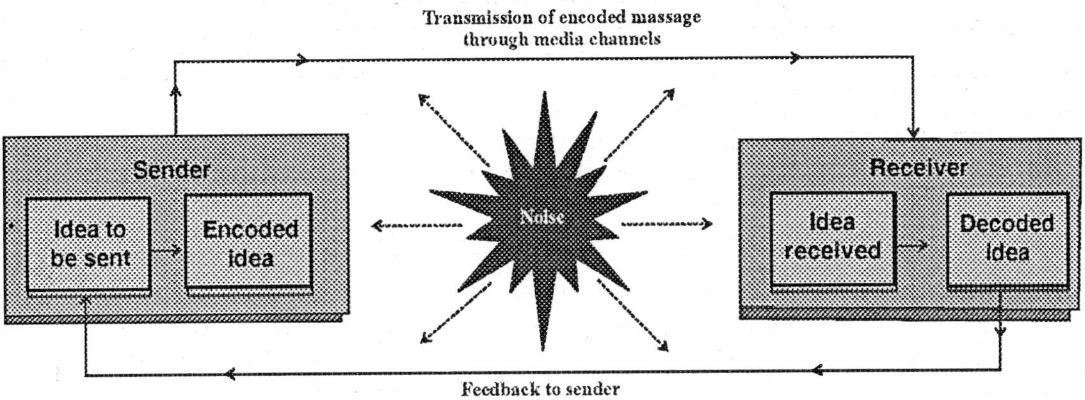

Source **: Jerald Greenberg & Robert A. Baron,** *Organizational Behaviour,* Pearson Education Inc., New Delhi, 7th Edition, 2003, p 293.

4.2 BASIC INGREDIENTS OF ANY COMMUNICATION SITUATION

Condition: In any communication situation, there exists at least the following four elements of communication:

(*i*) There must be a person (= **sender**) desirous of transmitting a message;

(*ii*) There must be another person (= **receiver**) who will receive the said message;

(*iii*) There must be proper **understanding** of the message by the receiver;

(*iv*) There must be some kind of **response** or **feedback** from the receiver's side.

Example: If two persons greet each other with folded hands, it constitutes a communication situation because —

(*i*) There is a person (= **sender**) who desires to pass on a message (i.e. *greeting*);

(*ii*) There is another person (= **receiver**) who receives the said message (i.e. *greeting*);

(*iii*) When the first person folds his hands, the second person **understands** that he is being greeted; and

(*iv*) The second person immediately **responds back** by folding his own hands.

Exception: If a Bengali-speaking person addresses a Marathi-speaking person in Bengali, the communication situation will not arise because even though the sender desires to transmit a message, the message is not understood by the receiver and consequently there is no feedback.

BOX 4.6 : THE BASIC COMMUNICATION CHAIN

Stage	*Process*	*Check points*
ENCODING	Deciding on the message. Selecting the right words. Understanding the other person.	Clarify your objectives. What will the other person want from the meeting? What will be the emotional impact of the message?
TRANSMITTING	Selecting the right medium. Sending the message. Giving non-verbal signals.	Make sure there are no more than approximately seven ideas to transmit. Are words and non-verbal signals consistent? Is the language suitable?
ENVIRONMENT	Coping with distractions. Dealing with distortions.	Avoid interruptions and noise. Is the seating right?
RECEIVING	Perceiving the message. Listening actively.	What phrases, facts and inferences am I looking for? How can I test my understanding of the message?
DECODING	Making sense of the message. Understanding the other person.	What do they mean? What is the *'hidden agenda'*? How will I handle it if it does not fit in with my beliefs?
FEEDBACK	Encoding the response. Starting the next message.	To keep the communication going, nod, smile, agree. To stop the communication, look uninterested, stop eye contact.

***Source* : D. Torrington** and **J. Weightman,** *Action Management,* Institute of Personnel Management, London, 1991.

Conclusion: It follows, therefore, that means of message (*here, it is language*) — whether in written or spoken version — must be known to and must match with both the receiver and the sender. Mutual understanding is, therefore, the most important basic ingredient to establish a communication situation. As **Shobhana Khandwala**[21] rightly says that basically communication is a two-way process and the two terminals should be concerned with mutual understanding if communication is to be purposefully effective.

LAUGH A LITTLE
THINK A LITTLE

WHO IS A SUCCESSFUL COMMUNICATOR ?

A woman was given an opportunity to meet two of the most famous men in England viz., William Gladstone and Benjamin Disraeli. Afterwards she was asked for impressions.

The woman said that after meeting Gladstone she was convined that she had been talking to the most important person in England. However, after meeting Disraeli, she said that she was convinced that she was the most important person in England.

Source : Not Known

SUMMARY

'Brevity is the soul of wit.'

➠ WILLIAM SHAKESPEARE

Communication begins when a *sender*, who may be an individual, group or organization, encodes an idea or thought which is to be sent to a particular *receiver*. A receiver can also be an individual, group or organization. *Encoding* translates mental thoughts into a code of language that can be understood by the receivers. The output of encoding is *message*. Messages are the signals and symbols which we use to convey what we mean. The intention of the message is the *purpose* in the sender's mind for sending it. Sometimes messages contain more than what meets the eye (e.g. *hidden agenda*). Messages need to match the channel used to transmit them. *Channel* describes both the *medium* and the *means* used to deliver messages. The means of communication may include face-to-face, telephone, e-mail, voice-mail, radio and video. Choosing the appropriate media depends on many factors such as nature of the message, its intended purpose, the type of audience, proximity to the audience, time horizon for disseminating the message, personal preference and the complexity of the problem/situation at hand. *Decoding* is the receiver's version of encoding. It divulges receiver's interpretation of the message sent by the sender. Decoding messages accurately is often a major challenge in communicating. *Feedback* is the receiver's *response* to the message. It lets the sender know how accurately his message is understood. *Noise* represents anything that interferes with the transmission and understanding of a message. It affects all linkages of the communication process.

KEY TERMS & CONCEPTS

'Most of the disputes in the world arise from words.'

➡ **WILLIAM MURRAY**

- Communicator/Sender
- Communicatee/Receiver
- Encoding
- Decoding
- Message
- Visual Message
- Auditory Message
- Tactile Message
- Olfactory Message
- Aim/Purpose
- Channel/Medium
- Response/Action
- Feedback
- Noise
- Physical Noise
- Psychological Noise
- Semantic Noise
- Effective Communication

REVIEW & DISCUSSION QUESTIONS

'Questions clarify the concepts.'

➡ **ANON**

Group A : OBJECTIVE TYPE QUESTIONS :

1. Fill in the blanks :

(a) A communicator is the source which may be ________, ________ or ________.

(b) A communicatee is the ________ of the message.

(c) Messages are ________ and ________ which we use to convey what we mean.

(d) Channel is the ________ through which a message is transmitted from the ________ to the ________.

(e) Noise is an element in the process of communication that ________ the ________ of a message.

2. State whether the following statements are True (T) or False (F), and JUSTIFY your answer:

(i) Two people can receive a similar signal and yet interpret it differently. The same people can receive a similar signal later in life and yet interpret it differently again.

(ii) Be sure that your brain is not engaged before putting your mouth in gear.

(iii) The errors and flaws that abound in business situations are basically the result of over-effusive feedback.

(iv) The company grapevine is a formal means of communication.

(v) Mutual understanding is the most important basic ingredient to establish a communication situation.

Group B : SHORT ANSWER TYPE QUESTIONS :

1. Enlist the ten elements of communication.
2. Differentiate 'encoding' from 'decoding.'
3. Illustrate the four types of communication messages.

4. Describe with examples four major communication channels.
5. Describe the basic ingredients of any communication situation.

Group C : ESSAY TYPE QUESTIONS :

1. 'The efficacy of any communication will depend in part on the quality of the communicator, just as music varies with its performer.' Explain this statement with suitable examples.
2. 'Success at communicating depends not only on the purpose and content of the message but also just as important on how skilful you are communicating, how well you know your audience, and how much you hold in common with your audience.' Illustrate the statement with examples.
3. Both encoding and decoding processes involve two steps. Elucidate.
4. What are the "human" elements required to be considered during feedback?
5. What do you mean by the term 'noise'? Describe different types of noises with appropriate illustrations.

REFERENCES & NOTES

1. Owen Hargie, David Dickson & Danish Tourish, *Communication in Management*, Gower Publishing House, Hampshire, England, 1999, p. 15.
2. Dr. Scot Ober, *Contemporary Business Communication*, Biztantra, New Delhi, 5th Edition, 2004, p. 7.
3. John Adair, *Training for Communication*, Macdonald & Co., London, 1973, p. 26.
4. Dr. Keith Davis, *Human Behaviour At Work*, Tata McGraw-Hill, New Delhi, 5th Edition, 1979, p. 373.
5. David K. Berlo, *The Process of Communication,* Holt, Rinehart & Winston, New York, 1960, p. 54.
6. Dr. Scot Ober, *op. cit.,* p. 8.
7. John Adair, *op. cit.,* p. 26.
8. Dr. Scot Ober, *op. cit.,* pp. 8-9.
9. D.A. Level, "Communication Effectiveness : Methods & Situation", *Journal of Business Communication,* Vol. 28, 1972, pp. 18-25.
10. Walter St. John, "In-House Communications Guidelines," *Personnel Journal*, Vol. 60, No. 11, November 1981, p. 872.
11. Dr. Scot Ober, *op. cit.,* p. 7.
12. John Adair, *op. cit.* p. 30.
13. G.C. Heaviside, "The Principles of Communication," *Personnel Management,* September, 1966.
14. Dale Yoder, *Personnel Management & Industrial Relations,* Prentice Hall, Englewood Cliffs, 1970.
15. John M. Pfinner & Frank F. Sherwood, *Administrative Organization*, Prentice Hall, New Jersey, 1964.
16. David K. Berlo, *The Process of Communication,* Holt, Rinehart & Winston, New York, 1960.

17. "Essentials of Feedback," *A Seven-day Leadership Development Course,* Centre for Creative Leadership, Greensboro, N.C., 1976, pp. 77-78, as cited in Phillip V. Lewis, *Organizational Communication : The Essence of Effective Management,* Prentice Hall, Englewood Cliffs, N.J., 2nd Edition, 1980, pp. 157-158.
18. Kathryn M. Bartol & David C. Martin, *Management*, McGraw-Hill, New York, 2nd Edition, 1994, p. 446.
19. Brent C. Oberg, *Interpersonal Communication*, Jaico Publishing House, Mumbai, 2nd Impression, 2006, pp. 8-9.
20. Owen Hargie et. al., *op. cit.,* pp. 16-17.
21. Shobhana Khandwala, "Industrial Communication — Need for a Balanced Technique," in *Industrial Times,* September 01, 1964, p. 19.

❑ ❑ ❑

CHAPTER

5

COMMUNICATION — ITS FUNDAMENTALS

CONTENTS

QUOTABLE QUOTES

1. "Give everyman thine ear, but few thy voice.
   Take each man's censure, but reserve thy judgement."

   ➡ **WILLIAM SHAKESPEARE**

2. "A wise old bird sat on an oak;
   The more he saw, the less he spoke;
   The less he spoke, the more he heard;
   Why aren't we like that wise old bird?"

   ➡ **EDWARD HERSEY RICHARDS**

3. Here's an excellent example how people interpret or perceive whatever they see or hear with altogether different frames of reference — a process known as selective perception:

   Rhea entered into the cabin of her boss, Susan. Susan was busy in reading an important report. After noticing a bunch of beautiful flowers on the table of her boss, Rhea, pointing the flowers on the table, said, "Susan, those I'm sure are fragrant." Susan suddenly stopped reading the report, immediately looked up at Rhea with disgust and asked in a coarse voice: "Who told you I am pregnant?"

   ➡ Based on **STAN KOSSEN**, "The Human Side of Organizations"

4. "If a man has a talent and can't use it, he has failed.
   If he has a talent and uses one-half of it, he has partly failed.
   If he has a talent and learns somehow to use the whole of it,
   He has gloriously succeeded, and won a satisfaction and triumph,
   Few persons will know."

   ➡ **THOMAS WOLFE**

LEARNING OBJECTIVES

After going through this chapter, you should be able to —

- Recognize communication effectiveness is limited to the recipient's range of perception;
- Understand people perceive, see and hear largely what they expect to perceive, see and hear;
- Identify communication makes a demand on the recipient in terms of his emotional preference or rejection;
- Explain communication and information, though essentially different, are practically interdependent.

According to **Peter F. Drucker,**[1] there are four fundamentals of communication *viz.* **P**erception, **E**xpectation, **D**emands and **I**nformation.*

*		
	Acronym	: **PED1**
	Mnemonic	: **P**ublic **E**motion **D**ies **I**nstantly.

These fundamentals have been diagrammatically illustrated in ***Diagram 5.1*** as under :

DIAGRAM 5.1 : FUNDAMENTALS OF COMMUNICATION

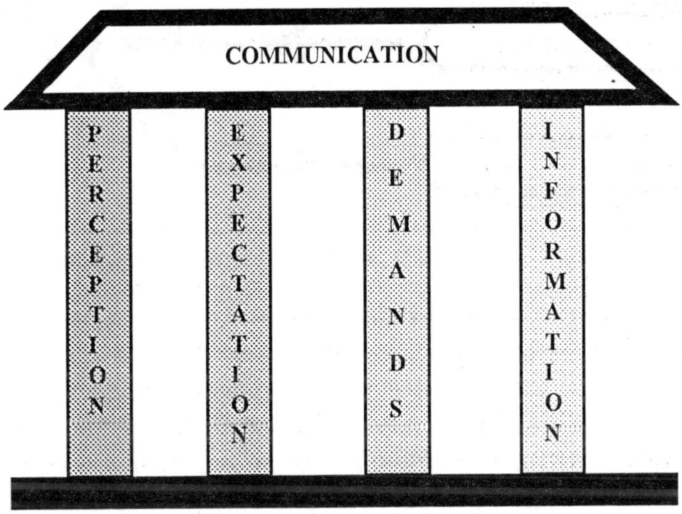

Source : Based on **Peter F. Drucker.**
Diagram : Exclusively designed by the Author **(Dr. Roy).**

5.1 COMMUNICATION IS PERCEPTION

This implies that it is only the recipient who communicates, because if he does not perceive what is transmitted, no communication takes place. The effectiveness of communication is limited to the recipients' range of perception. In **Plato's** *"Phaedo",* **Socrates**, therefore, rightly points out that one has to talk to people in terms of their own experience, that is, that one has to use carpenters' metaphors when talking to carpenters and so on.

According to **Dr. Rue & Dr. Byars**[2], perception in the communication process is primarily dependent on three factors, viz.,

(i) Individual Personality,
(ii) Previous Experience, and
(iii) A Stimulus (*cf.* ***Diagram*** *5.2*)

DIAGRAM 5.2 : PERCEPTION DEVELOPMENT IN COMMUNICATION

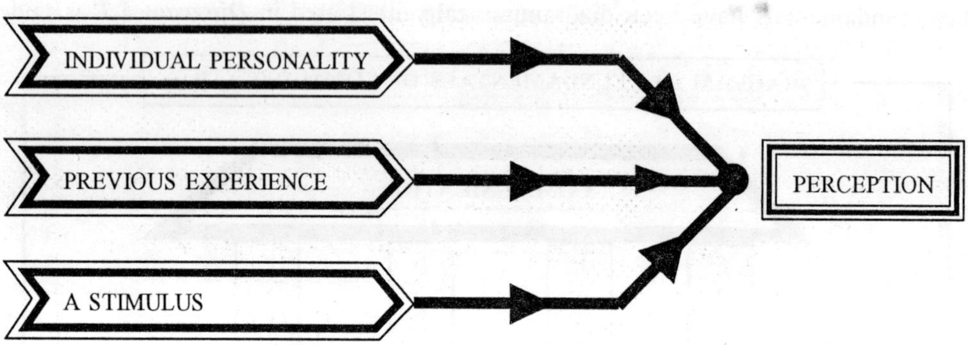

Source : **Dr. Leslie W. Rue & Dr. Lloyd L. Byars**, p. 286.
Diagram : Exclusively designed by the Author (**Dr. Roy**)

The combination of these factors creates perception which is unique for each individual. In perception development, the stimulus refers to the information received whether it be written, oral or otherwise. The individual receives the information and modifies it based on individual personality and previous experience. ***Because of different perceptions, teenagers perceive things differently than do their parents; college deans perceive academic problems differently than do faculty members; marketing managers view marketing problems differently than do production managers; the nurses interpret efficiency problems in a hospital differently than do the physicians.*** In any situation, individuals choose the part of their own past experiences that relate to the current experience and that help them form conclusions and judgements.[3]

5.2 COMMUNICATION IS EXPECTATION

People perceive only what they expect to perceive. They see largely what they expect to see, and they hear largely what they expect to hear. The unexpected is ignored or misunderstood. Before we communicate, we must, therefore, know what the recipient expects to see and hear. Only then can we know whether communication can utilize his expectations — and what they are — or whether there is need for the *"shock of alienation,"* for an *"awakening"* that breaks through the recipient's expectations and forces him to realize that the unexpected is happening.

In the Second World War, writes **John Adair,** more than one commander noted that intelligent soldiers fought much better when they were told what was going to happen. The conditions of modern warfare made close control impossible, and the soldier who knew the plan could use his initiative in carrying it out, even though he was separated from his officers. Moreover, ***it was noted that the simple act of telling men what was the task and the problems involved in it had a profound motivational effect.***

Now-a-days, majority of men and women at work expect not only to be told what they are doing but also why it has to be done that way. In addition, they expect to be consulted much more often, if not about the aims — at least about the objectives and methods of their daily work. ***Managers, supervisors, foremen, shop stewards and work people expect their leaders to communicate with them on a regular and thorough basis, just as they recognize the increasing demands made on them to communicate with others both within and without the organization.***

BOX 5.1 : A CLASSIC CASE OF *"OFFICIALESE"* OR *"GOBBLEDYGOOK"*

There is a story told around Washington about a not-too-bright inventor who wrote the Bureau of Standards that he made a great discovery : Hydrochloric acid is good for cleaning clogged drains.

He got this response,' "The efficacy of hydrochloric acid is indisputable, but the chlorine residue is incompatible with metallic permanence."

Believing that these big words indicated agreement, this not-so-bright inventor wrote back telling how pleased he was that the Bureau liked his discovery.

The Bureau replied with a note of alarm: "We cannot assume responsibility for the production of toxic and noxious residues with hydrochloric acid and suggest that you use an alternate procedure."

The inventor was even more gratified. He again expressed his appreciation to the Bureau for agreeing with him.

This time the Bureau got the message. It now avoided jargons and replied in plain English words that any inventor would be certain to understand: "Don't use hydrochloric acid. It'll eat hell out of pipes."

➡ *Stuart Chase*

5.3 COMMUNICATION MAKES DEMANDS

Experiments have shown that words with unpleasant emotional charges or threats tend to be suppressed while those with pleasant associations are retained longer. In other words, ***communication makes a demand on the recipient in terms of his emotional preference or rejection. It also demands him to become somebody or do something or believe something.***

The urge to communicate is sometimes triggered by a powerful feeling or emotion. If the sender does not communicate the emotional context of the message alongwith the specific content of the message, the receiver is not likely to respond or react in the manner desired by the sender.

For example, imagine a team leader who has just been told by superiors that unless team productivity increases sharply, the unit will be disbanded. Fearing for his job and the jobs of subordinates, the leader announces the need to become more productive. If the announcement communicates the leader's real anxieties about not satisfying top management, workers will respond differently from the way they would if they thought the manager was simply trying to get them to work harder.

The above example suggests another aspect of this problem — that is, a sender must be honest. A common misinterpretation/distortion of communication occurs when a person attempts to say something by asking an indirect question instead of making a straight forward statement.

For instance, a manager is courting communication problems when he or she asks, "How is the postal clerk working out ?" When the manager really wants to say, "I've noticed unnecessary mail delays. What's causing the problem ?" The listeners would be in a much better position to respond appropriately if the manager stated the message directly.

By the same token, the manager is more likely to receive the information he or she is looking for when the workers know what is being asked of them.[5]

5.4. COMMUNICATION AND INFORMATION DIFFERENT — YET INTERDEPENDENT

Information is logical, formal and impersonal, while communication is perception. The less tied up information is with human factors, the more valid and reliable it becomes. However, both these are interdependent. Getting information from the environment is primarily a communication activity. People are the vehicle through which information is processed and transmitted within the organization. They take raw informational inputs from outside the organization and transmit these inputs inside the organization. Processing information means being attuned to what is happening in the environment, transferring the relevant information to decision points within the organization, and then formulating an appropriate response to the informational inputs. Later, the information will be used in some of the tasks, e.g. goal setting, identification etc. ***To***

put it precisely, communication provides information for making decisions. Such information facilitates to identify and evaluate various alternatives.

LAUGH A LITTLE
THINK A LITTLE

THE OLDEST PROFESSION

Three friends — a surgeon, an engineer and a politician — were discussing which of their professions was the oldest. The surgeon said, "Eve was created from Adam's rib — a surgical procedure." The engineer replied, "Before Adam and Eve, order was created out of chaos, and that was an engineering job." The politician said, "Yes, my dear friends, but did you ever think who had created that chaos ?"

Source : Not Known

SUMMARY

'Brevity is the soul of wit.'

➡ WILLIAM SHAKESPEARE

Fundamentals of communication are four in number. Effectiveness of communication is subservient to the recipients' range of perceptions as also to his expectations. People perceive only what they expect to perceive, see what they expect to see, and hear what they expect to hear. Communication also makes a demand on the recipient in terms of his emotional preference or rejection. Communication and information, though basically different, are interdependent in that communication provides information for making decisions.

KEY TERMS & CONCEPTS

"Most of the disputes in the world arise from words."

➡ WILLIAM MURRAY

- Perception
- Metaphors
- Personality
- Experience
- Stimulus
- Expectation
- Shock of Alienation
- Awakening
- Emotional Threats
- Team Productivity
- Distortion of Communication
- Information
- Informational Inputs
- Goal Setting
- Decisions

REVIEW & DISCUSSION QUESTIONS

'Questions clarify the concepts.'

➡ ANON

Group A : OBJECTIVE TYPE QUESTIONS :

1. Fill in the blanks :

(a) It is only the ________ who communicates, because if he does not ________ what is transmitted, no ________ takes place.

(b) People perceive only what they expect to ________, ________ what they expect to see, and hear what they expect to ________.

(c) An individual receives the ________ and modifies it based on individual ________ and previous ________.

(d) If the sender does not communicate the ________ ________ of the message alongwith the specific ________ of the message, the receiver is not likely to ________ or ________ in the manner desired by the sender.

(e) Processing information means being attuned to what is happening in the ________, transferring the relevant information to ________ points within the organization, and then formulating an appropriate ________ to the ________ inputs.

2. State whether the following statements are True (T) or False (F), and JUSTIFY your answer:

(i) One has to use carpenters' metaphors when talking to carpenters.

(ii) Before we communicate, we need not know what the recipient expects to see and hear.

(iii) The urge to communicate is always triggered by a powerful feeling or emotion.

(iv) Nowadays, majority of men and women at work expects not only to be told what they are doing but also why it has to be done that way.

(v) Communication provides information for making decisions.

Group B : SHORT ANSWER TYPE QUESTIONS :

1. Name the four fundamentals of communication.
2. It is only the recipient who communicates. Justify.
3. The unexpected is ignored or misunderstood. Why?
4. Words with unpleasant emotional charges or threats tend to be suppressed. Is it so? Justify.
5. How does communication provide information for making decisions?

Group C : ESSAY-TYPE QUESTIONS :

1. How would you prove that communication is perception?
2. Illustrate with at least two examples that communication is expectation.
3. Justify why a sender, while communicating, must be honest.

4. Cite examples to show that communication and information are different.
5. Prove that despite being different, communication and information are interdependent.

REFERENCES & NOTES

1. Peter F. Drucker, *Management Tasks, Responsibilities, Practices,* Allied Publishers Pvt. Ltd., Bombay, 1975, pp. 483-489.
2. Dr. Leslie W. Rue & Dr. Llyod L. Byars, *Management Theory & Applications,* Richard D. Irwin, Inc., Homewood, Illinois, USA, 1977, p. 286.
3. James L. Gibson, John M. Ivancevich, James H. Donnelly, Jr., *Organizations: Behaviour, Structure Processes*, Richard D. Irwin, Inc., Boston, 7th Edition, 1991, p. 553.
4. John Adair, *Training for Communication*, Macdonald & Co., London, pp. 48-49.
5. Samuel D. Deep, *Human Relations in Management,* Glencoe Publishing Co., Inc., California, 1978.

❒ ❒ ❒

CHAPTER

6

COMMUNICATION — ITS CLASSIFICATIONS

CONTENTS

QUOTABLE QUOTES

1. An old codger and a young whipper snapper are on a mule trip. The youngster is having trouble getting his mule across a creek and asks the oldster for help. The wily veteran grabs a big stick and whacks the mule across the head. The mule trots meekly across the creek. The tenderfoot looks amazed and the old guy just says, "First you gotta get their attention."

   ➡ *Quoted by* **Dr. ALESSANDRA & Dr. HUNSAKER**

2. "Much of the time people spend communicating involves interpersonal communication. But in studying human communication, we are also concerned with contexts in which a great many parties are involved, feedback is limited, and messages are transmitted through such media as newspaper, radio, and television. We are interested, therefore, in the principles of human communication as they apply not only to the two-person setting and the interview, but to small group, public, organizational and mass communication."

   ➡ **Dr. TUBBS & Ms. MOSS**

3. **Pace & Baron** (1973) in their treatise *'The Human Transaction'* has cited a fine example of communication breakdown. He has stated that 'messages in serial production, like water in a great river, change through losses, gains, absorptions and combinations along the route from the headwaters to their final destinations.' A well-known example is the famous First World War communication allegory in which an officer in a trench asks the soldier next to him to pass on down the line of soldiers the following message for headquarters:

   "WE ARE GOING TO ADVANCE.
   SEND REINFORCEMENTS."

   By the time the message has passed along the line, it has become distorted to:

   "WE'RE GOING TO A DANCE.
   SEND THREE OR FOUR PENCE!"

   ➡ ***Based on*** **TIM HANNAGAN *'Management, Concepts & Practices'***

4. 'Knowledge may be power, but communication skills are the primary raw materials of good client relationships.' ➡ **ANON**

LEARNING OBJECTIVES

After going through this chapter, you should be able to —

- Define different types of communication;
- Diagnose special features of each type of communication;
- Differentiate one type of communication from the others.

Communication can be classified into the following seven categories. viz., **I**nterpersonal, **I**ntrapersonal, **G**roup, **O**rganizational, **M**ass **M**anagement and **B**usiness.*

*			
	Acronym	:	**IIGO – MMB**
	Mnemonic	:	**I**'m **I**n **G**old & **O**thers in **M**ulti-**M**edia.

These seven categories have been diagrammatically illustrated in ***Diagram 6.1*** :

DIAGRAM 6.1 : CLASSIFICATION OF COMMUNICATION

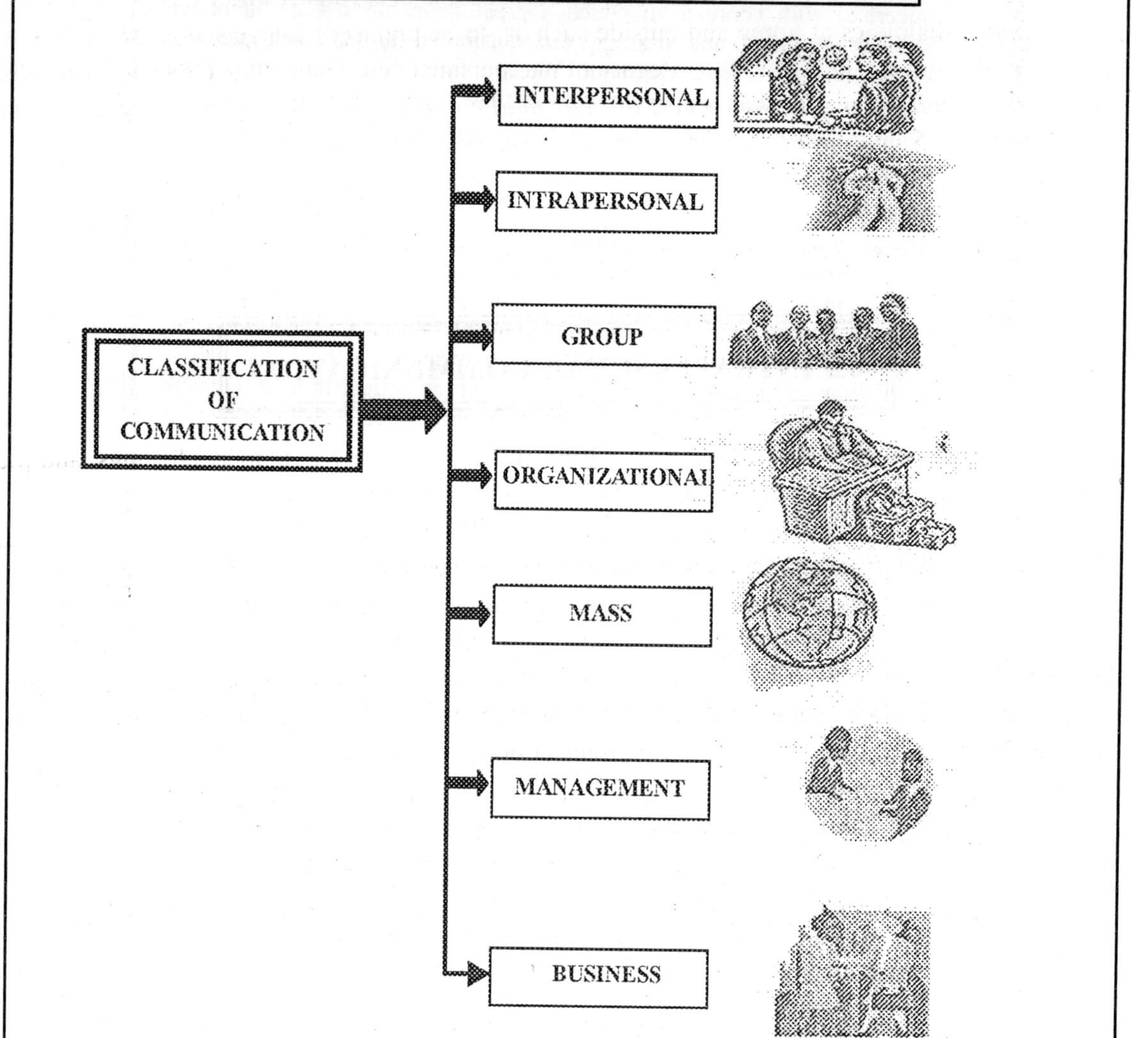

Source : Based on different Communication Theorists.
Diagram : Exclusively designed by the Author (**Dr. Roy**).

6.1 INTERPERSONAL COMMUNICATION

It means **person-to-person communication.** *As an interstate highway runs between two or more states, interpersonal communication is interaction that runs between two or more people.* **The basic level of interpersonal communication is a dyad,** which describes one-on-one communication, but it can include communication among larger number of individuals as well, where all participants interact face to face.[1] Observation in a variety of settings ranging from playgrounds, train depots, and shopping malls to other settings shows that most communication is **dyadic** in nature.[2] **The nature of this communication is oral, direct and behavior-oriented.** *For example,* dialogues at home and outside such as, to be precise, a conversation, an interview, a business dealing etc. belong to the category of interpersonal communication. ***One study revealed that college students spend almost half of their total communication time interacting with one other person.***[3] Some times **dyadic** *communication* (i.e. interaction between two persons) is considered identical to interpersonal communication. But not all two-person interactions can be considered interpersonal in the fullest sense of the word. *The qualities that characterize interpersonal communication are not limited to two-somes. They can be present in three-somes or even in small groups.*[4]

6.2 INTRAPERSONAL COMMUNICATION

It is concerned with **communication within the self**. It involves thoughts, feelings, and the way we look at ourselves. **Diagram 6.2** shows some of the things that make up the self and, hence, intrapersonal communication. It is actually a ***self-talk*** which takes place within a person. *People's self-talk influences the communication with others that they initiate and receive, since attitudes and mindsets have already been formed prior to the exchange of ideas between individuals.*[5] ***For example,*** if a manager believes that workers are inherently lazy and dishonest and need to be constantly scrutinized, this belief system will inevitably affect how the actions of individual are interpreted. Similarly, soliloquies or asides in dramatic works, day-dreaming or reverie, fantasies etc. are all examples of intrapersonal communication.

DIAGRAM 6.2 : INTRAPERSONAL COMMUNICATION

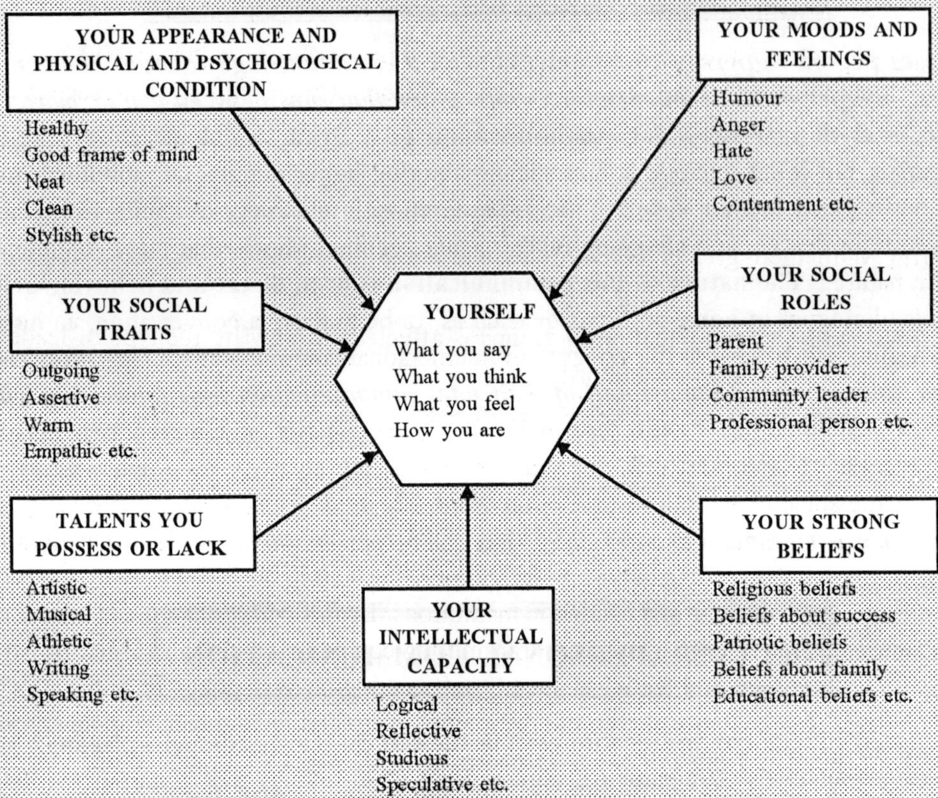

Source : **Saundra Hybels & Richard L. Weaver II,** *Communicating Effectively,* Random House Inc., New York, 1989, 2nd Edition, p. 17.

6.3 GROUP COMMUNICATION

It refers to *communication among more than two people*. It is defined as ***"the process by which three or more members of a group exchange verbal and non-verbal messages in an attempt to influence one another.***[6] Since this context involves three or more people, the degree of intimacy, participation, and satisfaction tends to be lower than in two-person communication. Groups are usually formed, *because the combined efforts of a number of people result in greater output than the individual efforts of the same number of people.* ***For example,*** conversations of members in a family, many people in a committee, or in a club, or among all the students enrolled in a class belong to this category.

Some communication theorists like **Adler & Rodman**[7] are of the opinion that groups possess certain characteristics that are not present in a dyad. ***For instance,*** (*i*) Two or more members of a group can form a coalition to defend their position against other members, whereas in a dyad the members face each other on their own, without support from others.

(*ii*) In a group, the majority of members can put pressure on those in the minority to conform, either consciously or unconsciously, whereas in a dyad no such pressures exist.

(*iii*) Conformity pressures can also be comforting, leading group members to take risks that they would not dare if they were alone or in a dyad.

(*iv*) With their greater size, groups also have the ability to be more creative than dyads.

(*v*) Finally, communication in groups is affected strongly by the type of leader who is in a position of authority.

6.4 ORGANIZATIONAL COMMUNICATION

Organizational communication is defined as *"the flow of messages within a network of interdependent relationships.*[8] This definition fits not only businesses but also hospitals, government agencies, military organizations, and academic institutions. **Leon C. Megginson** has described the process of communication in organizations as transmitting company policies and orders downward; getting suggestions, opinions, and feelings upward; and securing interest, goodwill, and co-operation from all employees.[9] Organizational communication involves sending and receiving messages, the generation of meaning and attribution of meaning in the context of organizational aspects of performance of tasks, meeting the deadlines, fulfilling the objectives, observing the rules and systems. It is an on-going process of interaction among organization members. According to **Wilson, Goodall & Waagen,**[10] *organizational communication is an evolutionary, culturally dependent process of sharing information and creating relationships in environments designed for manageable, goal-oriented behaviour.*

BOX 6.1 : A TO Z GOLDEN RULES TO FOLLOW IN YOUR ORGANIZATION & ALSO AT HOME

A : Always avoid deliberate confrontation at place of work & at home.

B : Before you write → think,

Before you speak → listen, and

Before you criticize → Wait.

C : Cultivate cheerfulness.

D : Don't do such things which will excite the present & harm the future.

E : Every assigned task, duty & job must be treated as worship.

F : Every assigned task, duty & job must be treated as worship.

F : Familiarize yourself with your self-strengths & weaknesses.

G : Give your mind to God and hands to the assigned job.

H : Have always a firm handshake.

I : Improve your behaviour with colleagues, subordinates & boss.

J : Jealously should always be shunned, curbed & overcome.

K : Kindness must always be promoted.

L : Jealously should always be shunned, curbed & overcome.

K : Kindness must always be promoted.

L : Learn to get along with people & to respect others' ideas & opinions.

M : Man must know what he is & what he ought to be.

N : Never think what the world has given you, instead what you can give to the world.

O : One cannot get anything beyond one's fate & before the right time.

P : Progress & develop yourself through continuous learning & knowledge.

Q : Quest always for acquiring & improving knowledge, attitude & skills.

R : Refrain from highlighting others' mistakes & hiding yours own.

S : Sow a character & reap your destiny.

T : Take regular physical exercise to stay fit & active.

U : Unselfishness gets always rewarded — sooner or later.

V : Vice is but a nurse of agencies.

W : X-ray & analyse, examine & solve your problems both at office & home.

Y : You pray to God for success in life but work hard to achieve it.

Z : Zealous pursuit must be imbibed to achieve individual mission statement.

Source : Unknown

6.5 MASS COMMUNICATION

Mass communication is the most formal and also the most expensive. It involves *communication that is mediated.* That means the source of a message communicates through some print or electronic medium. According to **Charles R. Wright,**[11] in *mass communication* the **audience** is relatively large, heterogeneous, and anonymous to the source. The **experience** is public, rapid, and fleeting. The **source** works through a complex organization rather than in isolation, and the **message** may represent the effort of many different people. Feedback in mass communication is limited and not as complete as it is in interpersonal communication.

It occurs when an organization reaches out to its public to achieve its goals. ***For example,*** television, radio, films, newspapers, etc. are the most common instruments of mass communication. Even a corporate web-site can be launched and/or utilized to reach a large intended audience. **Mass communication differs from the interpersonal, small group, and public varieties in several ways :**[12]

First, mass messages are aimed at a large audience without any personal contact between sender and receivers.

Second, most of the messages sent via mass communication channels are developed, or at least financed, by large organizations. In this sense, mass communication is far less personal and more of a product than the other types we have examined so far.

Finally, mass communication is almost always controlled by many gatekeepers who determine what messages will be delivered to consumers, how they will be constructed, and when they will be delivered. Sponsors (whether corporate or governmental), editors, producers, reporters, and executives all have the power to influence mass messages in ways that don't affect most other types.

Because of these and other unique characteristics, the study of mass communication raises special issues and deserves special treatment.

6.6 MANAGEMENT COMMUNICATION

Communication within the management group is called **management or intra-management communication.** It is essential for managers to make sound decisions.[13] **A. Forrest** has identified five directions in which managers must employ their skills — upwards, downwards, across, outwards and self[14] (*cf. **Diagram** 6.3*). Communication is necessary in each of the first four. Managers have to communicate effectively in writing, meeting face to face, and on the telephone with superiors, subordinates, peers and people outside the organization. Furthermore, different forms of interaction will be required for each direction. **An air of confidence** is needed when managing staff, **a more deprecating style** may be appropriate when reporting to senior managers,

a co-operative approach is best with colleagues, and **a professional manner** should be displayed with customers.[15]

DIAGRAM 6.3 : THE FIVE DIRECTIONS OF MANAGEMENT COMMUNICATION

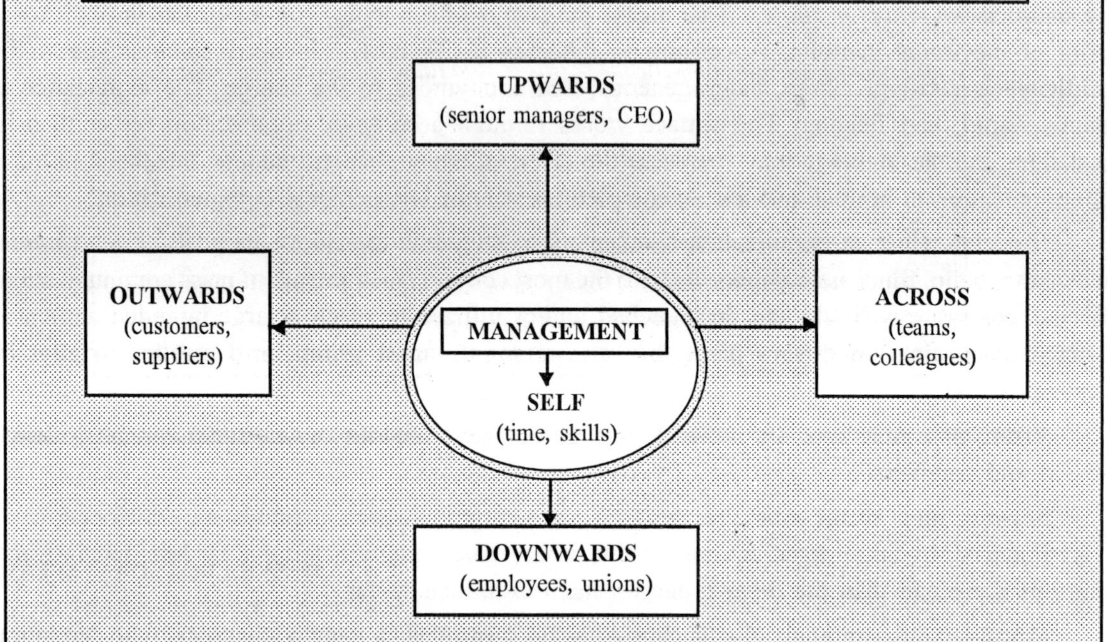

Source : Based on **A. Forrest** & Designed by **Hargie, Dickson & Tourish,** p. 8.

6.7 BUSINESS COMMUNICATION

Communication which takes place in any business enterprise to accomplish business objectives is termed as **business communication**. It is actually not a separate category of communication *per se*; rather it is typically organizational communication having mixed ingredients of categories already discussed. **Business communication as a separate discipline of study is receiving greater recognition recently** *due to increasing complexity of the business structure, increasing need for meeting customer aspirations, increasing demands upon the organization to communicate with its customers, the general public and the vast number of governmental agencies on the local, state and national level.* **Communication is to the business organization what electrical current is to a wiring system.** Communication makes the business organization alive, effective as also dynamic.

LAUGH A LITTLE
THINK A LITTLE

A WORKER & HIS EMPLOYER

A worker who was being paid by the week-end approached his employer and held up his last pay-cheque. "This is two hundred dollars less than we agreed on," he said.

"I know", the employer said. "But last week, I overpaid you two hundred dollars, and you never complained."

"Well, I don't mind an occasional mistake," the worker answered, "but when it gets to be a habit, I feel I have to call it to your attention."

Source : Not Known

SUMMARY

'Brevity is the soul of wit.'

➡ **WILLIAM SHAKESPEARE**

There are different kinds of communication viz. interpersonal, intrapersonal, group, organizational, mass, management and business. **Interpersonal Communication** occurs when you communicate on a one-to-one basis — usually in an informal, unstructured setting. **Intrapersonal communication** occurs within your own self, where you are both the *sender* and the *receiver*, where the *message* is made up of your own thoughts and feelings and where the *channel* is your brain which processes what you are thinking and feeling. **Group communication** occurs when a small number of people meets to solve a problem. Research indicates that groups can solve problems more easily than individuals. Motivation increases and most people seem to learn faster when they are in groups. **Organizational communication** involves human communication that occurs within the context of organizations — for it is people, who do the communicating, not organizations. In **mass communication**, the audience is relatively large, heterogeneous and anonymous to the source. The experience is public, rapid and fleeting. **Management communication** is about the acquisition and transmission of information up and down the line. Managers should possess three essential skills — technical, human and conceptual — to some degree according to their level of hierarchies within the organization in order to get things done through people. And at every step, communication is intricately linked to managerial performance. Managers with good human skills i.e., skill to communicate, motivate, lead and inspire, can get the best out of their people. Management communication is, therefore, mainly conversational. **Business Communication** is a specialized branch of general communication which is specifically concerned with well-defined business activities. It provides an insight into what makes one excel over his/her business rivals and how to build and showcase a positive image of oneself to his/her competitors across the length and breadth of the globe.

KEY TERMS & CONCEPTS

'Most of the disputes in the world arise from words.'

➡ **WILLIAM MURRAY**

- Interpersonal
- Dyadic
- Dialogue
- Intrapersonal
- Monologue
- Soliloquy
- Reverie
- Self-talk
- Group Communication
- Group Characteristics
- Organizational Communication
- Generation of Meaning
- Attribution of Meaning
- Mass Communication
- Gate-keepers
- Management Communication
- Business Communication
- Business Rivals / Competitors

REVIEW & DISCUSSION QUESTIONS

'Questions clarify the concepts.'

➡ **ANON**

Group A : OBJECTIVE TYPE QUESTIONS :

1. Fill in the blanks

(a) The nature of interpersonal communication is _______, _______, and behaviour-oriented.

(b) Intrapersonal communication occurs within your _______ _______, where you are both the _______ and the _______, and where the message is made up of your _______ and _______.

(c) Research indicates that groups can solve problems more _______ than individuals.

(d) In mass communication, the audience is relatively _______, _______, and _______ to the source.

(e) Communication within the management group is called _______ _______, whereas communication which takes place in any _______ enterprise to accomplish _______ objectives is termed as _______ _______.

2. State whether the following statements are True (T) or False (F) and JUSTIFY your answer:

(i) Interpersonal communication is always dyadic.

(ii) Intrapersonal communication is actually a self-talk.

(iii) Group communication believes that two heads are better than one.

(iv) Mass communication differs from interpersonal, small group and public varieties in several ways.

(v) Business communication is a variety of management communication.

Group B : SHORT ANSWER TYPE QUESTIONS :

1. Not all dyadic communication can be considered interpersonal. Why?
2. Distinguish between intrapersonal and interpersonal communication. Give suitable examples.

3. When does a group communication occur? What are its benefits?
4. Management communication is mainly conversation. Why?
5. Business communication is all about business activities. Do you agree? If so, why? If not, why not?

Group C : ESSAY-TYPE QUESTIONS :

1. Enlist different types of communication. Illustrate at least any two of them with appropriate examples.
2. "Groups possess certain characteristics that are not present in a dyad." Enumerate five such characteristics.
3. How does mass communication differ from interpersonal, small group and public varieties? Illustrate with examples.
4. According to A. Forrest, "managers must employ their skills towards five directions." Name all the five directions and enlist the reasons for employing managers' skills towards those directions.
5. "Communication is to the business organization what electric current is to a wiring system." Justify the validity of the statement.

REFERENCES & NOTES

1. Brent C. Oberg, *Interpersonal Communication — An Introduction to Human Interaction*, Jaico Publishing House, Mumbai, 2nd Impression, 2006, p. 6.
2. J. John, "The Distribution of Free-Forming Small Group Size," *American Sociological Review*, Vol. 18, 1953, pp. 569-570.
3. L. Wheeler & J. Nelek, "Sex Differences in Social Participation," *Journal of Personality & Social Psychology,* Vol. 35, 1977, pp. 742-754.
4. Ronald B. Adler & George Rodman, *Understanding Human Communication*, Oxford University Press, New York, 9th Edition, 2006, p. 7.
5. Lehman & Dufrene, *Business Communication,* South Western, Ohio, USA, 13th Edition, 2002, p. 19.
6. Stewart L. Tubbs, *A System Approach to Small Group Interaction,* McGraw-Hill, New York, 7th Edn., 2001, p. 5.
7. Ronald B. Adler & George Rodman, *op. cit.,* p. 8.
8. Gerald M. Goldhaber, *Organizational Communication,* Dubuque IA : Brown, 5th Edn., 1990, p. 11.
9. Leon C. Megginson, *Personnel: A Behavioural Approach to Administration,* Homewood, III, Richard D. Irwin, Inc., 1967, p. 519.
10. Gerald L. Wilson, H. Llyod Goodall & Christopher L. Waagen, *Organizational Communication,* Harper & Row, New York, 1986.
11. Charles R. Wright, *Mass Communication — A Sociological Perspective,* Random House, New York, 1986, pp. 6-9.

12. Ronald B. Adler & George Rodman, *op. cit.,* p. 8.
13. Keith Davis, *Human Behaviour At Work,* Tata McGraw Hill, New Delhi, 1979, p. 394.
14. A. Forrest, *5-Way Management*, The Industrial Society, London, 1977.
15. Owen Hargie, David Dickson & Dennis Tourish, *Communication in Management,* Gower Publishing House, Hampshire, England, 1999, p. 8.

❒ ❒ ❒

CHAPTER

7

COMMUNICATION — ITS POSTULATES OR ATTRIBUTES

CONTENTS

QUOTABLE QUOTES

1. Communicating is the art of being understood."

➡ PETER USTINOV

2. "Let thy speech be better than silence or be silent."

➡ DIONYSIUS, THE ELDER

3. "If your employee relations program is a sound one, if your intent is true, if your people believes in that intent, and in that truth, then and only then are you successfully communicating."

➡ PAUL ARNOLD, ***President of Arnold Bakeries, USA***

4. "Effective communication skills benefit organizations as also individuals. In a recent survey, human resource managers of large and small companies rated communication skills as the most important asset of a newly hired employee – ranking even above education and experience. Similarly, in a survey of 1000 employees, 79 per cent rated communication skills or interpersonal relationship skills as the most important skill set in a good boss. People enhance their own status by letting others know about their contributions, and they help their co-workers by co-operating in achieving mutual goals. A person who engages in clear, helpful communications becomes trusted, liked and respected. Thus, effective communicators benefit the organization, they also benefit their own careers."

➡ Dr. RICHARD L. DAFT & Prof. RAYMOND A. NOE

LEARNING OBJECTIVES

After going through this chapter, you should be able to —

- Identify various postulates or attributes of communication;
- Understand characteristic features of each of them;
- Differentiate one postulate/attribute from the others.

Edmund R. Gray & Larry R. Soneltzer[1] have identified four postulates of human communication. viz., **Process**, **Systematic**, **Interactional** and **Transactional**, **Intentional** or **Unintentional**.*

* *Acronym*	:	**PS–I&T– I or U**
Mnemonic	:	**P**olice **S**tation at **I.T.** hub resembles **I**nferno or **U**topia.

All these four postulates have been diagrammatically illustrated in ***Diagram 7.1***.

DIAGRAM 7.1 : POSTULATES OR ATTRIBUTES OF COMMUNICATION

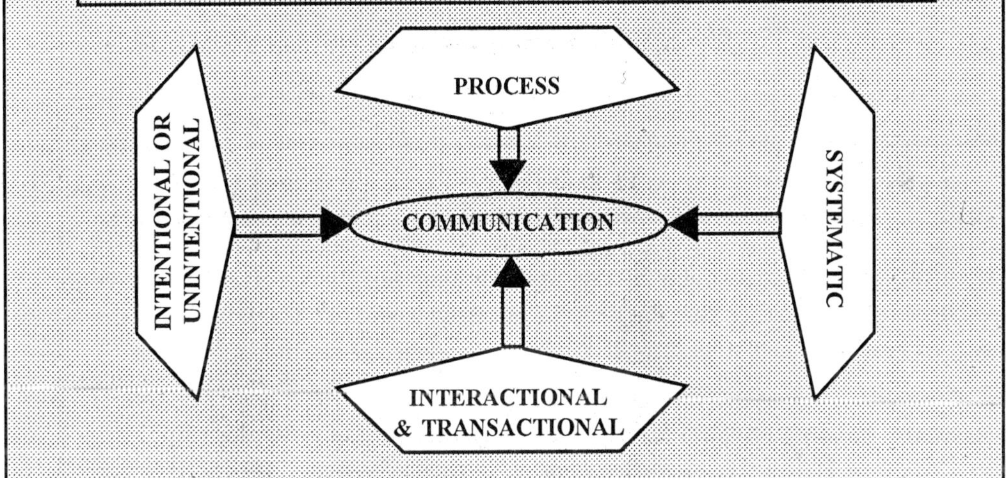

Source : Based on **Gray & Soneltzer.**

Diagram : Exclusively designed by the *Author* (**Dr. Roy**).

7.1 COMMUNICATION IS A PROCESS

The statement implies that communication is **continuous** and **dynamic**. It is **continuous because** it does not have a definite starting and stopping time but rather continues both **verbally** and **non-verbally**. It is **dynamic because** it includes words, gestures, facial expressions, special arrangements, and so on.

7.2 COMMUNICATION IS SYSTEMATIC

The components of the communication process (*viz., a source, a message, a channel, a receiver* and *feedback*) **are interdependent. Communication occurs when the components within it interact and affect one another.** The elimination of any one of those components could either prevent communication from occurring or at least make it less effective.

BOX 7.1 : THE EXECUTIVE'S MOST NEEDED SKILL

As soon as you move one step up from the bottom, your effectiveness depends on your ability to reach others through the spoken or the written word. And the further away your job is from manual work, the larger the organization of which you are an employee, the more important it will be that you know how to convey your thoughts in writing or speaking. In the very large organization, whether it is the government, the large business corporation, or the Army, this ability to express oneself is perhaps the most important of all the skills a man can possess.

➡ *PETER F. DRUCKER, "How to be an Employee." Fortune Magazine, May, 1952.*

7.3 COMMUNICATION IS INTERACTIONAL & TRANSACTIONAL

Interaction is the exchange of messages among people involved in the communication process. **Transaction** implies that the persons involved in the communication process share in the **encoding** (= *creating*) and **decoding** (= *interpreting*) of messages.

For example, an **interaction** occurs when two managers meet and say *'hello'* to each other. If one manager begins to extend his hand, he may be indicating his desire to shake hands. The second manager perceives this *non-verbal cue* and extends his hand. This is a **transaction** because the two managers are simultaneously sharing information.

7.4 COMMUNICATION CAN BE INTENTIONAL OR UNINTENTIONAL

Communication can occur, whether it is intended or not. Given the intent or lack of it, there are **four ways to categorise messages :**

- *A person intends to send a message to another person who wishes to receive it* (***This is the ideal situation***). ***For instance,*** one person asks for directions and the other person gives them.
- *A person unintentionally sends a message to a person who is intentionally trying to receive it* (***This may be termed as eavesdropping***). ***For instance,*** a salesman will watch for non-verbal signs from buyers to determine how interested they are in various products.
- *A person intends to send a message, but the receiver reacts only unconsciously or unintentionally.* ***For instance,*** during a meeting, the speaker may smile to an audience to attract that person's attention. That person may

unintentionally react to the smile and pay closer attention to the speaker's message.

- *Neither party may intend for communication to occur.* An exchange of this type often involves non-verbal communication, such as appearance. ***For instance,*** a person who wears a kurta-pyjama in a sitting where most others are formally dressed is communicating, and the other employees are receiving a message even when they don't concentrate on it.

According to **Dean C. Barnlund,**[2] there are other three attributes tied to human communication. viz., Complexity, Irreversibility/Unrepeatability, and involvement of Total Personality.*

* ***Acronym***	: **C – I&U – TP**
Mnemonic	: **Can Ice melt Under low Temperature & Pressure ?**

All these attributes have been discussed as under :

7.5 COMMUNICATION IS COMPLEX

Someone once said that whenever there is communication, **there are at least six "people" involved:**

(i) *The person you think yourself to be;*

(ii) *the man your partner thinks you are;*

(iii) *the person you believe your partner thinks you are;* **plus**

(iv) to (vi) *the three equivalent "persons" at the other end of the circuit.*

If, with as few as four constants, mathematicians must cope with approximately fifty possible relations, then we, in studying communication, where an even greater number of variables is concerned, ought to expound with considerable humility. **In this age of Freudian and non-Freudian analysts, of information theory specialists, of structural linguists, and so on,** *we are just beginning to unravel the mysteries of this terribly involved, and therefore fascinating, puzzle.*

7.6 COMMUNICATION IS IRREVERSIBLE AND UNREPEATABLE

The distinction being suggested here is between systems that are deterministic and mechanical, and those that are spontaneous and evolutionary. *One can start a motor, beat a rug or return a book. But you cannot start a man thinking, beat your son; or return a compliment with the same consequences.* **The words of a teacher, even when faithfully repeated, do not produce the**

same effect, but may lead to new insight, increased tension, or complete boredom. A moment of indifference or interest, a disarming or tangential remark, leave indelible traces.

7.7 COMMUNICATION INVOLVES THE TOTAL PERSONALITY

Despite all efforts to divide body and mind, reason and emotion, thought and action, meanings continue to be generated by the whole organism. *This is not to say that some messages do not produce greater or lesser dissonance, or shallower or deeper effects on the personality; it is only to hold that eventually every fact, conclusion, guilt, or enthusiasm must somehow be accommodated by the entire personality.* **The deeper the involvement produced by any communication, the sooner and more pervasive its effects upon behaviour.**[3]

LAUGH A LITTLE THINK A LITTLE

COMPUTER — WHETHER MASCULINE OR FEMININE ?

In a language class, there arises a confusion as to whether the word 'computer' is a masculine or feminine gender. The teacher did not know the right answer. So, for fun she split the class into two groups by gender, and asked both the groups to decide the gender of computer citing four reasons supporting the decision.

The men's group decided that computers should definitely be of the feminine gender because —

(a) No one but their creator understands their internal logic.

(b) The native language they use to communicate with other computers is incomprehensible to everyone else.

(c) Even the smallest mistakes are stored in long-term memory for possible later retrieval.

(d) As soon as you make a commitment to one, you find yourself spending half your pay cheque on accessories for it.

The women's group, however, concluded that computers should be masculine because —

(i) In order to get their attention, you have to turn them on.

(ii) They have a lot of data, but are still clueless.

(iii) *They are supposed to help you solve problems, but half the time they are the problem.*

(iv) *As soon as you commit to one, you realize that if you'd waited a little longer, you could have gotten a better model.*

However, the women won.

Source : The Times of India, Pune Edition. 'Gag Bag' Column, December 16, 2001.

SUMMARY

'Brevity is the soul of wit.'

➡ WILLIAM SHAKESPEARE

According to communication theorists, there are in all seven postulates or attributes of communication. Communication is a continuous and dynamic process. It changes with changes in the moods and thinking of both receivers and senders. It is systematic in that the elimination of any element of communication makes communication ineffective. It is both interactional and transactional, intentional or unintentional. Communication is complex. It is also irreversible and unrepeatable. And finally, communication involves total personality. The deeper the involvement produced by any communication, the sooner and more pervasive its effects upon behaviour.

KEY TERMS & CONCEPTS

'Most of the disputes in the world arise from words.'

➡ WILLIAM MURRAY

- Communication Process
- Interactional
- Transactional
- Intentional
- Eavesdropping
- Irreversible
- Unrepeatable
- Evolutionary
- Personality
- Pervasive

REVIEW & DISCUSSION QUESTIONS

'Questions clarify the concepts.'

➡ ANON

Group A : OBJECTIVE TYPE QUESTIONS :

1. Fill in the blanks :

(a) Communication is a _______ and _______ process.

(b) The elimination of any one of the components of communication could either _______ communication from _______ or at least make it less _______.

(c) Transaction implies that the persons involved in the communication process share in the _______ and _______ of messages.

(d) Whenever there is _______, there are at least _______ people involved.

(e) One can start a motor, beat a rug or return a book. But you can't start a man _______, beat your _______, or return a _______ with the same consequences.

2. State whether the following statements are True (T) or False (F) and JUSTIFY your answer :

(i) Interaction is the exchange of messages among people involved in the communication process.

(ii) As soon as you move one step up from the bottom, your effectiveness depends on your ability to reach others through the spoken or the written word.

(iii) A salesman never watches for non-verbal signs from buyers to determine how interested they are in various products.

(iv) A moment of indifference or interest, a disarming or tangential remark leave indelible traces.

(v) The deeper the involvement produced by any communication, the sooner and more pervasive its effects upon behaviour.

Group B: SHORT ANSWER TYPE QUESTIONS :

1. Name the four postulates of human communication.
2. What does it mean when we say that communication is a process?
3. How would you prove that communication is systematic ?
4. *"Communication is both interactional and transactional."* Elucidate the statement with examples.
5. *"Communication involves the total personality."* Substantiate the view.

Group C: ESSAY TYPE QUESTIONS :

1. How many ways are there to categorise messages? Describe each of them in details
2. Dean C. Barnlund has prescribed three more attributes to human communication What are they? Write a brief note on each of them.
3. Prove that communication can be intentional or unintentional.
4. *"Communication is irreversible and unrepeatable."* Justify.
5. Do you think communication is complex? If yes, cite reasons therefor.

REFERENCES & NOTES

1. Edmund R. Gray & Larry R. Soneltzer, *Management — The Competitive Edge,* Macmillan Publishing Co., New York, pp. 545-546.
2. D.C. Barnlund, "Toward a Meeting-Centred Philosophy of Communication", *Journal of Communication,* 11 (1962), pp. 198-202, reprinted in K. Giffin & B.R. Patton, eds. *Basic Readings in Interpersonal Communication,* New York, pp. 9-10.
3. *Ibid*.

❒ ❒ ❒

CHAPTER

8

COMMUNICATION — ITS LEVELS

CONTENTS

QUOTABLE QUOTES

1. An organization that lacks communication is like a football team without a quarterback — no one knows what the play is or when to start moving."

➡ DAVID D. VANFLEET

2. "A critic is a legless man who teaches running."

➡ CHANNING POLLOCK

3. "Listen to a story about empowering. These were four people named **EVERYBODY, SOMEBODY, ANYBODY** and **NOBODY**. There was an important job to be done and **EVERYBODY** was sure that **SOMEBODY** would do it. **ANYBODY** could have done it but **NOBODY** did it. **SOMEBODY** got angry about that, because it was **EVERYBODY's** job. **EVERYBODY** thought **ANYBODY** could do it but **NOBODY** realized that **EVERYBODY** wouldn't do it. It ended up that **EVERYBODY** blamed **SOMEBODY** when **NOBODY** did what **ANYBODY** could have done!"

➡ ANON

4. "The influence an executive has with other executives is partly a matter of his position in the hierarchy, partly a question of his competence, and partly dependent upon a complete and sensitised communication system."

➡ DIMOCK

LEARNING OBJECTIVES

After going through this chapter, you should be able to —

- Define and identify different levels of communication;
- Understand basic natures of each of them;
- Diagnose distinguishing features of each of the levels of communication;
- Practice more uses of the best level in your day-to-day communication.

There are four levels of communication.[1] They are Conventional, Exploratory, Participative and Conformative*.

* ***Acronym*** : **CEPC**
Mnemonic : **Come & Eat Pizza & Cola.**

All the four levels have been diagrammatically illustrated in ***Diagram 8.1.***

DIAGRAM 8.1 : LEVELS OF COMMUNICATION

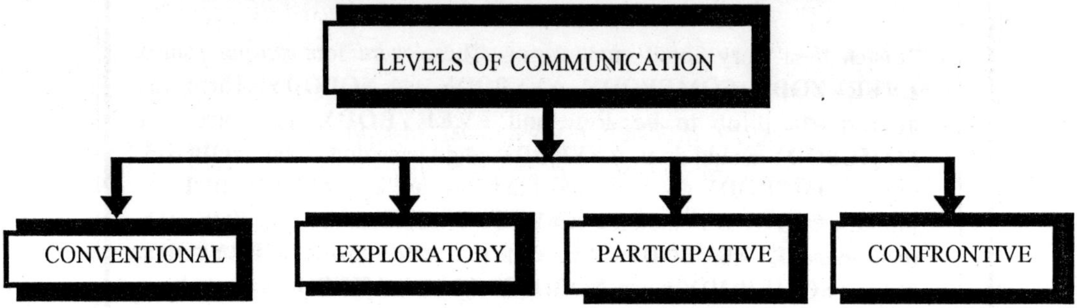

Source : Based on **Dr. C.B. Mamoria.**
Diagram : Exclusively designed by the Author (**Dr. Roy**).

8.1 THE CONVENTIONAL LEVEL

Communication at this level is fairly impersonal, as with strangers and casual acquaintances. Remarks like *"Hello, how are you ?", "Good morning, Sir"* etc. are conventional attempts to be polite or to get acquainted, to fill silences, or to seek or convey incidental information.

BOX 8.1 : A SENIOR MANAGER SPEAKS

Management cultures are changing. In order to be a fast moving company today, you have to be a people company. The old concept of "Familiarity breeds contempt" is long gone. People are expected to work harder than ever before so they need to be supported by management. I believe strongly in the importance of making staff feel valued. In the end of the day, they are the people making it happen, not the directors sitting in their ivory towers. If your staff are happy and motivated, they will do a better job and customers will be happy. In the end of the day, we are a business and we need to show growth and profitability.......... I have worked for companies where staff were in awe of management and spent most of their working day stressed out about their jobs or worried about their future because they didn't know what was going on. Cable Tel's approach is very informal and refreshing. A combination of focusing on the customer by focusing on each other. ***Communication is key to good management****........... The communication must be a two-way thing; that's why we have initiatives like breakfast with the boss. Once a month we pick eight people at random to go for breakfast and just talk about how the company is doing, how they are doing and what the company should be doing. Our associates (staff) are the people at the coal face. They are the ones that know if something is wrong and management need to get this feedback. At the same time if an associate has a problem with some part of his or her role, it is an opportunity to discuss it and get it fixed.......... Yes, we have a budget for our initiatives, but it is directly related to our success. I am not sitting here throwing money at schemes just for the sake of it......... In any case it doesn't cost a lot to take the time to know your staff by their first names and to take an interest in their well being, which is the main thrust of our approach.*

Source **: Owen Lamont**, Managing Director, Cable Tel, interviewed by **Jacqui Quinn** in *News Letter*, October 7, 1997, Business Section, p.3.

8.2 THE EXPLORATORY LEVEL

Communication at this level, though usually impersonal, is basically fact and problem-oriented. Discussions about things, people, theories, definitions, accidents as also classroom lectures fall into this level.

8.3 THE PARTICIPATIVE LEVEL

At this level people talk about themselves and engage in self-disclosure. By the term **'self-disclosure'** here we mean *'intentionally making known information about oneself.'* A variety of research studies, pioneered by **G.J. Chelune**[2], et al., links self-disclosure with intimacy and marital satisfaction. A recent analysis of disclosure studies conducted by **Kathryn Dindia**[3] confirms that *self-dsiclosure causes liking, liking causes self-disclosure, and that self-dsiclosure is reciprocal.* **However, at the participative level, people express their own feelings, describe their own experiences and discuss their own ideas.** Though these are personal subjects, they are expressed in a fairly safe way: *"I feel happiest with people of my own age."*

LAUGH A LITTLE
THINK A LITTLE

ONE METER OR TWO METERS ?

In exchange for some U.S.-controlled land in West Germany, the German government agreed to construct a new facility at another military installation controlled by the U.S. army. After the preliminary drawings were completed, a meeting was held with the German and the American engineers and one translator. When a German engineer asked a question, the translator repeated the question in English; the American's answer was then translated back into German.

A German asked a question about the maximum distance allowed between two points he indicated in the drawing. The question was translated and an American engineer quickly raised his hand with his index finger pointing upward and answered "one meter." The translator, thinking no translation was necessary, remained silent. The German engineers wrote two meters in their notes; the Americans wrote one meter.

The funny thing in the issue is the socio-cultural diversity. Whereas the Americans, when using fingers to show a number, begin counting with the index finger as number one, the Germans do the same with the thumb as number one. Therefore, the index finger, being the second finger from the thumb, was considered by the Germans as the number two. Hence, the difference in their notings.

Source : Based on **Cheryl Hamilton & Cordell Parker,** *Communicating for Results,* Wadswords Publishing Co., Bolmont, California, 2nd Edition, 1987, p. 9.

8.4 THE CONFRONTIVE LEVEL

Communication at this level reveals intimate relationships between people. 'Intimacy' has been defined by **Sternberg**[4] as *'feelings that promote closeness, bondedness, and connectedness'.* Intimate relationships have at their centre a mutual process like finely choreographed dancers in which a balance of movement of sharing occurs. Such intimate relationship does arise out of deeply-felt mutual understanding, but is at times fraught with risk. **This type of communication is rare in organizations** *but it is common among close friends, lovers and married couples.*

BOX 8.2 : BALANCE YOUR BUDGET — REACH IN, REACH OUT

Many corporate executives invest all their time and effort in pursuing their careers and climbing the professional ladder. When they reach the summit, however, most realize it wasn't really worth all the toil. ***They discover that their victory is empty and that they won it at an irreparable loss to their health, family and psyche :*** *incurring obesity, heart disease and fatigue on the physiological front; separated spouse, estranged children and uncared - for parents on the* ***familial front;*** *frustration, depression and stress on the* ***psysio-psychological front.*** *In the U.S.A., Canada, China and Japan, this phenomenon has resulted in a tragic burgeoning of suicides and cardio-vascular and cancer-related deaths.* ***The Royal Bank of Canada*** *devoted one of its monthly letters to this problem with the title "LET's SLOW DOWN." 'We are victims of mounting tension', it enunciated. 'We have difficulty in relaxing : we are not living fully.'*

➡ **SADHU VISHWAMURTIDAS**

Source **:** The Times of India, Pune Edition, March 01, 2002.

SUMMARY

'Brevity is the soul of wit.'

➡ **WILLIAM SHAKESPEARE**

There are four levels of communication viz., conventional, exploratory, participative and confrontive. At the conventional level, communication is usually impersonal, whereas at the exploratory level, communication is basically fact and problem oriented. People divulge personal subjects a bit safely at the participative level while they boldly bring face-to-face intimate relationships at the confrontive level.

KEY TERMS & CONCEPTS

'Most of the disputes in the world arise from words.'

➡ **WILLIAM MURRAY**

- Conventional level
- Impersonal
- Casual acquaintance
- Exploratory level
- Problem-oriented
- Participative level
- Self-disclosure
- Personal
- Confrontive level
- Mutual understanding

REVIEW & DISCUSSION QUESTIONS

'Questions clarify the concepts.'

➡ ANON

Group A : OBJECTIVE TYPE QUESTIONS :

1. Fill in the blanks :

(a) Communication at the ________ level is fairly impersonal.

(b) Communication at the ________ level is basically fact and ________.

(c) People talk about themselves and engage in ________ at the ________ level.

(d) Communication at the ________ level reveals ________ relationships between people arising out of deeply-felt ________ ________.

(e) The confrontive level of communication is rare in organization but it is common among close ________, ________ and ________ ________.

2. State whether the following statements are True (T) or False (F) and JUSTIFY your answer:

(i) According to communication technology, levels of communication are four in number.

(ii) Communication at the conventional level attempts to get acquainted or to fill silences among close friends and lovers.

(iii) Discussions about things, people, theories, definitions, accidents as also class-room lectures fall into the participative level of communication.

(iv) People express their own feelings, describe their own experiences and discuss their own ideas at the explorative level of communication.

(v) Communication at the confrontive level reveals strained relationships among married couples, lovers and friends.

Group B : SHORT ANSWER TYPE QUESTIONS :

1. How many levels of communicaion are there? Name them.
2. What do you mean by the conventional level of communication? Illustrate with examples.
3. Define the exploratory level of communication.
4. *"I feel happiest with people of my own age."* At which level does this statement belong to and why?
5. Explain the confrontive level of communicaiton. Enlist the situations or environs where it is used most.

Group C : ESSAY TYPE QUESTIONS :

1. Compare and contrast the conventional level of communicaiton with exploratory level of communication.
2. *"The confrontive level of communication is rare in organizations, but is common among close friends, lovers and married couples."*
   (*a*) Explain, citing suitable reasons, why confrontive level of communication is rare in organizations.
   (*b*) Elucidate with examples the confrontive level of communication among close friends.
3. Identify the level of communication in the following statements:
   (*a*) Hello, Priyanka, how are you? How is your brother, Pritam and your sister, Poonam? It's a long time since I saw you. Where had you been?
   (*b*) My partner fits my ideal standards of physical beauty / handsomeness. Our friendship merged gradually into love over time. I can't be happy unless I place my partner's happiness before my own.
   (*c*) I tell you, all a man wants to get on in the world, is some brains, plain common sense and plenty of push. And you can't learn these things from books. And while you are developing your "so-called intellectual faculties" by being a book-worm, you are spoiling your health. You will soon be a thin, white, narrow-chested, half-blind weakling if you stick to your beloved books like this. Look at my broadchest and feel my biceps! Anyway, I am developing my physical powers with my games and athletics.
   (*d*) Radhika : Hi, Pooja, what's the matter? Why have so many people gathered here?
   Pooja : A few minutes ago, a bus and a motor cycle collided here with each other. People are saying the bus driver was drunk and was driving very rashly.
   (*e*) 1st Passenger : Excuse me, could you please tell me which bus goes to Gateway of India?
   2nd Passenger : There are only two buses from here to Gateway of India via Churchgate Railway station.
   (*f*) In **Jhumpa Lahiri**'s short story "**Interpreter of Maladies** (1999), Mina and Raj Das, a young couple from the United States, and their three children are touring and visiting family in India. Mrs. Das takes an interest in Mr. Kapasi, their driver and tour guide for the day .... Later in the day Mrs. Das stays behind in the car while her husband goes on with the children to do more sight-seeing. Watching as Bobby, the younger son, passes a stick back and forth to a monkey, Mr. Kapasi comments on what a brave little boy he is : Mrs. Das tells him it's not surprising because he's not her husband's son, that he's the child of one of her husband's colleagues, with whom she had a brief affair. "No one knows, of course," she tells an astonished Mr. kapasi. "No one at all. I've kept the secret for eight whole years" (p. 62). Further disclosures about her feelings, but we know that Mina Das and Mr. Kapasi will never meet again.

REFERENCES & NOTES

1. Dr. C.B. Mamoria, *Personnel Management,* Himalaya Publishing House, Mumbai, 2000, pp. 754-755.
2. G.J. Chelune, et. al., "Self-Disclosure & Its Relationships to Marital Intimacy." *Journal of Clinical Psychology,* 40, 1984, pp. 216-219.
3. Kathryn Dindia, "Self-Disclosure, Identity, and Relationship Development : A Dialectical Perspective" in Kathryn Dindia & Steve Duck, eds., *Communication & Personal Relationships,* John Willey & Sons, New York, 2000, pp. 147-161,
4. Robert J. Sternberg, *The Triangle of Love : Intimacy, Passion, Commitment,* Basic Books, New York, 1998, p. 6.
5. Valerian J. Derlega & J. Grzelal, "Appropriateness of Self-Disclosure," in G.J. Chelune, ed., *Self-Disclosure,* Jossey-Bass, San Francisco, 1984, p. 29.

❒ ❒ ❒

CHAPTER

9

COMMUNICATION — ITS NATURE

CONTENTS

QUOTABLE QUOTES

1. "In the old days of barbarism, the people fought with hatchets. Civilized men bury the hatchets and now fight with gossips."

➠ **EDGAR WATSON HOWE**

2. "One fallacious assumption frequently made by management is that grapevine generally carries only gossip and is not very reliable. The grapevine does carry gossip, but its reliability may be better than is generally thought. Recent research by **Dr. Keith Davis** has revealed that between 75 and 95 per cent of grapevine information is correct, even if most of the messages are incomplete in detail."

➠ **Dr. RUE & DR. BYARS**

3. "Of all those arts in which the wise excel,
Nature's chief masterpiece is writing well."

➠ **DUKE OF BUCKINGHAM:** *Essay on Poetry*

4. "Three words *'I love you'* have changed lives miraculously. While the three dreaded words *'I hate you'* have often triggered off violence. *'Sorry', 'please'* and *'thank you'* have worked wonders. Some words can give you ulcers, heart-burns or bruised egos, ... *'Blind man's son is blind too'*, laughed Draupadi, when Duryodhana slipped and fell in the palace of the Pandavas, mistaking the glass-floor for water. Draupadi's words of mockery set the stage for battle in the Mahabharata."

➠ **ANON**

LEARNING OBJECTIVES

After going through this chapter, you should be able to —

- ❖ Understand the multiple natures of communication;
- ❖ Distinguish one nature of communication from the others.

Nature of communication is very complex. However, an attempt is made in the following paragraphs to enlist some of the salient natures of communication.*

* ***Acronym*** : **HASAS – IPPT – MCU**

Mnemonic : (i) **H**umayun, **A**kbar, **S**hahjahan, **A**urangzeb, **S**hershah **I**nflated **P**ublic **P**erception **T**owards **M**anaging **C**ommon **U**tilities.

(ii) **H**on'ble **A**dvocate **S**amaj **A**dat **S**udhar approached **I**ndian **P**olice **P**enal **T**ribunal to release **M**oney-**C**heat **U**ndertrials.

All these salient natures of communication have been diagrammatically presented in ***Diagram 9.1. (cf. Page. 125)***.

9.1 A HUMAN PROCESS

Communication is a human process. Right from birth till death, a human being is spontaneously engaged in sending , receiving , listening, understanding and acting upon messages. Communication is a vital tool for getting things done through people in any organization.Communication is ***effective*** when both sender and receiver interpret a message in the same way. It is **efficient** when messages are trasferred at a low cost in terms of resources expended.[1] Communication is the ***'nervous system'*** which makes organizations cohere and permits their members to co-operate and co-ordinate.[2]

9.2 NOT A NATURAL BUT AN ACQUIRED ACTIVITY

Communication is not a normal and natural human activity but is an acquired or a learned one. Research findings reveal that newly-born babies separated from their mothers right from the date of birth and kept under the care of nurses who were instructed not to speak even a single word in presence of those babies were unable to utter a single word in any language. Communication, therefore, requires deliberate effort and deliberate thought[3] (*cf.* ***Box 9.1***).

BOX 9.1 : COMMUNICATION — A DELIBERATE & NOT A NORMAL, NATURAL HUMAN ACTIVITY

In ancient times about a century ago an European King decided to make an experiment to find out whether communication is a normal and natural human activity or a learned one. For this, he isolated a number of newly-born babies in a quiet, calm room and instructed those who were taking care of them not to speak even a single word in the infant's presence. When the babies began to talk, the king thought that the world's languages were the one natural to persons and such languages will automatically come out from the lips of those babies. But the records of these experiments showed that not even a single unfortunate infant ever said even a single word in any language of the world. In fact, most of them died.

Communication, therefore, requires a deliberate effort and also deliberate thought.

Source : Wendell Johnson[3]

9.3 A SOCIAL PROCESS

Communication is a social process in the sense that it enables everyone in society to express and satisfy his needs and desires as also to get along and grow with other people harmoniously and thus acts as a powerful means of social advancement. Through communication, we create myths, stories, rituals, ceremonies, rules, and other aspects of our social reality. It is communication that provides us with meaning and expectations about people and situations. Because the way we communicate is responsible to a large extent for creating our social worlds.[4]

9.4 BOTH AN ART AND A SCIENCE

Communication is an art because it, like any other art, is practice-oriented and creative involving certain skills or craftsmanship — particularly human behavioral dynamics which cannot be reduced to a common formula because even the same man may express or behave differently in different circumstances. **Communication is also a science because it, like any other discipline of science, is based on certain principles, methods, and techniques** which are getting more pronounced and systematized with the emergence of sophisticated communication technologies.

9.5 AN INTERDISCIPLINARY HERITAGE

Unlike most subjects, communication has captured the interest of scholars from a wide range of fields.[5] Ever since classical times, **philosophers** have studied the meaning and significance of messages. In the twentieth century, **social scientists** have joined the field. **Psychologists** examine the causes and effects of communication as it relates to individuals. **Sociologists and anthropologists** examine how communication operates within and between societies and cultures. **Political scientists** explore the ways communication influences governmental affairs. **Engineers** use their skill to devise methods of conveying messages electronically. **Zoologists** focus on communication between animals. Communication has thus been the professional concern of philosophers, scientists (social, biological and physical), poets, politicians and entertainers. Responding to this diversity, **Brent Rubin** asked, "How does *'being interested in communication'* differ from *'being interested in life?"*

9.6 A PSYCHOLOGICAL PROCESS

Communication involves the psychological condition of the individual. Sometimes our external style of interaction is influenced by what is going on inside us. **People often communicate for important psychological reasons, and when we communicate with someone, we must feel some degree of reciprocity with that person.** Otherwise serious problem may result.

9.7 A PERSUASIVE MEANS

All employees cannot be dealt with by force, coercion and repression. The management must make them work by the gentle art of persuasion. **Persuasion is an effective means of communication by which an employee, even a problem employee, is encouraged to work voluntarily** (*cf.* ***Box. 9.2***).

BOX 9.2 : SEQUENTIAL STAGES IN PERSUASION

Persuasive communication follows twelve sequential stages :

(i) Exposure to the message.
(ii) Attending to the message.
(iii) Becoming interested in it.
(iv) Understanding it.
(v) Learning how to process and use it.
(vi) Yielding to it.
(vii) Memorizing it.
(viii) Retrieving it when required.
(ix) Using it when making decisions.
(x) Carrying out these decisions.
(xi) Reinforcing the actions.
(xii) Consolidating the decision based upon the success of the actions.

Source : Adapted from **W.J. McGuire**, 'Theoretical Foundations of Campaigns' in **R. Rice & W. Paisley** (eds.) *Public Communication Campaigns*, Beverley Hills, Sage.

9.8 A TRANSACTIONAL PROCESS

Communication is a transactional process in the sense that while communicating, the sender and the receiver are continuously involved to construct meanings, develop expectations and exchange symbols. According to **Myers and Myers**, communication is a transactional process in which you are both cause and effect of whatever is happening.[6] The transactional nature of communication shows up in school, where teachers and students influence one another's behaviour. ***For example***, teachers who regard some students negatively may treat them with subtle or overt disfavour. As a result, these students are likely to react to their teachers' behaviour negatively, which reinforces the teachers' original attitudes and expectations.[7]

9.9 MULTI-DIMENSIONAL

Communication occurs on many levels simultaneously. It is not merely downward but can be upward and also horizontal, which means communication can be inter-scalar, intra-scalar or extra-organizational. **Inter-scalar communication** refers to communication between different scalar levels, e.g. communication between superior and subordinates. **Intra-scalar communication** suggests communication between the same levels e.g. communication between two departmental heads. **Extra-organizational communication** means communication between the management and the external world.

9.10 COMPLEX

Communication is far from simple, primarily because it is human beings who do the communicating. People make communication complex because people themselves are complex and unpredictable.

BOX 9.3 : COMMUNICATION IS LIKE DANCING

Communication is rather like dancing — at least the kind of dancing we do with partners. Like dancing, communication depends on the involvement of a partner. And like good dancing, successful communication isn't something that depends just on the skill of one person. A great dancer who does not consider and adapt to the skill level of his or her partner can make both people look bad. In communication and dancing, even two talented partners don't guarantee success. When two talented dancers perform without co-ordinating their movements, the results feel bad to the dancers and look foolish to an audience. The way you dance probably varies from one partner to another because of its co-operative, transactional nature. Likewise, the way you communicate almost certainly varies with different partners.

Source **: Ronald B. Adler & George Rodman**[8]

9.11 UNIVERSAL

The principles and skills of communication are universal in application because all the persons regardless of their positions use the same communication skills and principles throughout the globe.

DIAGRAM 9.1 : NATURE OF COMMUNICATION

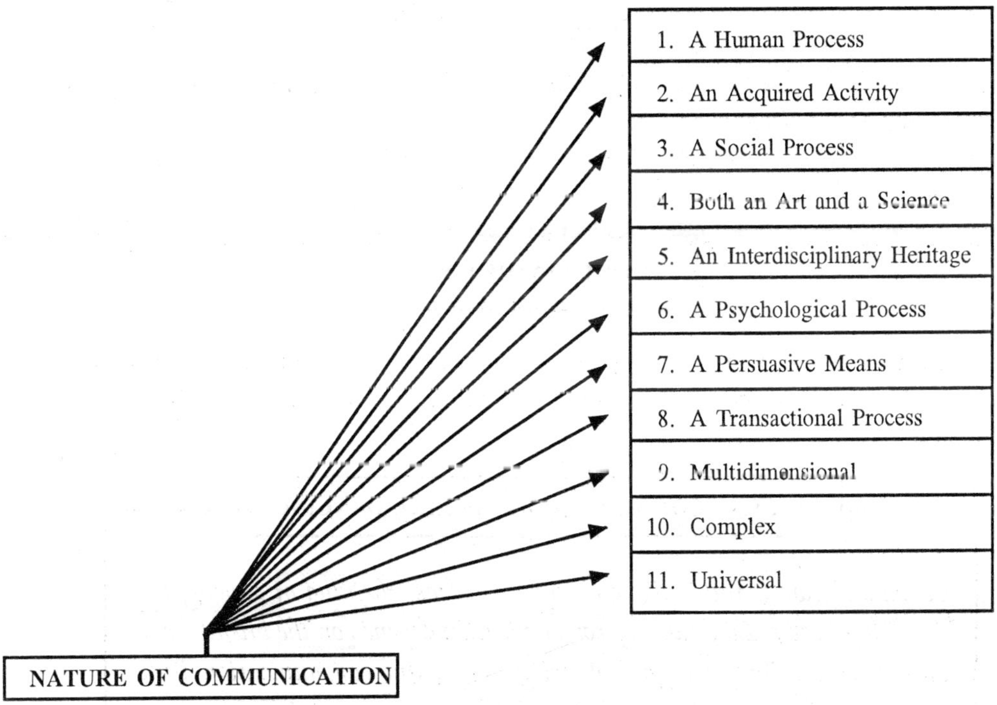

Source : Based on different **Communication Theorists.**

Diagram : Exclusively designed by the Author (**Dr. Roy**).

LAUGH A LITTLE, THINK A LITTLE

[A] CUT MY ORDER IN HALF!

1. *A merchant ordered 350 turkeys for the 'thanksgiving' holiday season one year. A few weeks before 'thanksgiving', his sales dropped sharply. Afraid that he won't be able to sell all of the turkeys, he phoned the distributor and said, "Cut my order in half!" When his order arrived, guess what it contained ? Three hundred and fifty turkeys, each cut in half !*

[B] TAKE-OFF POWER

2. *On final approach, just short of touchdown, the pilot of a military plane determined that the runway was too short to land and that the landing must be aborted. He yelled to his engineer, "Takeoff power." The engineer immediately reached up and turned off the engines, and the plane crashed off the end of the runway. The pilot had wanted the engineer to give him extra power for takeoff.*

Source : **Cheryl Hamilton & Cordell Parker,** *Communicating for Results,* Wadsworth Publishing Company, Belmont, California, 2nd Edition, 1987, pp. 9-10.

SUMMARY

'Brevity is the soul of wit.'

➡ WILLIAM SHAKESPEARE

Nature of communication is very complex, because human beings themselves are complex. Communication is a human process, a persuasive means for getting things done. It's an acquired quality, a social and psychological process. It has an interdisciplinary heritage. It is both an art and a science — art because it is practice-oriented and science because it is based on certain principles, methods and techniques. It is transactional, multidimensional and universal in application.

KEY TERMS & CONCEPTS

'Most of the disputes in the world arise from words.'

➡ WILLIAM MURRAY

- Acquired Quality
- Social Process
- Craftsmanship
- Behavioural Dynamics
- Communication Technologies
- Psychological Process
- Reciprocity
- Coercion & Repression
- Transactional Forces
- Multi-dimensional
- Interdisciplinary
- Universal

REVIEW & DISCUSSION QUESTIONS

'Questions clarify the concepts.'

➡ ANON

Group A : OBJECTIVE TYPE QUESTIONS :

1. Fill in the blanks :

(a) Right from birth till death, a human being is spontaneously engaged in sending, _______, _______, understanding and _______ upon messages.

(b) Communication requires deliberate _______ and deliberate _______.

(c) Human _______ dynamics cannot be reduced to a _______ formula because even the same man may express or behave _______ in _______ circumstances.

(d) Persuasion is an _______ means of communication by which an employee, even a _______ employee, is encouraged to work _______.

(e) Communication is not merely _______ but can be upward and also _______, which means communication can be interscalar, _______ or _______.

2. State whether the following statements are True (T) or False (F) and JUSTIFY your answer:

(i) Communication is a normal and natural human activity.

(ii) Communication is an art, and not a science.

(iii) When we communicate with someone, we must feel some degree of reciprocity with that person.

(iv) All employees can be dealt with by force, coercion and repression.

(v) Communication occurs on many levels simultaneously.

Group B : SHORT ANSWER TYPE QUESTIONS :

1. Why is it said that nature of communication is complex?
2. Why is communication called an acquired or a learned activity?
3. Explain why communication is said to have an interdisciplinary heritage.
4. Show reasons why communication is called a branch of science.
5. "*Communication is Universal.*" Do you agree? If so, why? If not, why not ?

Group C : ESSAY TYPE QUESTIONS :

1. *"Communication can be inter-scalar, intra-scalar or extra-organizational."* Explain the statement with suitable examples.
2. *"Communication is a transactional process in which you are both cause and effect of whatever is happening."* Examine the validity of this statement. Cite appropriate examples.
3. Prove whether communication is an art or a science, or both.
4. *"Communication has been the professional concern of philosophers, scientists (social, biological and physical), poets, politicians, and entertainers."* Do you support the view? Give suitable examples.

5. "*The principles & skills of communication are universal in application.*" Examine the veracity of the statement.

REFERENCES & NOTES

1. John R. Schermerhorn, Jr., James G. Hunt, & Richard N. Osborn, *Managing Organizational Behaviour,* John Wiley & Sons, Inc., New York, 5th Edition, 1994, pp. 565-566.
2. J. Daue & W. Lord, Jr., *Functional Business Communication,* Englewood Cliffs, N.J., Prentice Hall, 1968.
3. Wendell Johnson, 'The Fateful Process of Mr. A. Talking to Mr. B, *Harvard Business Review,* Jan.-Feb. 1953, Vol. 31, No. 6, pp. 52-62.
4. Sherwyn P. Morreale, Brian H. Spitzberg & J. Kevin Barge, *Human Communication : Motivation, Knowledge & Skills,* Wadsworth-Thomson Learning, Inc., Belment, USA, 2001, p. 15.
5. Ronald B. Adler, *Understanding Human Communication*, Oxford University Press, New York, 9th Edition, 2006, p. 5.
6. M.T. Myers & G.E. Myers, *Managing by Communication,* McGraw-Hill International Book Company, 1982.
7. T.P. Mottet & V.P. Richmond, "Student Non-Verbal Communication & Its Influence on Teachers & Teaching : A Review of Literature" in J.C. McCroskey, eds. *Communication for Teachers,* Allyn & Bacon, 2001.
8. Ronald B. Adler & George Rodman, *Understanding Human Communication,* Oxford University Press, New York, 9th Edition, 2006, p. 16.

❒ ❒ ❒

CHAPTER

10

COMMUNICATION — ITS SCOPE & NEEDS

CONTENTS

QUOTABLE QUOTES

1. "Communication is as necessary to an organization as the bloodstream is to a person."

   ➡ **Dr. KEITH DAVIS**

2. "The real value of an organization will be in its people's ability to think and learn."

   ➡ **PETER F. DRUCKER**

3. "The optimist sees the rose and not its thorns;
   The pessimist stares at the thorns oblivious of the rose."

   ➡ **KAHLIL GIBRAN**

4. "Yesterday is but a cancelled cheque,
   It'll not return at call or beck.
   Tomorrow is just a promissory note,
   On this I will not dream and gloat.
   Today alone is legal tender,
   To this I pledge my best to render.
   'Now' is the only time we live,
   To this I pledge my best to give."

   ➡ **MERLYN CUNDIFF,**
   Today Is Your Day

LEARNING OBJECTIVES

After going through this chapter, you should be able to —

- Identify different components of scopes of communication;
- Understand specific functions of each component;
- Differentiate one scope-components from others;
- Diagnose the reasons for which need for communication is felt;
- Explain distinguishing features of one need for communication from others.

10.1. SCOPE OF COMMUNICATION

The scope of communication is very much wider. It includes mainly the following: **I**nformation sharing, **M**otivating and influencing, **P**roblem-solving, **D**ecision making, **R**egulating and controlling, providing **F**eedback, **G**roup-building and **G**ate-keeping.*

*		
	Acronym	: IMP–DR–FGG ;
	Mnemonic	: I'M the Problem Detector, Regulator, Feedback-giver to Gents & Girls.

All these components have been diagrammatically illustrated in ***Diagram 10.1***. *(cf.* ***Page 134****)*.

10.1.1 Information Sharing

Chris Argyris said that the most important resource an organization has is valid information. Various types of information are transmitted in the organization *viz.,* policies and rules, changes and developments, settlements and awards etc. **By communication, we transmit such information from a source to target groups or individuals.**

10.1.2 Motivating and Influencing

Modern work problems are related more to attitudes than to fundamental skills and job-knowledge. **Through communication, the manager has, therefore, to provide in his employees the right attitudes necessary for motivation, co-operation and job-satisfaction.** Hence, the manager motivates and influences employees in a right way so as to create a good working climate, right attitudes, and congenial working relationships. By communication alone, the manager can know the needs and wants of his employees and can accordingly motivate them to better their job-performance.

10.1.3 Problem Solving

Communication helps in solving problems. Negotiations between management and employee unions are a means aiming at finding a solution to a number of vexatious issues. **Sometimes seminars, group meetings are conducted to brainstorm alternative solutions for a problem and to evolve a consensus.**

LAUGH A LITTLE
THINK A LITTLE

PROBLEM SOLVING

An engineer after serving his company over thirty years happily retired. Several years later, the company contacted him regarding a seemingly impossible problem they were having with one of their multi-million dollar machines. They had tried everything and everyone also to get the machine fixed, but to no avail. In desperation, they called on the retired engineer who had solved so many problems in the past.

The Engineer reluctantly took the challenge. He spent a day studying the huge machine. At the end of the day, he marked a small 'X' in a chalk on a particular component of the machine and proudly stated, "This is where your problem is."

The part was replaced and the machine worked perfectly again. Next day the company received a bill of $ 50,000/- from the engineer for his service. The company demanded an itemised accounting of his charges. The engineer responded briefly :

(i) Putting chalk-mark : $ 1.

(ii) Knowing where to put the chalk-mark : $ 49,999

Source : Unknown

10.1.4 Decision Making

Communication helps a great deal in making logical decisions. In the process of decision making, several kinds of communication are needed *viz.,* exchange of information, attitudes and feelings, views and ideas, available alternatives, favourable or unfavourable points of each alternative etc.

10.1.5 Regulating & Controlling

By communication the behavior of members of an organization can be regulated and controlled. Persons in different roles and positions at different hierarchial levels need to communicate in order to see that organizational tasks get fulfilled. Organizational life becomes orderly through clear communication. Both the subordinate and the superior know what to expect, when and why.

10.1.6 Providing Feedback

Communication is a two-way transmission of messages. **Feedback enables the sender to check that his message has been conveyed successfully and effectively.** Difficulties encountered in the communication of feedback help in taking corrective measures and making necessary adjustments.

BOX 10.1 : TWO-WAY COMMUNICATION IS LIKE PLAYING THE GAME OF TENNIS

Engaging in two-way communication can be compared to playing the game of tennis. Consider the process that must go on in the mind of one of its powerful young stars, ***Venus Williams****. As Venus serves the ball, she cannot tell herself, "My next shot will be a crosscourt forehand. Her next shot, to be effective, must depend on feedback from the receiver, that is, on where and how her opponent returns the serve. Venus undoubtedly has an overall strategy for the match, but each of her shots must be contingent on the way the ball is returned to her — its force, spin, and placement — and on the position of her opponent on the opposite side of the court. If Venus fails to match her shots to her opponent's game, she will find that her game is not as effective as it could have been that day. As is the case in communication, ignoring feedback limits the likelihood that the exchange will be successful.*

Source : Dr. John W. Newstrom[3]

10.1.7 Group Building

Communication develops understanding necessary for group formation. If communication breaks down, the group may disintegrate. Communication provides the necessary lubrication for the proper functioning of a group.

BOX 10.2 : BUILDING STRONG GROUPS & TEAMS

The ability to create strong groups & teams depends on communication. The last decade has seen an explosion in the use of groups in social and work settings. Over 40 million people in the United States currently participate in support groups such as ***Alcoholics Anonymous, Cancer Survivor Groups,*** *and* ***Consciousness-Raising Groups.*** *Moreover, in an era of increased domestic and international competition and corporate* *downsizing, organizations increasingly rely on work teams to maintain a competitive edge. In both our social and work lives, groups are becoming a more powerful presence. When group members choose forms of communicating that allow the creation of collective goals, the blending of individual members' knowledge, and the promotion of learning, they are more likely to be successful.*

Source : Morreale, Spitzberg & Barge[4]

10.1.8 Gate-Keeping

Communication plays an important role in building linkages of the organization with the outside world. It helps in developing rapport, creating confidence, winning goodwill, building moral support and establishing mutual understanding with the external world. The organization can use its environment to increase its effectiveness.

DIAGRAM 10.1 : SCOPE OF COMMUNICATION

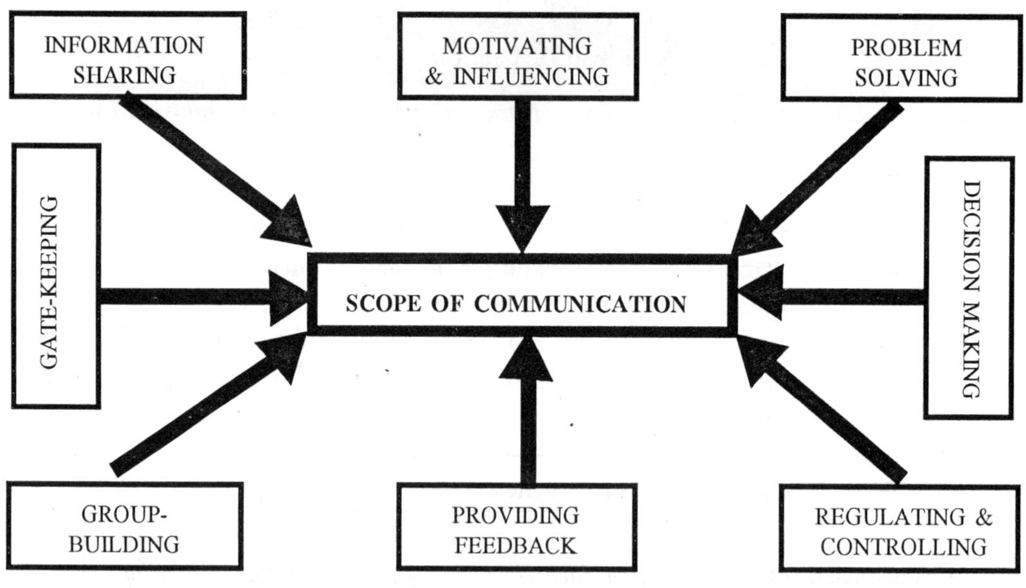

Source : Various authors on the subject
Diagram : Exclusively designed by the Author (**Dr. Roy**).

BOX 10.3 : A GLASS — HALF EMPTY OR HALF FULL ?

Two shoe companies, viz. Company A & Company B, sent their salespersons one each to Africa, instructing them to check out the market there. One informed his company A, ***"Here, there's no scope for shoe-market because everyone is barefoot."*** *The other salesperson from Company B wired headquarters of his company,* ***"Incredible scope for shoe-market. Everyone is barefoot here."*** *The first salesperson behaved just like a personnel from an ageing organization, whereas the second represented a growing organization.*

Source : Unknown

10.2. NEED FOR COMMUNICATION

"An organization that lacks communication
is like a football team without a quarter back —
no one knows what the play is or when to start moving."

➡ **David D. Vanfleet**, *Behaviour in Organizations*

'Communication is as necessary to an organization as the bloodstream is to a person.'[5] It is a *'sine qua non'* for any kind of business. Success of every human venture depends on clear-cut and accurate communication. Need for communication can be best explained by the fact that an idea, no matter how great, is useless until it is transmitted and understood by others.

Need for communication stems from certain interpersonal needs. All of us feel the urge to express, to know, to participate, to understand, to contribute, to share etc. Employees at lower levels have a number of communication needs. Managers think that they understand employees' needs, but often their employees don't think so.[6] This fundamental difference in perception tends to exist at each level in organizations, thereby making communication more difficult.

BOX 10.4 : NEEDS FOR COMMUNICATING

Researchers & theorists have identified a range of needs we satisfy by communicating :

(i) ***Pleasure*** *e.g.* *"because it's fun,"*
"to have a good time," etc.

(ii) ***Affection*** *e.g.* *"to help others,"*
"to let others know I care," etc.

(iii)	***Inclusion*** *e.g.*	*"because I need someone to talk to or be with,"* *"because it makes me less lonely," etc.*
(iv)	***Escape*** *e.g.*	*"to put off doing something I should be doing", etc.*
(v)	***Relaxation*** *e.g.*	*"because it allows me to unwind," etc.*
(vi)	***Control*** *e.g.*	*"because I want someone to do something for me,"* *"to get something I don't have," etc.*

Source : R.B. Rubin, E.M. Perse, & C.A. Barbato[7]

However, need for communication is usually felt for the following reasons viz., Self-expression, Affection, Inclusion, Control and Co-ordination*:

* *Acronym* : SAICC
Mnemonic : Sachin & Adam Gilchrist are considered as Ishwar of International Cricket Club.

10.2.1 Need for Self-expression

This is the need to express one's views, feelings, likings, preferences etc. **Need for self expression acts like a meta-message behind all other messages.**

10.2.2 Need for Affection

This is the need to maintain a satisfactory relation between the self and the other people with regard to love and affection. **In the business setting, this need takes the form of friendship.**

10.2.3 Need for Inclusion

This is the need to maintain a satisfactory relation between the self and the other people with regard to belongingness or interaction. Some people like to be with other people most of the time as also want to interact and mingle. On the contrary, some other people prefer to be alone, to interact minimally and stay out of groups.

BOX 10.5 : GLASS CEILING SYNDROME — BLATANT INFRINGEMENT ON DEMOCRATIC RIGHTS

Getting hired is merely an initial step for women and minorities as well. Getting promoted within a company often proves a more imposing challenge. ***For senior positions, promotions are very hard to achieve. This is commonly refers to as the Glass Ceiling Syndrome.*** *Women and minorities can see opportunities above for senior management positions, but they cannot reach there despite having more than required competencies and expertise,* ***because they are blocked by seemingly invisible barriers from climbing to those higher levels.*** *Much of the decision to promote someone to a senior position is based on such tangibles as how comfortable the senior team is with that person. It is quite normal to be more comfortable with those who are similar to the team-members of higher-ups in their interests and background.*

Source : Adapted from **James A.F. Stoner, R. Edward Freeman, Daniel R. Gilbert, Jr., Management** (6th Edition), Prentice Hall of India, New Delhi, 1999, p. 193.

10.2.4 Need for Control & Co-ordination

This is the need to maintain a satisfactory relation between the self and the other people with regard to power and influence. Every individual has a need to control his situation and his environment to some extent. Ordinarily this amounts to controlling other people involved in a given situation as also co-ordinating efforts of those people towards higher productivity.

BOX 10.6 : FUTURE SUCCESS

Future success depends on enabling everyone, regardless of gender, ethnic background or disability, to use their abilities to the full. When staff typically constitute the biggest item in the cost base, when know-how and innovation are the stock-in-trade, it makes an excellent commercial sense to invest in human assets and to engender a maximum return on that investment.

Source : Lord Alexander of Weedon QC, Chairman, National Westminster Bank plc.

SUMMARY

'Brevity is the soul of wit.'

➡ WILLIAM SHAKESPEARE

The scope of communication is very much wider. It includes *information sharing, motivating and influencing, problem-solving, decision making, regulating and controlling, giving and receiving feedback, group-building and gate-keeping.*

All of us feel the urge to express, to know, to participate, to understand, to contribute, to share etc. Need for communication, therefore, stems from certain interpersonal needs viz. *self-expression, affection, inclusion, control and co-ordination.*

KEY TERMS & CONCEPTS

'Most of the disputes in the world arise from words."

➡ WILLIAM MURRAY

- Information sharing
- Influencing
- Problem-solving
- Decision making
- Regulation & Control
- Group-building
- Gate-Keeping
- Rapport
- Self-expression
- Affection
- Inclusion
- Co-ordination

REVIEW & DISCUSSION QUESTIONS

'Questions clarify the concepts.'

➡ ANON

Group A : OBJECTIVE TYPE QUESTIONS :

1. Fill in the blanks :

(a) By communication, we transmit ________ from a source to ________ or individuals.

(b) Communication helps in developing ________, creating ________, winning ________, building ________ support and establishing ________ understanding with the external world.

(c) Need for self-expression acts like a ________ behind all other messages.

(d) In the business setting, need for affection takes the form of ________.

(e) Need for control and co-ordination is the need to maintain a ________ relation between the ________ and the other people with regard to ________ and influence.

2. State whether the following statements are True (T) or False (F) and JUSTIFY your answer:

(i) By communication alone, the manager can know the needs and wants of his employees and can accordingly motivate them to better their job-performance.

(ii) Negotiations between management and employee unions are the ends aiming at finding a variety of vexatious issues.

(iii) Communication develops misunderstanding among various groups.

(iv) Communication plays the role of a gate-keeper.

(v) Need for communication stems from certain personal needs.

Group B : SHORT ANSWER TYPE QUESTIONS :

1. Enlist the main components under scope of communication.
2. How does communication help in making logical decisions?
3. Write short notes on the role of communication for
   (a) Group-building,
   (b) Gate-keeping.
4. Why is there any need for communication?
5. Compare and contrast between 'need for affection' and 'need for inclusion.'

Group C : ESSAY TYPE QUESTIONS :

1. Describe in detail the main components under scope of communication.
2. "Organizational life becomes orderly through clear communication." Explain the staement with appropriate examples.
3. "By communication alone, the manager can know the needs and wants of his employees and can accordingly motivate them to better their job-performance." How far does this statement prove right? Elucidate with examples.
4. "Communication is as necessary to an organization as the bloodstream is to a person." Justify.
5. "An idea, no matter how great, is useless until it is transmitted and understood by others." In the light of the above statement, explain the role of feedback in communication process.

REFERENCES & NOTES

1. "Conversation with Chris Argyris", *Organizational Dynamics,* Summer 1974, p. 62.
2. Dr. Keith Davis, *Human Behaviour At Work,* Tata-McGraw Hill, New Delhi, 5th Edition, 1979, p. 375.
3. Dr. John W. Newstrom, *Organizational Behaviour*, McGraw-Hill, New York, 12th Edition, 2007, pp. 48-49.
4. Sherwyn P. Morreale, Brian H. Spitzberg & J. Kevin Barge, *Human Communication: Motivation, Knowledge & Skills,* Wadsworth-Thomson Learning, Inc., Belmont, USA, 2001, p. 20. Also see R. Wuthnow, *Sharing the Journey: Support Groups & America's New Quest for Community,* Free

Press, New York, 1994; I.R. Katzenbach & D.K. Smith, *The Wisdom of Teams,* Harper Business, New York, 1994; P.M. Senge, *The Fifth Discipline,* Doubleday, New York, 1991.

5. Dr. Keith Davis, *op. cit.,* p. 371.
6. For a retrospective analysis of a classic study in misperception of employee needs by supervisors, see Stephen A. Rubenfeld, John W. Newstrom & Thomas Duff, "Caveat Emptor: Avoiding Pitfalls in Data-Based Decision-Making", *Review of Business,* Winter 1994, pp. 20-23.
7. R.B. Rubin, E.M. Perse & C.A. Barbato, "conceptualizatin & Measurement of Interpersonal Communication Motives", *Human Communication Research,* Vol. 14, 1988, pp. 602-628.

❐ ❐ ❐

CHAPTER 11

COMMUNICATION — ITS OBJECTIVES

CONTENTS

QUOTABLE QUOTES

1. "An objective is what we intend to achieve either by individual effort or by group efforts or by both. It is the purpose with which we undertake an activity. By communication, we organize human, economic and other resources effectively, and develop plans and policies towards attainment of both individual as also institutional goals."

   ➡ **ADAPTED**

2. 'Discovery consists of seeing what every one has seen and thinking what nobody has thought."

   ➡ **ANON**

3. "A successful person is one who can lay a firm foundation with the bricks that others throw at him."

   ➡ **ANON**

4. "Little drops of water
   Little grains of sand
   Make the mighty ocean,
   And the pleasant land.

   Little deeds of kindness
   Little words of love
   Make this world we live on
   Like the heaven above."

   ➡ **ANON**

LEARNING OBJECTIVES

After going through this chapter, you should be able to —

- Identify different objectives of communicaiton prescribed by different communicaiton theorists;
- Understand the implications of each objective;
- List out major objectives of communication as understood by you;
- Differentiate nature and function of each objective that communication processes serve within organizations.

An objective is what we intend to achieve either by individual effort or by group efforts or by both. It is the purpose with which we undertake an activity. Every organization has its own objectives or goals. **By communication, we establish and disseminate organizational goals.** By communication, we sense customers' needs and expectations, market competitions and business operations. *By communication, we organize human, economic and other resources effectively, and develop plans and policies towards attainment of both individual and institutional goals.* Communication has, therefore, specific objectives in every organization.

11.1 SCOTT & MITCHELL'S VIEW

According to **Scott & Mitchell,** there are four major objectives that communication processes serve within organizations[1] :

1. ***To increase acceptance of organizational rules by subordinates*** in allowing them to discuss attitudes, resolve ambiguities about their jobs and settle conflicts among groups and individuals.
2. ***To gain greater commitment to organizational objectives*** by motivating, controlling and evaluating the performance of organizational personnel.
3. ***To provide data necessary for decision making.***
4. ***To clarify task responsibilities, identify authority positions and provide accountability for performance.***

11.2 WILLIAM SCHOLZ'S VIEW

According to **William Scholz,** communication in any business organization has the following five objectives[2] :

1. To help in ***achieving operating objectives*** of the business.
2. To help in ***improving performance and job satisfaction*** of all categories of employees.
3. To ***enhance company image*** with the employee as also with the public.
4. To ***win understanding, approval and support of the organization's position*** on vital social, political and economic issues.
5. To ***keep management informed of attitudes, trends and reactions among employees and other appropriate 'publics'*** as an aid to decision-making and control.

11.3 S.M. CUTLIP et. al.'s VIEW

According to **Cutlip et al,**[3] the goals of employee communication are to identify, establish and maintain mutually beneficial relationships between the organization and the employees on whom its success or failure depends. ***They identify four stages of employment where effective communications are vital:***

1. **The Start** : attracting and inducting new employees.
2. **The Work** : where instructions, news and job-related information should be disseminated.
3. **The Rewards & Recognition** : promotions, special events, awards.
4. **The Termination** : breakdown of equipment, lay-offs, dismissals.

Employee-awareness of operations, problems, goals and developments will increase their effectiveness as ambassadors, both on-and-off the job. Top management should, therefore, demonstrate a real interest in the employees' concerns by organising attitude surveys, suggestion schemes and stimulating the upward flow of communication. *The most common failing in employee communication, according to* **Cutlip et al.,** *is that it is too busy selling a management view downward. It neglects to stimulate an equivalent upward flow.*

11.4 A HOLISTIC VIEW

From the foregoing, we may list out the following objectives of communication :

1. Conveying the Right Message

An important objective of communication is to ***convey the right message to the right person in the right perspective so as to evoke a right response from the receiver.*** In any progressive organizations, top management always keeps the employees well informed about goals and policies, procedures and priorities, tasks and responsibilities.

2. Building up Image of the Organization

Communication is used to build up image-consciousness among employees. ***Bright image of the organization helps its continuous existence, unblemished survival and unfettered growth.***

3. Employee Orientation

Management uses communication ***to make new employees familiarized with the goals and policies of the organization*** and also keep its existing employees well informed about any change in this regard at regular periodical intervals.

4. Employee Appraisal

Management ***appraises the contribution of their subordinates to the organization*** and employees are apprised of such performance of theirs by means of communication.

5. Providing Advice

In order to better performance, employees need advice from their higher-ups or even specialised advice from the experts in the related areas. ***Advice should be both man-centred and work-centred. Advice is most effective when given orally, confidentially, in a sympathetic tone and in informal manner.***

6. Counselling

Almost all professionally managed business organizations have counselling centres for their employees ***where services of specialists viz., psychiatrists, doctors, lawyers etc. are made freely available to the employees*** who require counselling and vocational guidance. Counselling may be communicated orally or in writing.

7. Issuing Orders and Instructions

Orders and instructions are issued by superiors to subordinates to get things done. ***Order is the assignment of a task while instruction specifies the way the task is to be performed.*** An order may be written or verbal, general or specific, procedural or operational, definite or sequential, mandatory or discretionary. Instruction about transfer of an employee from one branch of an organization to another is an order. ***Instructions are meant to be followed whereas orders are meant to be compulsorily complied with.***

BOX 11.1 : JOB INSTRUCTION

Here is an example of an inadequate job instruction and its disastrous consequence :

A manufacturer of small tools hired a new sales representative, gave him a tour of the plant and a copy of the product catalog, and assigned him to a territory. In a few weeks, the representative jubilantly sent in an order for 1,00,000 units of a multipurpose tool. Only then did the company realize it had neglected to tell him that that product was never promoted to its customers because the tool was priced well below the company's cost of producing it in order to match a competitor's price. The result was that the company lost over $ 10,000/- on this one order !

Source **: Dr. John W. Newstrom**[4]

8. Issuing Warning

When advice and counselling fail to achieve results, warning is given either orally or in writing. A written warning is often called a memo. ***Warming is a forceful form of communication and it demands immediate action*** failing which severe disciplinary action may follow. Warning is communicated confidentially.

9. Enforcing Discipline

Employees recognise the need for discipline in organized activities. The objective of communication, whether oral or written, is to acquaint employees with the rules and regulations of the organization.

10. Imparting Education and Training

All kinds of education and training are imparted with the help of communication. Both executives and workers sharpen their knowledge and skills as also improve their efficiency and potential through education and training. ***Different kinds of communication are used for training*** e.g., lectures, case studies, audio-visual methods, seminar, symposium, group meetings, conferences etc.

11. Promoting Human Relations

Communication promotes and maintains human relations by improving mutual understanding between the management and the workers. ***It helps the management understand the needs, attitudes, feelings of the workers and simultaneously it helps the workers better realise their duties, responsibilities towards achievement of organizational goals.***

12. Developing Good Industrial Relations

Communication aims at developing good labour-management relations by keeping both in contact with each other. Through exchange of ideas, opinions and viewpoints, labour-unions and management understand each other and dispel any misunderstanding between them.

13. Fostering Co-ordination & Teamwork

Communication serves as an effective tool to co-ordinate the efforts of all who are involved in running a business. Communication assists all the employees in understanding and accepting the reasonableness of the status and authority of everyone in the organization.

BOX 11.2 : BENEFIT OF CO-ORDINATION AND TEAM-WORK

A man was lost while driving through the country. As he tried to read a map, he accidentally drive off the road into a ditch. Though he wasn't injured, his car was stuck deep in the mud. So, the man walked to a nearby farm and asked for help.

"Warwick can get you out of that ditch," said the farmer, pointing to an old mule standing in a field. The man looked at the haggard mule doubtfully, but figured he had nothing to lose. The two men and Warwick made their way back to the ditch.

The farmer hitched the mule to the car. With a snap of the reins he shouted, "Pull Fred !
Pull, Jack !
Pull, Ted !
Pull, Warwick !"

And the mule pulled the car from the ditch with very little effort. The man was amazed. He thanked the farmer, patted the mule, and asked, "Why did you call out all of those other names before you called Warwick?"

The farmer grinned and said, "Old Warwick is just about blind. As long as he believes he's part of a team, he doesn't mind pulling."

Source : Adapted from **James W. Moore,** *Some Folks Feel the Rain : Others Just Get Wet,* Nashville, TN : Dimensions for Living, 1999.

14. Effecting Persuasion

Persuasion means making efforts to change or influence the behavior and attitude of others. A great deal of communication in a workplace is persuasive. ***When employees have to be convinced of the need for greater efforts, when goods have to be sold despite competition, when dues have to be collected from an unwilling customer — all these situations call for persuasive efforts.*** Skill and ability to use words, both spoken and written, are essential in effecting effective persuasion.

15. Discouraging Mis-information

One of the important objectives of communication ***is to avoid distortions in communications.*** Communication is used to discourage the spread of mis-information, rumours, gossip and to release the emotional tensions of workers.

16. Encouraging Suggestions and Complaints

In any organization, suggestions are like the moving force of all actions or decisions. Employees are encouraged to give constructive suggestions for the betterment of organization. Complaints are essentially requests made to seek redressal of grievances. ***Both suggestions and complaints are a useful means of feedback and represent a subtle form of communication.***

17. Making Appeals and Representations

Appeals and representations are a special category of requests made by employees and supported by facts and figures in order to seek favours like leave, promotion etc. ***An appeal may be written or oral but a representation is always in writing.*** An employee may appeal to his superior for a foreign training. A group of aggrieved employees may represent to seek a change in the place of their posting or transfer.

18. Facilitating Decision Process

Decision is the triggering mechanism of communication. All decisions are based on communication of information to the management. Every communication contains information but all sorts of information may not have communicative value. ***Meaningful decisioning depends entirely on accuracy and adequacy of necessary information possessing only communicative values.*** **Management Information System (MIS)** has, therefore, assumed unique importance in modern management.

19. Stimulating Motivation

Another important objective of communication is motivation. ***To motivate means to supply a motive and a motive means an impelling power that incites a person to work. In organizations, managers put their communication skills to good use to improve employees' sense of self-worth*** by showing recognition, appreciating good work and providing a measure of support. A positively motivated employee is really an asset to the organization.

20. Boosting Morale

Morale refers to the condition of mental well-being of an individual. It is an attitude towards work, employer and fellowmen. ***According to behavioral scientists, morale is a lubricant to human relations.*** When morale is low, the performance is poor and when morale is high, the mood is upbeat and the outlook optimistic. Effective system of communication raises morale of employees.

Nelson's oft-quoted statement ***"England expects every man to do his duty"*** or **Netaji Subhas Bose**'s strong emotive appeals ***"Give me blood, I shall give you freedom"*** are fine examples of morale-boosting communications during freedom struggle.

BOX 11.3 : TRUE RELIGION

"My heart has become capable of every form;
It's a pasture of gazelles,
And a convent for christian monks,
And a temple for idols,
And the pilgrim's Ka'ba,
And the tables of the Tora,
And the book of Koran.
I follow the religion of Love, whichever way His camels take."

Source : IBN' ARABI

11.5 OBJECTIVES OF COMMUNICATION VIS-A-VIS DIRECTIONS OF COMMUNICATIONS

There exists a definite linkage between the directions of communication flows and the specific objectives of communication.

(A) Objectives of Downward Communication (i.e. Superior to Subordinate/Superior-initiated Communication)

1. Conveying information about goals and policies, procedures and priorities, tasks and responsibilities,
2. Projecting image of the organization,
3. Employee Orientation,
4. Employee Appraisal,
5. Providing Advice & Counselling,
6. Issuing orders & Instructions,
7. Giving Warning,
8. Enforcing Discipline,
9. Imparting Education & Training,
10. Promoting Human as also Industrial relations,

11. Fostering Co-ordination and team work,
12. Discouraging Misinformation,
13. Facilitating Decision-making,
14. Stimulating Motivation,
15. Boosting Morale.

(B) Objectives of Upward Communication (i.e. Subordinate to Superior/Subordinate-initiated Communication)

1. Providing Feedback,
2. Making Requests for seeking permission & concessions,
3. Preferring Appeals for favours,
4. Making Demands,
5. Filing Complaints,
6. Making Representations,
7. Reporting at periodical intervals,
8. Offering Suggestions,
9. Expressing Empathy or Sympathy,
10. Facilitating the flow of information as a part of the Management Information System (MIS).

(C) Objectives of Lateral or Horizontal Communication

1. Establishing and maintaining mutual understanding and trust between peers (i.e., individuals/groups of equal rank/status),
2. Facilitating interdepartmental co-operation,
3. Promoting team work,
4. Settling interdepartmental as also intradepartmental differences without intervention of the management,
5. Lending effectiveness by removing duplication of work procedures and thereby minimizing wastage of time, money, materials and labour,
6. Solving problems at lower levels,
7. Co-ordinating efforts of different departments and persons at the same level of authority,
8. Facilitating unrestricted free flow of factual information because of absence of status-barriers.

(D) Objectives of Cross-wire or Diagonal Communication

1. Expediting transfer/exchange of information by cutting across departmental hierarchies,
2. Improving understanding among persons at different levels having no direct reporting relationships with one another,
3. Speeding up action so vital for protecting organizational interests,
4. Inducing cost effectiveness,
5. Bringing about all-round efficiency towards accomplishment of organizational goals.

BOX 11.4 : "HUMANITY" MODEL OF COMMUNICATION

The Basic fundamentals of communication revolve around a sense of "HUMANITY" toward one's fellow human beings. And what does "HUMANITY" stand for in communication transmission ?

H ⟶ Honesty with other people.
U ⟶ Understanding of their problems.
M ⟶ Mutual respect.
A ⟶ Awareness of their limitations.
N ⟶ Negotiability.
I ⟶ Identification with their feelings.
T ⟶ Trust.
Y ⟶ "You" orientation, and not "I".

Source : **Schneider, Donaghy & Newman**, *Organizational Communication*, McGraw-Hill Kogakusha Ltd., Tokyo, 1975, p. 69.

SUMMARY

'Brevity is the soul of wit.'

➡ **WILLIAM SHAKESPEARE**

Different communication theorists have prescribed different objectives that communication processes serve within organization. **Scott & Mitchell** have suggested four objectives; **William Scholz** have enlisted five objectives; **S.M. Cutlip et al.** have suggested several others. We may, for the sake of convenience, listed out some major objectives of communication in organizations such as conveying right message, building up bright image of the organization, orienting and appraising employees, providing advice and counselling, using orders and warning, enforcing discipline, imparting education and training, promoting human as well as good industrial relations, fostering coordination and teamwork, encouraging suggestions and complaints, facilitating decision process, stimulating motivation, boosting morale etc.

KEY TERMS & CONCEPTS

'Most of the disputes in the world arise from words.'

➡ **WILLIAM MURRAY**

- Organizational objectives
- Image of the organization
- Rewards & recognition
- Termination
- Attitude survey
- Suggestion Scheme
- Flow of communication
- Employee orientation
- Employee appraisal
- Employee Counselling
- Employee discipline
- Education and training
- Human relations
- Industrial relations
- Motivation & morale

REVIEW & DISCUSSION QUESTIONS

'Questions clarify the concepts.'

➡ **ANON**

Group A : OBJECTIVE TYPE QUESTIONS :

1. Fill in the blanks :

(a) According to Scott & Mitchell, one of the objectives of communication is to clarify ________ responsibilities, identify ________ positions, and provide ________ for performance.

(b) According to William Scholtz, communication, helps in achieving ________ objectives of the business and improving ________ and ________ of all categories of employees.

(c) According to Cutlip et. al., the goals of employee communication are to identify, ________ and ________ mutually ________ relationships between the organization and the employees on whom its success or failure depends.

(d) Instructions are meant to be ________, whereas orders are meant to be compulsorily ________ ________.

(e) To motivate means to supply a ________ and a ________ means an impelling ________ that incites a person to ________.

2. State whether the following statements are True (T) or False (F) and JUSTIFY your answer:

(i) By communication, we organize human, economic and other resources effectively, and develop plans and policies towards attainment of both individual and institutional goals.

(ii) Employee awareness of operations, problems, goals and developments will jeopardise their effectiveness as ambassadors, both on-and-off the job.

(iii) Instruction is the assignment of a task, while order specifies the way the task is to be performed.

(iv) Almost all professionally managed business organizations have counselling centres for their employees where services of specialists viz. psychiatrists, doctors, lawyers etc. are made available to the employees at a reasonable cost.

(v) Decision is the triggering mechanism of communication.

Group B : SHORT ANSWER TYPE QUESTIONS :

1. What are the four major objectives of communication suggested by Scott & Mitchell?
2. Name the five objectives of communication listed out by William Scholtz.
3. Cutlip, Center & Broom identified four stages of employment where effective communication is vital. Describe those four stages in brief.
4. Why is it necessary to build up a good image of the organization?
5. How does communication stimulate motivation and boost morale of employees?

Group C : ESSAY TYPE QUESTIONS :

1. "An important objective of communication is to convey the right message." To whom the right message is conveyed and why?
2. How does communication help in employee orientation and training?
3. Differentiate:

   (a) The term *'order'* from the term *'instruction'*.

   (b) The term *'advice'* from the term *'counselling.'*

   How does communication play effective roles in both the above cases.
4. "Decision is the triggering mechanism of communication." Elucidate with suitable examples.
5. Write short notes on the objectives of the following directional flow of communication :

   (a) Superior-initiated communication,

   (b) Subordinate-initiated communication,

   (c) Lateral communication,

   (d) Cross-wire/Diagonal communication.

REFERENCES & NOTES

1. William G. Scott & Terrence R. Mitchell, *Organizational Theory: A Structural & Behavioural Analysis,* Homewood III, Richard D. Irwin, 1976.
2. William Scholtz, *Communication in Business Organization,* Prentice Hall, New Jersey, 1963.
3. S.M. Cutlip, A.H. Center, & G.M. Broom, *Effective Public Relations,* Prentice Hall, 6th Edition, 1985, pp. 315-317.
4. Dr. John W. Newstorm, *Organizational Behaviour,* McGraw-Hill, New York, 12th Edition, 2007, p. 56.

❐ ❐ ❐

CHAPTER

12

COMMUNICATION — ITS FUNCTIONS

CONTENTS

QUOTABLE QUOTES

1. "Communication serves mainly four functions viz., the informative function, the command and instructive function, the influence and persuasive function and the integrative function.

   ➨ **LEE THAYER**

2. What you hear, you forget;
   What you see, you know;
   What you do, you understand

   ➨ **ADAPTED**

3. "But the fact that some geniuses were laughted at does not imply that all who are laughed at are geniuses. They laughed at Columbus, they laughed at Fulton, they laughed at the Wright Brothers. But they also laughed at Bozo, the clown."

   ➨ **CARL SAGAN**

4. "During the process of light-bulb invention, Thomas Alva Edison initially failed innumerable times. On being asked by his detractors, Edison gave a polite but witty reply: 'I have not failed, friend; I have just found 10,000 ways that won't work.'

   And we all know, he succeeded to invent light-bulb in his next attempt."

   ➨ **ADAPTED**

LEARNING OBJECTIVES

After going through this chapter, you should be able to —

❖ Identify and understand various functions of communication;

❖ Explain different views of communication theorists on functions of communication;

❖ List out and illustrate, with examples, the similarities and dissimilarities among their views.

12.1 STEPHEN P. ROBBINS' VIEW

Communication performs multipurpose functions. According to **Stephen P. Robbins**[1], communication serves the following four major functions within a group or organization. viz. **C**ontrol, **M**otivation, **E**motional Expression and **I**nformation*.

*		
Acronym	:	**CMEI**
Mnemonic	:	**C**amel **M**oves to **E**gypt & **I**ran.

All these functions have been diagrammatically illustrated in ***Figure 12.1*** as under :

FIG. 12.1 : FUNCTIONS OF COMMUNICATION: S.P. ROBBINS' VIEW

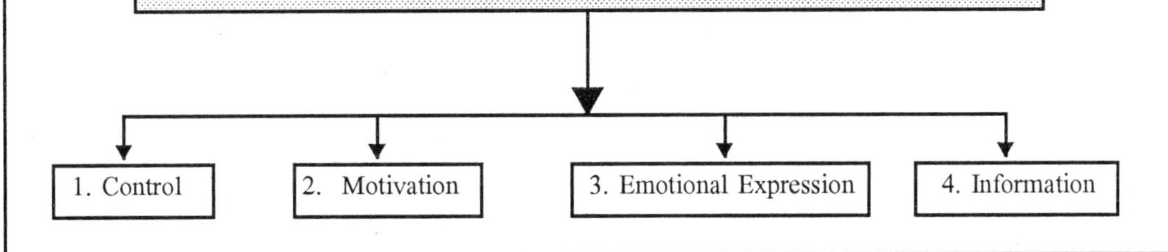

Source : **Stephen P. Robbins,** *Organizational Behavior,* Ninth Edition, Prentice Hall of India Pvt. Limited, New Delhi, 2000, p. 284.

1. Control

Communication acts to control member-behavior in several ways. Organizations have authority hierarchies and formal guidelines that employees are required to follow. ***When employees, for instance, are required to first communicate any job-related grievance to their immediate boss, to follow their job-description, or to comply with company policies, communication is performing a control function.***

2. Motivation

Communication fosters motivation by clarifying to employees what is to be done, how well they are doing, and what can be done to improve performance if it's subpar. The formation of specific goals, feedback on progress towards the goals, and reinforcement of desired behavior — all stimulate motivation and require communication.

3. Emotional Expression

For many employees, their work group is a primary source for social interaction. The communication that takes place within the group is a fundamental mechanism by which members show their frustrations as also feelings of satisfaction. ***Communication, therefore, provides a release for the emotional expression of feelings and for fulfilment of social needs.***

4. Information

The final function that communication performs relates to its role in facilitating decision making. ***It provides the information that individuals and groups need to make decisions by transmitting the data to identify and evaluate alternative choices.***

12.2 LEE THAYER'S VIEW

Lee Thayer[2] has divided the functions of communication into the following four specific categories viz. **I**nformative, **C**ommand & **I**nstructive, **I**nfluence & **P**ersuasive, and **I**ntegrative*.

* ***Acronym***	:	**IC – II – PI**
Mnemonic	:	**I**ndia & **C**hina **I**nspected **I**guana in **P**acific **I**slands.

All these categories have been diagrammatically presented in ***Figure 12.2*** as under :

FIG. 12.2 : FUNCTIONS OF COMMUNICATIONS: LEE THAYER'S VIEW

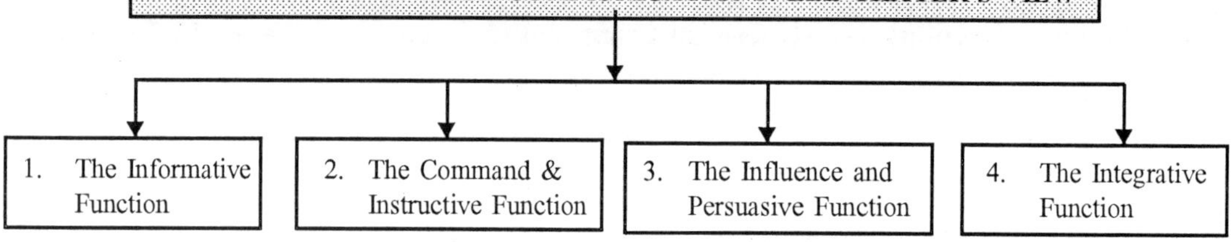

Source : **Lee Thayer**, *Communication and Communication Systems*, pp. 187-289.
Figure : Exclusively designed by the Author (**Dr. Roy**).

1. The Informative Function

This function serves to provide knowledge to the individual's need for guidance in their actions. It also fulfils workers' desires for awareness of things that affects them.

2. The Command & Instructive Function

This function serves to make the employee aware of his obligations to the formal organization and to provide him with additional guidance on how to perform his duties adequately.

3. The Influence and Persuasive Function

This function is also termed as motivational function and is mainly concerned with the influencing of behaviors and attitudes of the people through persuasion and encouraging them to person or to exhibit a certain behaviour necessary for achieving organizational objectives.

4. The Integrative Function

This function advocates that the communication of messages/ideas, if properly handled, should help to relate the activities of the workers to their efforts compliment rather than detract from each other. ***Work efforts are unified rather than fragmented as a result of properly integrative communication.***

12.3 C. CONRAD'S VIEW

C. Conrad[3] identified three functions communication performs in our organizations viz. **C**ommand function, **R**elational function, and **A**mbiguity-**M**anagement function*.

* *Acronym*	: **CRAM**
Mnemonic	: **C**ar **R**ental begets **A**mple **M**oney.

All the three functions have been diagrammatically presented in ***Figure 12.3*** as under :

FIG. 12.3 : FUNCTIONS OF COMMUNICATION : C. CONRAD'S VIEW

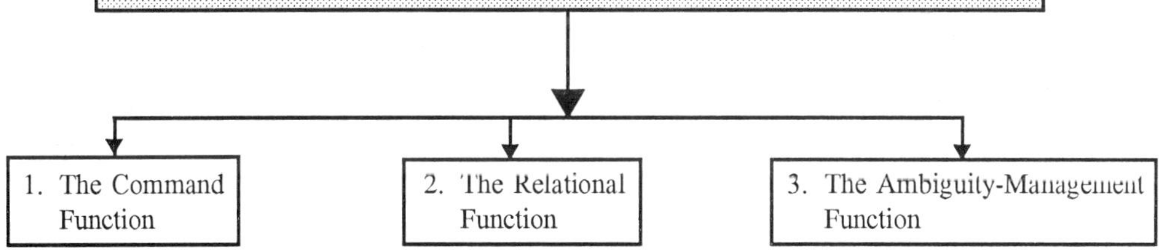

Source : **C. Conrad**, *Strategic Organization Communication : Cultures, Situations & Adaption*, pp. 7-8.
Figure : Exclusively designed by the Author (**Dr. Roy**).

1. The Command Function

Communication allows members of the organization ***to issue, receive, interpret, and act on commands.*** The two types of communication that make up this function are ***directions*** and ***feedback***, and the goal is the successful influence of other members of the organization. *The outcome of the command function is co-ordination among the many interdependent members of the organization.*

2. The Relational Function

Communication allows members of the organization ***to create and maintain productive business and personal relationships with other members of the organization.*** Relationships on the job affect job performance in many ways, ***for example***, job satisfaction, the flow of communication both down and up the organizational hierarchy, and the degree to which commands are followed. The importance of good interpersonal skills is highlighted on the job when you consider that many of the necessary relationships are not chosen but forced by organizational circumstances, making the relationships less stable, more prone to conflict, less committed, and so on.

3. The Ambiguity-Management Function

Choices in an organizational setting are often made in highly ambiguous circumstances. ***For example,*** multiple motivations exist since choices affect co-workers and the organization, as well as oneself, the organization's objectives may not be clear, and the context within which the choice needs to be made may be unclear. ***Communication is the means for coping with and reducing the ambiguity inherent in the organization.*** Members talk with each other in an effort to structure the environment and make sense of new situations, which entails gaining and sharing information.

BOX 12.1 : LIFE OF SIR RICHARD BURTON

"He who knows not and knows not he knows not,
— HE IS A FOOL, SHUN HIM.
He who knows not and knows he knows not,
— HE IS SIMPLE, TEACH HIM.
He who knows and knows not he knows,
— HE IS ASLEEP, AWAKE HIM.
He who knows and knows he knows,
— HE IS WISE, FOLLOW HIM."

Source : Lady Burton

12.4 A HOLISTIC VIEW

In addition to the above, communication also serves the following seven functions. viz. **E**valuating, **I**mage-projecting, **W**elfare, **T**eaching, **E**xecutive, **O**rientation and **I**ncidental-Neutral functions*.

* *Acronym* : **EIW – TEO – I**

Mnemonic : **E**mperor of **I**reland **W**ent to **T**hailand to **E**at **O**range **I**cecream.

1. The Evaluating Function

This function evaluates one's own inputs, or another's outputs or some ideological schemes. The dynamic nature of a functioning organiszation demands that ***constant evaluation be made of the activities to measure progress towards the desired objectives***. Feedback often tells the effects of communication or action.

2. Image Projecting Function

The image which an enterprise creates for itself is very much significant. It helps its existence, growth and survival. ***Communication is used for not only building up image consciousness among employees but also projecting goodwill or image of the enterprise in the society.***

3. Welfare Function

Both sociologists and psychologists consider ***communication to be a means of attaining the welfare of an enterprise.***

4. Teaching Function

By communication, the organization educates workers about personal safety on the jobs, particularly during work situations at machines. This is essential to reduce accidents, to lower compensation and legal costs, as also to decrease recruitment and training costs for replacements.

5. Executive Function

According to **Chester I. Barnard**, the first executive function is to develop and maintain a system of communication. ***Pertinent information consisting of facts, feelings and ideas must therefore, be communicated for taking prompt and proper decisions.***

6. Orientation Function

One of the important functions of communication ***is to make people acquainted with subordinates, peers and superiors with policies, objectives, rules and regulations of the organization.***

7. Incidental Neutral Function

According to **Lee Thayer**, many communications within organizational contexts have no direct connection with accomplishment of the objectives of the organization. ***However, as auxiliary or contributing communications, they may contribute indirectly to organizational objectives and directly to satisfaction of individual needs that are compatible with organizational goals.*** Providing social contact within the organization is an apt example in this regard.

LAUGH A LITTLE
THINK A LITTLE

ART OF INTERPRETATION

The wife chewed out her husband at the company picnic a while back: "Doesn't it embarrass you that people have seen you go upto the buffet table five times?"

"Not a bit", The husband replied. "I just tell them I'm filling up the plate for you!"

Source : Not Known

SUMMARY

'Brevity is the soul of wit.'

➠ WILLIAM SHAKESPEARE

Communication performs multipurpose functions. According to **Stephen P. Robbins,** communication serves four major functions viz. to control, to motivate, to express emotion and to provide information. **Lee Thayer** divides functions of communication into four specific categories such as informative function, command function, persuasive function and integrative function. **C. Conrad,** identifies three functions of communication : command function, relational function and ambiguity-management function. To sum up, following are the major functions of communication : to evaluate, to teach, to execute, to orient employees and to project image, to obtain welfare of the enterprise as also to provide incidental neutral function within the organization.

KEY TERMS & CONCEPTS

'Most of the disputes in the world arise from words.'

➠ WILLIAM MURRAY

- Control
- Motivation
- Emotional Expression
- Information
- Instruction
- Persuasion
- Integration
- Evaluation
- Image Projection
- Orientation
- Exeuctive Function
- Incidental Neutral Function

REVIEW & DISCUSSION QUESTIONS

'Questions clarify the concepts.'

➠ *ANON*

Group A : OBJECTIVE TYPE QUESTIONS :

1. Fill in the blanks :

(a) Organizations have ________ hierarchies and formal _______ that employees are required to follow.

(b) Communication fosters motivation by ________ to employees what is to be ________, how ________ they are doing, and what can be done to ________ performance if it is ________.

(c) Work efforts are ________ rather than ________ as a result of properly integrative communication.

(d) Communication is used for not only building up image ________ among employees but also projecting ________ or ________ of the enterprise in the society.

(e) Communication is used for not only building up image ________ among employees but also projecting ________ or ________ of the enterprise in the society.

(e) Communication makes people acquainted with subordinates, ________ and ________ with policies, ________ and rules and ________ of the organization.

2. State whether the following statements are True (T) or False (F) and JUSTIFY your answer:

(i) The influence and persuasion function can also be termed as relational function.

(ii) The first executive function is to develop and maintain a system of communication.

(iii) Communication teaches workers about personal safety even at the cost of image of the enterprise.

(iv) The two types of communication that make up the command function are motivational and evaluative.

(v) Communication is the means for coping with and reducing the ambiguity inherent in the organization.

Group B : SHORT ANSWER TYPE QUESTIONS :

1. What, according to **Stephen P. Robbins**, are the major functions of communication within a group or an organization?
2. What are the specific categories to which **Lee Thayer** has divided major functions of communication?
3. List out and discuss the major functions of communication identified by **Conrad**.
4. What do you mean by 'Relational Function' of communication suggested by Conrad.
5. Write short notes on :

   (a) The 'Integrative Function' of communication.

   (b) The 'Ambiguity-Management Function' of communication.

   (c) The 'Incidental Neutral Function' of communication.

Group C : ESSAY TYPE QUESTIONS :

1. *"Within a group or an organization, communication acts to control member behaviour in several ways."* How? Cite examples.
2. How does communication facilitate decision-making by providing information?
3. Compare *'teaching function'* of communication with *'orientation function.'* Bring out the contrast between them.
4. *'The importance of good interpersonal skills is highlighted on the job when you consider that many of the necessary relationships are not chosen but forced by organizational circumstances.* Justify citing appropriate examples.
5. Do you find any similarities between the views of *Robbins, Thayer & Conrad* as regards functions of communication? Discuss analytically.

REFERENCES & NOTES

1. Stephen P. Robbins, *Organizational Behaviour,* Prentice Hall of India, New Delhi, 9th Edition,. 2000, p. 284.
2. Lee Thayer, *Communication and Communication System,* Richard D. Irwin, Inc., 1968, pp. 187-239.
3. The thematic discussion, ideas and examples in this section are drawn from C. Conrad, *Strategic Organizational Communication: Cultures, Situations and Adaption*, Holt, Rinehart & Winston, New York, 1985, pp. 7-8; Dr. Tubbs & Ms. Moss, *Human Communication : Principles & Contexts,* McGraw-Hill, New York, 9th Edition, 2003, p. 454.

❒ ❒ ❒

CHAPTER

13

COMMUNICATION — ITS PURPOSES

CONTENTS

QUOTABLE QUOTES

1. "True ease in writing comes from art, not chance;
   As those move easiest who have learnt to dance."

   ➡ **ALEXANDER POPE**

2. "Genius is one percent inspiration and ninety-nine percent perspiration."

   ➡ **THOMAS ALVA EDISON**

3. General Eisenhower used to teach leadership with a simple piece of string. He would put it on a table and say, "Pull it and it will follow wherever you wish. Push it and it will go nowhere at all. It is just that way when it comes to leading people. Don't push people into doing things. Pull (=motivate) them."

   ➡ **ADAPTED**

4. "I know you believe you understand
   What you think I said,
   But I am not sure you realize that
   What you heard is not what I meant!"

   ➡ **ROBERT McCLOSKEY**

LEARNING OBJECTIVES

After going through this chapter, you should be able to —

- Identify and understand many different purposes of communication;
- Explain different opinions of communication theorists as regards purposes of communication;
- Compare & contrast various views and select the best ones as per your own understanding of the theme.

13.1 MICHAEL A. HITT et. al's VIEW

According to **Hitt, Middlemist & Mathis,**[37] purposes of communication can be sorted into *three* primary categories:

(1) **To express an opinion, idea, or attitude:** The sender who simply expresses does not intend for the listener to do anything more than listen to the statement. *For example,* the purpose of financial reports to stockholders is often just to express the information.

(2) **To prompt action from the listener:** *For example,* a manager may attempt to improve an employee's performance by communicating displeasure with the employee's current performance.

(3) **To support actions initiated by other mechanisms:** *For example,* management of a firm may decide to implement a *"communication council"* to co-ordinate policy and help business units improve communication. To support this action, management also may implement a new training program in communication skills.

BOX 13.1 : STRATEGY — WHAT & WHY?

Alice : Would you tell me, please, which way I ought to go from here?
Cheshire Cat : That depends a good deal on where you want to get to.
Alice : I don't much care where ....
Cheshire Cat : Then, it doesn't matter which way you go.

Source : **Lewis Carroll,** *'Alice in Wonderland'*

13.2 KEITH DAVIS'S VIEW

According to **Dr. Keith Davis,**[2] there are *two* purposes of communication as a management activity :

(1) **The *skill* to work:** One purpose of communication is to provide the information and understanding necessary for group effort.

(2) **The *will* to work:** Another purpose of communication is to provide the attitudes necessary for motivation, co-operation and job satisfaction.

According to **Dr. Davis,** the second purpose is extremely important, *because there is increasing evidence that modern work problems are related more to attitudes than to fundamental skills and job knowledge.* And when both the skills and the wills to work are combined, the result is the joint achievement of high productivity and high job satisfaction through teamwork.

13.3 JOHN ADAIR'S VIEW

John Adair[3] has usefully defined the purpose of communication in organizations through a model of three over-lapping circles:

(*i*) to achieve the common task,

(*ii*) to maintain the unity of the whole body, and

(*iii*) to meet individual needs.

DIAGRAM 13.1 : PURPOSES OF COMMUNICATION — JOHN ADAIR'S MODEL

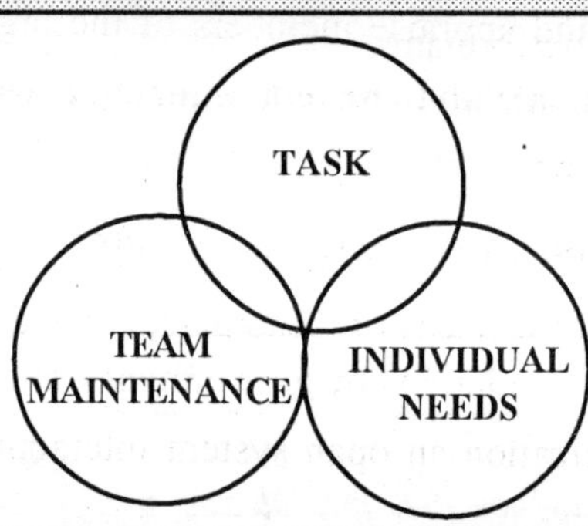

Source : **John Adair**, *'Training for Communication'*, London, 1973, p. 50.

Success or failure in the *Task circle* helps to build up or break down group unity (the *Team Maintenance* need). Also it affects the *Individual* for good or ill, because in a large part his own higher needs (*physical, social, esteem, achievement and self-actualisation*) and values are bound up with the common advance or corporate progress, as well as the quality of the common life. Yet performance rests on the knowledge and skills of individual members, just as the social life of the team rests upon the humour and courage which individuals export into it. The circles are thus interacting.

BOX 13.2 : COMMUNICATION — AN ART

Communication is an art. It is here where you win or lose a friend. After conversing with Gladstone and Disraeli, Madam Ezabella remarked, "When Gladstone talked to me, I felt that he was the most important person in England. But when Disraeli spoke to me, he made me feel that I was the most important person in England."

Source : *Unknown*

13.4 KOONTZ & WEIHRICH'S VIEW

Dr. Koontz & Dr. Weihrich[4] have listed the purposes of communication both within the organization (*i.e. internal*) and outside the organization (*i.e. external*) in the following way:

(A) Purposes of Internal Communication

1. To establish and disseminate goals of an enterprise;
2. To develop plans for their achievement;
3. To organise human and other resources in the most effective and efficient way;
4. To select, develop and appraise members of the organization;
5. To lead, direct, motivate and create a climate in which people want to contribute;
6. To control performance.

(B) Purposes of External Communication

1. To become aware of the needs of customers, the availability of suppliers, the claims of stakeholders, the regulations of governments, and the concerns of a community;
2. To make any organization an open system interacting with its environment.

13.5 KATZ & KAHN'S VIEW

In any organization, downward communication i.e. *superior-initiated communication* is more dominant than upward communication. i.e. *subordinate-initiated communication.* **Katz & Kahn**[5] have identified five general purposes of superior-initiated communication in an organization :

1. To give specific task directives about job instructions;
2. To give information about organizational procedures and practices;
3. To provide information about the rationale of the job;
4. To tell subordinates about their performance;
5. To provide ideological information to facilitate the indoctrination of goals.

BOX 13.3 : THE PARABLE OF A SOWER

Once there was a man who was sent out to sow corn. As he scattered the seeds in the field, some of them fell along the path, and the birds ate them up. Some of then fell on rocky ground, and when the plants sprouted, they dried up because the soil had no moisture. Some of the seeds fell among thorn bushes, which grew up with the plants and choked them. And some seeds fell in good soil, the plants grew and produced corn, some produced a hundred grains, others sixty and others thirty.

Source : **Mathew, 13, 1-9, Luke 8, 4-8.**

13.6 GERALD M. GOLDHABER'S VIEW

According to recent research findings, one of the major dimensions of communication is *interactive communication.* **Gerald M. Goldhaber,**[6] basing his inquiry on several research studies, has summarized *four* of the most important purposes of *interactive communication :*

1. **Task Co-ordination:** The Department heads may meet monthly to discuss how each department is contributing to the system's goals.
2. **Problem-solving:** The members of a department may assemble to discuss how they will handle a threatened budget cut; they may employ ***brainstorming techniques.***
3. **Information-sharing:** The members of one department may meet with the members of another department to give them some new data.
4. **Conflict Resolution:** The members of one department may meet to discuss a conflict inherent in the department or between departments.

The examples for each of the major purposes are mainly departmental or inter-depepartmental meetings.

13.7 DAVID D. VANFLEET'S VIEW

According to **David D. Vanfleet**[7], *organizational communication* serves mainly three purposes:

DIAGRAM 13.2 : PURPOSES OF ORGANIZATIONAL COMMUNICATION — DAVID D. VANFLEET'S MODEL

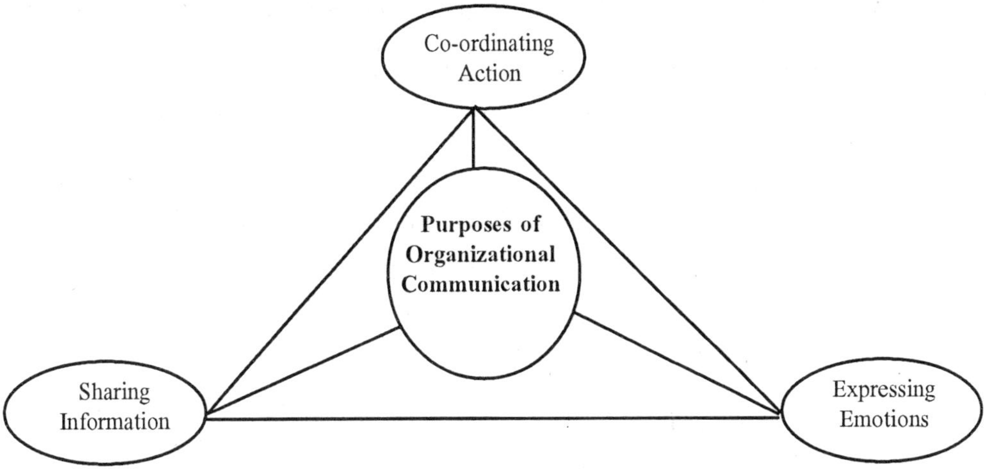

***Source* :** **David D. Vanfleet,** Behaviour in Organizations, pp. 213-215.
***Diagram* :** Exclusively designed by the Author (**Dr. Roy**).

1. **Co-ordinating Action:** *Just as the human nervous system responds to stimuli and co-ordinates responses by sending messages to the various parts of the body, communications co-ordinate the actions of the parts of an organization.* Communication transforms a group of unrelated individuals into a team that knows what its goals are and how it will try to reach them.
2. **Sharing Information:** The first type of an information that needs to be shared is what the goals of the organization are. People need to know where they are headed and why. They also need directions for their specific tasks. To keep its employees working well, an organization must also communicate with them about how well they are performing. Communication is essential to the decision-making process as well. *Information-sharing is needed to define problems, generate and evaluate alternatives, implement decisions and evaluate results.*
3. **Expressing Emotions:** Communication also allows people to express their emotions. Some people think that expressions of emotion have no place in the organization, but in fact communication about feelings can be very important to employee morale and productivity. *Employees who feel they cannot vent their anger or express their joy on the job may feel frustrated and repressed and may distance themselves from the organization.*

LAUGH A LITTLE

THREE ECONOMISTS & THREE MATHEMATICIANS

Three economists and three mathematicians were going for a trip by train. Before the journey, the mathematicians bought three tickets but the economists bought only one. The mathematicians were glad their studpid colleagues were going to pay a fine. Howevr, when the T.T.E. was approaching their compartment to check the tickets, all three economists went to the nearest toilet. The T.T.E. noticing that somebody was in the toilet, knocked on the door. In reply, he saw a hand with one ticket. He checked it and left. Thus, the economists saved 2/3rd of the ticket price.

The next day, the mathematicians decided to use the same strategy. They bought only one ticket, but the three economists did not buy tickets at all! When the mathematicians saw the T.T.E., they all hid in the toilet, and when they heard knocking, they handed in the ticket for T.T.E.'s checking. But they didn't get the ticket back.

Why? – The economists took it and went to the other toilet.

Source : **Not Known**

13.8 JOHN G. GLOVER'S VIEW

John G. Glover[8] has advocated the following purposes of communication for the organization:

(*a*) To keep employees informed of company's progress;

(*b*) To provide employees with orders and instructions in connection with their rights, duties and responsibilities;

(*c*) To solicit information from the employees which may aid management;

(*d*) To make each employee interested in his respective job and in the work of the company as a whole;

(*e*) To express management's interest in its personnel;

(*f*) To minimize or prevent labour turnover;

(*g*) To indoctrinate employees with ***'the will to work'*** and the benefits derived from their association with the company; and

(*h*) To instill each employee with personal prestige and pride in being a member of the company.

LAUGH A LITTLE
THINK A LITTLE

[A] MAGIC WITH NUMBER '9'

0 × 9 + 1 = 1
1 × 9 + 2 = 1 1
12 × 9 + 3 = 1 1 1
123 × 9 + 4 = 1 1 1 1
1234 × 9 + 5 = 1 1 1 1 1
12345 × 9 + 6 = 1 1 1 1 1 1
123456 × 9 + 7 = 1 1 1 1 1 1 1
1234567 × 9 + 8 = 1 1 1 1 1 1 1 1
123456678 × 9 + 9 = 1 1 1 1 1 1 1 1 1
123456789 × 9 + 10 = 1 1 1 1 1 1 1 1 1 1

[B] MAGIC OF ADDITION

1+2 = 3
4+5+6 = 7+8
9+10+11+12 = 13+14+15
16+17+18+19+20 = 21+22+23+24
25+26+27+28+29+30 = 31+32+33+34+35
36+37+38+39+40+41+42=43+44+45+46+47+48

SUMMARY

'Brevity is the soul of wit.'

➡ WILLIAM SHAKESPEARE

Broadly speaking, the purpose of communication in any organization is to effect changes — to influence actions towards the welfare of the organization. In this chapter, we have discussed in brief different opinions of reputed communication theorists on the purposes of communication. Most prominent among them are the views of Hitt, Middlemist & Mathis, Keith Davis, John Adair, Koontz & Weihrich, Katz & Kahn, Goldhaber, Vanfleet, Glover, etc. To sum up, we fulfil many different purposes through communication. It is said *'to live is to communicate'* and we communicate to understand others as also have others understand us. The better the understanding of others' thoughts and behaviour by the sender of the message, the more effective and purposeful the communication can be.

KEY TERMS & CONCEPTS

'Most of the disputes in the world arise from words.'

➡ WILLIAM MURRAY

- Attitude
- Stockholders
- Listener
- Mechanism
- Communication Council
- Strategy
- Skill to Work
- Will to Work
- Task
- Internal Communication
- External Communication
- Interactive Communication
- Organizational Communication
- Labour turnover
- Indoctrination

REVIEW & DISCUSSION QUESTIONS

'Questions clarify the concepts.'

➡ ANON

Group A : OBJECTIVE TYPE QUESTIONS :

1. Fill in the blanks :

(a) According to Dr. Keith Davis, there are two purposes of communication viz. the _______ to work and the _______ to work.

(b) According to Dr. Koontz & Dr. Weihrich, the two purposes of communication are _______ communication and _______ communication.

(c) In any organization _______ _______ communication is more dominant than _______ _______ communication.

(d) Four of the most important purposes of interactive communication suggested by Gerald M. Goldhaber are _______ _______, problem solving, _______ _______ and _______ _______.

(e) John Adair has defined the purposes of communication in organizations through a model of three overlapping circles. They are _______ circle, _______ _______ circle, _______ _______ circle.

2. State whether the following statements are True (T) or False (F) and JUSTIFY your answer:

(i) The 'will-to-work' is more important than 'skill-to-work.'

(ii) Success or failure in the 'task' circle builds up or breaks down group unity.

(iii) Communication within the organization is no longer as necessary as communication outside the organization.

(iv) Organizational communication serves mainly two purposes viz. co-ordinating action and expressing emotions.

(v) A manager may attempt to improve an employee's performance by communicating displeasure with the employee's past performance.

Group B : SHORT ANSWER TYPE QUESTIONS :

1. What, according to Hitt, Middlemist & Mathis, are the purposes of communication?
2. Prove, citing appropriate examples, why 'will-to-work' is more important than 'skill-to-work.'
3. What are the purposes of internal communication as suggested by Dr. Koontz & Dr. Weihrich?
4. Enlist three purposes of organizational communication.
5. Describe, after John G. Glover, the eight purposes of communication for an organization.

Group C : ESSAY TYPE QUESTIONS :

1. What are the major purposes of interactive communication? Can you add one or two more purposes to that list? You have to substantiate your contentions.
2. "In any organization, superior-initiated communication is more dominant than subordinate-initiated communication." Critically comment on the statement.
3. Compare and contrast the views expressed by John G. Glover and also by David D. Vanfleet on the purposes of communication.
4. "When both skills and wills to work are combined, the result is the joint achievement of high productivity and high job-satisfaction through teamwork." Do you agree with this statement? If so, give valid reasons therefor.
5. Why is external communication gaining growing importance in business organizations? Critically offer your views particularly in the context of on-going globalization, liberalisation and rapid technological advancements.

REFERENCES & NOTES

1. Michael A. Hitt, R. Dennis Middlemist & Robert L. Mathis, *Management: Concepts & Effective Practices,* 3rd Edition, 1989, pp. 411-412.
2. Dr. Keith Davis, *Human Behaviour A Work,* Tata McGraw-Hill, New Delhi, 1979, p. 375.
3. John Adair, *Training for Communication,* Macdonald & Co., London, 1973, p. 50.
4. Dr. Harold Koontz & Dr. Heinz Weihrich, *Essentials of Management,* Tata McGraw-Hill, New Delhi, 5th Edition, 1998, p. 367.
5. Daniel Katz & Robert Kahn, *The Social Psychology of Organizations,* Wiley, New York, 2nd Edition, 1978, p. 440.
6. Gerald M. Goldhaber, *Organizational Communication,* W.C. Brown, Dubuque, 1974, p. 121.
7. David D. Vanfleet, *Behaviour in Organizations,* Houghton Mifflin Co., Boston, USA, 1991, pp. 213-215.
8. John G. Glover, *Fundamentals of Professional Management*, Harper & Row, 1958, p. 167.

❒ ❒ ❒

CHAPTER

14

COMMUNICATION — ITS IMPORTANCE & SIGNIFICANCE

CONTENTS

QUOTABLE QUOTES

1. "Just as arteries and veins sustain the flow of life-giving blood to the vital organs of the body, so does the communication work as the very sap and life-blood of all our daily tasks. Without communication, almost all daily functions would cease and the world as it is known today would grind to a halt."

   ➡ ANON

2. "Communication is the essential 'flux' that binds individuals together in group activities. It proposes to ensure for continuing effectiveness of the binder."

   ➡ DALE YODER

3. "A committee is a group of men who individually can do nothing but as a group decide that nothing can be done."

   ➡ ANON

4. On being asked by Akbar, Birbal painted the emperor's portrait in six days. Akbar asked his other eight Navratnas to comment. Each one put a dot on the portrait wherever he felt it was not good.

   Akbar asked Birbal to explain. Birbal thought for a while and then called for eight blank canvases for his colleagues and asked them to do the portrait.

   No one came forward. Akbar, with drooping eyes, murmured.

   The moral of the story is that it's easy to find faults in what others do, but difficult to do it yourself."

   ➡ ADAPTED

LEARNING OBJECTIVES

After going through this chapter, you should be able to —

- Explain why communication is so much important in both organizational and individual contexts;
- List out and exemplify the notable contributions communication makes to get things done;
- Identify and discuss significant factors responsible for growing importance of communication in business.

14.1 : COMMUNICATION — ITS IMPORTANCE AND SIGNIFICANCE

For an organization, *Communication* has been portrayed variously by different authors as:

- its life blood
- its brain
- its arteries
- the mortar/glue which binds its parts together
- its oxygen
- its central nervous system
- the highways along which its business is transacted
- the fuel which drives its engine.

All these metaphors emphasize the important role of communication. According to **William Scholz**[1], communication is the only key that unlocks the door to increase personal effectiveness, enhances job satisfaction and improves 'on-the-job' performance. It is also an important tool in raising productivity, preventing conflicts and strikes, cutting costs, and contributing on the whole to the growth and profitability of any business.

Silence is, therefore, not golden. It breeds secrecy. Secrecy leads to misunderstanding and mistrust. Mistrust gives birth to suspicion. Suspicion prevents social cohesion and integration. Communication is, therefore, a basic pre-requisite for mutual understanding.

According to **Dale Yoder,**[2] communication is the essential 'flux' that binds individuals together in group activities. It proposes to ensure the continuing effectiveness of the binder. In the words of **David R. Hampton,**[3] what communication does for an organization resembles what the bloodstream does for an organism. The bloodstream supplies all the cells of the organism with oxygen; the communication system supplies all the units — departments and divisions — people of the organization with information. Deprived of oxygen, the cells malfunction and die; deprived of necessary information, individuals and departments with the organization malfunction, which can certainly lead to a sort of terminal ineffectiveness for them and for the organization as a whole. **Fred Luthans**[4] has even gone so far as to pinpoint communication as the explanation for lovers' quarrels, ethnic prejudice, war between nations, the generation gap, industrial disputes and organizational conflict.

The importance as also significance of communication can be judged from the following:

14.1.1 An Aid to Managerial Performance

According to **James A. Stoner,**[5] effective communication is important for managers for two reasons. ***Firstly,*** communication is the process by which the management functions of planning, organising, leading and controlling are accomplished. ***Secondly,*** communication is the activity to which managers devote an overwhelming proportion of their time.

14.1.2. A Tool of Supervision

In the words of **E.F.L. Brech**[6], communication is a tool of supervision which is in constant use and must always be in good condition. It is perhaps true that what makes leaders inspiring and outstanding, in addition to that vital spark of enthusiasm and an unshakable faith, is the ability to convey ideas and information clearly and vividly, and communicate them most appropriately to others.

14.1.3. A Basis of Co-ordination

Mary Cushing Nyles[7] remarked that good communications are essential to co-ordination. They are necessary upward, downward and sideways through all the levels of authority and advice for transmission, interpretation and adoption of policies, for the sharing of knowledge and information and for the more subtle needs of good morale and mutual understanding.

14.1.4. A Basic to an Organization's Existence

According to **Herbert A. Simon**,[8] without communication there can be no organization, for there is no possibility then of the group influencing the behavior of the individual. **Herbert G. Hicks**[9] is also of the opinion that communication is basic to an organization's existence — from the birth of the organization on through its continuing life. When communication stops, organised activity ceases to exist.

BOX 14.1 : PETER DRUCKER ON THE IMPORTANCE OF COMMUNICATION IN BUSINESS

"Colleges teach the one thing that is perhaps most valuable for the future employee to know. But very few students bother to learn it. This one basic skill is the ability to organize and express ideas in writing and speaking.

"As soon as you move one step from the bottom, your effectiveness depends on your ability to reach others through the spoken or the written word. And the further away your job is from manual work, the larger the organization of which you are the employee, the more important it will be that you know how to convey your thoughts in writing or speaking. In the very large organization .... this ability to express oneself is perhaps the most important of all the skills a person can possess."

Source : **Peter F. Drucker**, ***People & Performance***, Harper College Press, New York, 1977.

14.1.5. Eyes and Ears of Management

Management means dealing with people. Communication provides the key to such dealing. It facilitates exchange of ideas and information, the meeting of minds, and can, therefore, be aptly described as the eyes and ears of management. According to **John J. Corson,**[10] when two people work together, each must understand what the other is doing. They may talk to each other, or if they are deaf mutes, make signs with their hands. However, they must get their ideas from one to the other and vice-versa. **Peterson & Plowman,**[11] therefore, regard communication as an essential function of management.

14.1.6. A Promoter of Good Human Relations

In the words of **Charles E. Redfield,**[12] effective communication is an essential ingredient in management-employee relations. It may cement an organization or disrupt it. In western countries, it has worked as the lubricant of industry. It is the mechanism through which human relations have developed. **Robert D. Berth**[13] also opines that it is impossible to have human relations without communication and vice versa.

14.1.7. A Tool of Information

According to **Peter F. Drucker,**[14] the manager has a specific tool — *'information'*. He does not *'handle'* people; he motivates, guides, organises people to do their own work. *His tool — his only tool — to do all this is the spoken or written word or the language of numbers.* No matter whether the manager's job is engineering, accounting or selling, his effectiveness depends on his ability to listen and to read, on his ability to speak and to write. He needs skills in getting his thinking across to other people as well as skills in finding out what other people are after.

14.1.8. A Lubricant for Smooth Working

Communication makes possible the smooth and uninterrupted running of an enterprise. When objectives are desired, what activities are required, how they will be done, who will do what and when — all these depend upon both internal and external communication process of the organization. According to **George R. Terry,**[15] communication serves as the lubricant fostering for the smooth operation of the management process.

14.1.9. An Aid to Efficient Planning

The making of a plan requires facts, figures, reports of past performance, estimates of future trends, opinions of experts, suggestions from subordinates, and so on. All these are made available to the planners through communication network. The more accurate and up-to-date the communication network, the more efficient and successful the planning.

BOX 14.2 : WINNING STARTS WITH BEGINNING

A woman had five children to bring up on her own. She loved her children very much and was the best mother — helping them with their homework, cooking healthy meals for them, working at two jobs so she could provide for them. Each night she prayed that she would win the lottery so that she could buy her children all the little extras she would love to give them but couldn't afford.

Before she knew it, her children were grown. They'd all left home and she was alone. Reflecting on how much she had sacrificed for the sake of her family, she suddenly felt sad and a little angry. That night when she prayed she said : "God, I've done by best. I've been a good mother and a God-fearing woman. Why haven't you helped me out? Why haven't you let me win the lottery just once? Even a small win? After all, I've done my bit!"

Suddenly, the house shook. Thunder crashed and lightning flashed. A deep voice said : "The least you could have done was buy a lottery ticket!"

Source : ANON

14.1.10. A Vital Factor in Effective Decision Making

Quality of managerial decisions mainly depends on good communication processes. According to **Pfiffner & Sherwood**,[16] if decision making and communication processes are not identical, they are so interdependent that they become inseparable in practice.

14.1.11. An Important Tool for Effective Control

According to **Newman, Summer & Warren**,[17] to be assured of good control, we need a system of regular formal reports. Every manager should give some attention to whether the report system in his department and company provides the right kind of information, to the right people and at the right time to enable his controls to work effectively.

14.1.12. An Aid to Effective Leadership

A leader sells his ideas, removes misunderstanding, and influences mindset and behavior of his followers. All these are effectively done by successful leaders only through tactful and persuasive communication.

14.1.13. An Aid to Managerial Efficiency

By communication management conveys goals and targets, issues instructions and orders, allocates jobs and responsibilities, and looks after performance of subordinates. The yardstick for measuring managerial efficiency is judged by the flow and quality of communication.

14.1.14. A Contributor to Organizational Effectiveness

According to **Bavelas & Barrett,**[18] an organization may be viewed as an elaborate system of gathering, evaluating, recombining and disseminating information. It follows from this that the effectiveness of an organization depends very largely on the effectiveness of its communication — upon the quality and availability of information with the system.

14.1.15. A Saver of Time and Efforts

Effective communication results in saving time and efforts. Manager by sitting in his chamber can communicate easily to all his subordinates, and in turn the subordinates can convey their work reports, suggestions, grievances without personally visiting the chamber of their boss. Time and efforts are thus saved at both the ends.

14.1.16. A Promoter of Industrial Peace

Communication creates a meeting of minds as well as a meeting of hearts. It promotes good relations between management and employees as also between management and trade unions thereby improving mutual co-operation and understanding as also industrial peace and harmony.

14.1.17. A Tool for Maximum Productivity

A sound communication system helps the management in achieving maximum productivity with minimum cost. In the words of **William Scholz,**[19] it is an important tool in raising productivity, preventing conflicts and strikes, cutting costs and contributing on the whole to the growth and profitability of any business.

BOX 14.3 : FROZEN EVALUATION RUINS PRODUCTIVITY

MARY IS A POOR WORKER

A frozen evaluation of a person, object or event is judgement set in concrete. It occurs when one forgets the process of change. An employee of 1965 is not an employee of 1975. A few years bring changes in everyone. Yet we sometimes remember someone with whom we have had no contact for a number of years as the same person we "knew" last time we were with them. This assumption of "non-change" is fallacious because it implies rest, permanence, constancy, which is really not.

Suppose, Mary Adams is transferred from one department to another in a large bank. Her previous supervisor comments to her new superior that "Mary is a poor worker." At least two communication errors are made here. ***First,*** *Mary's former supervisor fails to be specific concerning what she means by the term "poor worker." Under what conditions, doing what sorts of work can Mary be called poor?* ***Second,*** *the statement implies that Mary is unable or unwilling to improve her performance regardless of any changed circumstances that may occur in the future. It is quite possible that with a new job assignment and a different supervisor Mary could become a satisfactory employee.*

To talk of Mary as if she is totally static & unchanging is to run the risk of misevaluating reality. Her new supervisor should withhold judgement until she has had a chance to prove herself on her new assignment. Her previous supervisor might have increased the accuracy of her statement by stating under what conditions Mary's performance was unsatisfactory and why it was judged to be so. In addition, the time period during which the unsatisfactory performance occurred might have been given.

Source: Based on **Herbet G. Hicks & C. Ray Gullett,** *Management*, pp. 515-16.

14.1.18. An Aid to Job Satisfaction

According to **A.J. Ayer,**[20] evil communication corrupts good manners. Good communication persuades human beings to make greater efforts towards their work performance. It is the only key, as **William Scholz**[21] puts it, that unlocks the door to increase personal effectiveness, enhanced job satisfaction, and improved on-the-job performance.

14.1.19. A Basic Tool for Morale Building and Motivation

Effective communication enables management to change the attitudes, to motivate, influence and satisfy the subordinates. It assists the workers in their adjustment with the physical and social aspect of work. **Dale Yoder**[12] observes that modern theory recognizes the influence of communication in every aspect of social or group activity. It is related to all levels of needs. Communication appears to be very close to primary creature needs of all, in part because the process of transmission and reception is pleasing and satisfying. It is the force that binds the people of the organization together.

LAUGH A LITTLE
THINK A LITTLE

THE FASTEST FATHER

Three boys are in the school yard bragging of how great their fathers are. The first one says, "Well, my father runs the fastest. He can shoot an arrow, and start to run; and I tell you, he gets there before the arrow."

The second boy says, "Ha ! you think that's fast. My father is a hunter. He can fire his gun and be there before bullet."

The third boy listens to the other two and shakes his head. He then says: "You two know nothing about fast. My father is a civil servant. He stops working at 4-30 and he is home by 3-45 !"

Source : **Adapted**

14.1.20. A Projector of Corporate Image

Communication develops, maintains and projects goodwill of the organization to the existing and potential customers, suppliers, stockholders, investors, dealers, governments and other sections of the society. By communicating necessary information on financial soundness, profitability and contribution of an organization in the social developments, public image towards the organization is created.Thus, the growth, stability and success of the organization mainly depends on how effectively the organization can handle its various means of communication.

Communication is, therefore, very vital for the existence and smooth sailing of any organization. That's why, **Chester I. Barnard**[23] has aptly remarked that the first executive function is to develop and maintain a system of communication.

BOX 14.4 : IMPORTANCE AND SIGNIFICANCE OF COMMUNICATION — POINTS AT A GLANCE

1. An aid to Managerial Performance	11. An important tool for effective Control
2. A tool of Supervision	12. An aid to effective Leadership
3. A basis of Co-ordination	13. An aid to Managerial Efficiency
4. A basic to Organization's existence	14. A contributor to Organizational Effectiveness
5. Eyes & ears of Management	15. A saver of Time and Efforts
6. A promoter of good Human Relations	16. A promoter of Industrial Peace
7. A tool of Information	17. A tool for maximum Productivity
8. A lubricant for Smooth Working	18. An aid to Job-satisfaction
9. An aid to efficient Planning	19. A basic tool for Morale building and Motivation
10. A vial factor in effective Decision-making	20. A projector of Corporate Image

14.2 A SPECIAL NOTE ON FACTORS RESPONSIBLE FOR GROWING IMPORTANCE OF COMMUNICATION IN BUSINESS

Following are the main factors which are usually responsible for growing importance of communication in business organizations:

14.2.1. Growth in Size of Organization

Modern business organizations are larger in size, employing thousands of persons, working at different places with different hierarchial levels in organization structure. Obviously, therefore, direct contacts are not possible. Hence, there is a need for an effective and efficient network of communication.

14.2.2 Growth of Trade Union Movement

Modern employees are more conscious of their rights and hence they are organised into trade unions. Management should develop and maintain healthy relations with the trade unions through an efficient system of communication.

14.2.3. Growing Specialisation

This being an age of sepcialisation, different activities of a business organization are being handled by different departments manned by specialists. The productivity gains of specialisation can be achieved only if there exists an effective system of communication in order to ensure mutual co-operation, co-ordination and understanding among various departments.

14.2.4. Growing Multinational and Multiple Business Activities

Multinational and multiple business activities across the world demand a strong communication link without which healthy growth of business comes to a complete halt.

14.2.5. Growing Cut-throat Competition

In this era of free and fierce competition resulted due to liberalisation and globalisation, the survival of a businessman depends upon his knowledge about his business rivals, the quality and prices of their products and also publicity strategies. A good businessman must, therefore, keep his all communication links alive in order to survive and also reach more and more customers to earn maximum profit thereby cutting a niche over their competitors.

BOX 14.5 : NEW GROWTH OPPORTUNITIES IN A GLOBAL MARKET PLACE

In the global market place, most natural boundaries and national borders are no longer the impassible barriers they once were. Domestic markets are opening to world-wide competition as businesses of all sizes look for new growth opportunities outside their own countries. Automotive giant, 'Ford' markets to customers in more than 125 countries with websites that offer local information, usually in the local language.

Even small companies in remote locations can sell and support their products on a global scale, thanks to e-mail, the internet, and world-wide delivery services. 'Pygmy boats' is a small manufacturer of Kayak kits in the equally small town of Port Townsend, Washington, and yet it reaches customers all over the world via its website. Similarly, 'Pens.it', an Italian retailer of fountain pens, sells its products globally online as well.

Source **: Bovee & Thill,** *Business Communication Today,* Pearson Education, Inc., Eighth Edition, 2008, p. 62.

14.2.6. Rapid Technological Advancements

Fast changes in science and technology lead to obsolescence of technology and knowledge. In order to overcome such situations, modern business organizations are adopting latest technologies and providing regular training to their staff-members through various advanced communication network e.g. telelecturing, video-conferencing and other computer-aided sophisticated devices.

14.2.7 Growing Emphasis on Human Relations

The significance of communication in business organization has been increased due to the growing importance of human relations in business and the desire of management to maintain good and healthy relations with the workers who are no longer treated as servants or commodities but as co-partners of the organization. Such treatment by the management develops in the minds of workers a sense of belongingness and loyalty to the organization.

14.2.8. Growing Need for Public Relations

The concept of social responsibilities of business implies that any business organization owes certain obligations to the society. As such the organization has to keep its owners. i.e. shareholders and the public viz. customers, employees, government and other sections of the society well-informed through a sound communication system about its contribution to society at large. Such relations with the public help business to improve its image in society.

LAUGH A LITTLE
THINK A LITTLE

A FORGETTFUL PATIENT

Doctor : *Was there anything troubling you ?*

Patient : *Well, to tell the truth, Doc, yes. You see, I seem to be getting forgetful. No, it' actually worse than that. I'm never sure I can remember where I put the can, or whether I answered a letter, or where I'm going, or what it is I'm going to do once I get there. So, I really need your help. What can I do ?*

The doctor looked at the patient minutely for half a minute, mused seriously for a moment, and then answered in his kindest tones, "Pay me in advance, please."

Source : Adapted

SUMMARY

'Brevity is the soul of wit.'

➡ **WILLIAM SHAKESPEARE**

Communication is the foundation for all human interactions. It is the only key that unlocks the door to increase personal effectiveness, enhanced job satisfaction and improved 'on-the-job' performance. It is also an important tool in raising productivity, preventing conflicts and strikes, cutting costs, and contributing on the whole to the growth and profitability of any business. Further, communication provides a common thread for the management processes of planning, organizing, leading and controlling. Managers at their organizations develop plans through communication with others and organize to carry out those plans by talking with people. Managers also know through regular exchange of information as to how and when to motivate, lead, form groups and teams, as also to exercise control, wherever necessary, to accomplish desired objectives. Certain factors are responsible for growing importance of communication in business such as growth in size of organization, growth in trade union movement, growing cut-throat competition due to liberalization, globalization, privatization, rapid technological advancements etc.

KEY TERMS & CONCEPTS

'Most of the disputes in the world arise from words.'

➡ **WILLIAM MURRAY**

- Job satisfaction
- On-the-Job performance
- Productivity
- Profitability
- Social cohesion
- Tool of supervision
- Organized activity
- Meeting of minds
- Communication network
- Effective leadership
- Managerial efficiency
- Persuasive communication
- Organizational effectiveness
- Industrial peace
- Corporate image

REVIEW & DISCUSSION QUESTIONS

"Questions clarify the concepts."

➡ **ANON**

Group A : OBJECTIVE TYPE QUESTIONS :

1. Fill in the blanks :

(a) Communication is the only key that unlocks the door to increase personal ________, enhanced job ________ and improved ________ performance.

(b) Silence is not golden because it breeds ________ and ________ leads to misunderstanding and ________, which eventually gives birth to ________.

(c) What communication does for an organization resembles what bloodstream does for an ________.

(d) Communication serves as the ________ fostering for the smooth operation of the ________ ________.

(e) Good communication creates a meeting of ________ as well as a meeting of ________.

2. State whether the following statements are True (T) or False (F) and JUSTIFY your answer:

(i) Evil communication corrupts good manners.

(ii) Communication is an important tool of effective supervision.

(iii) When communication pours in from all sides, organized activity ceases to exist.

(iv) Communication may cement the organization or disrupt it.

(v) Communication creates a meeting of minds but not a meeting of hearts.

Group B : SHORT ANSWER TYPE QUESTIONS :

1. How does communication help project a good image towards the organization ?
2. "Communication acts a basic tool for morale-building and motivation." Elucidate with examples.
3. "Good communication is an aid to job satisfaction." Justify.
4. Prove that effective communication promotes industrial peace.
5. "Quality of managerial decisions depends on good communication." Explain briefly.

Group C : ESSAY TYPE QUESTIONS :

1. Why do you think good communication in an organization resembles bloodstream in an organism?
2. "The yardstick for managerial efficiency is judged by the flow and quality of communication." Give reasons in support of the above statement.
3. "Effective communication results in saving time and efforts." Explain with the help of valid examples.
4. Write three small paragraphs on the importance and significance of communication in business organizations.
5. Discuss briefly the factors responsible for growing importance of communication in business.

REFERENCES & NOTES

1. William Scholz, *Communication in Business Organization,* Prentice Hall, New Jersey, 1963.
2. Dale Yoder, *Personnel Management and Industrial Relations,* Prentice Hall, New Delhi, 1976.
3. David R. Hampton, *Contemporary Management,* McGraw-Hill, New York, 1981, p. 399.
4. Fred Luthans, *Organizational Behaviour*, McGraw-Hill, Singapore, 6th Edition, 1992, p. 466.
5. James A. Stoner, *Management,* Prentice Hall, Englewood Cliffs, 1982.
6. E.F.L. Brech, *The Principles & Practice of Management,* p. 314.
7. Mary Cushing Nyles, *The Essence of Management,* pp. 390-391.
8. Herbert A. Simon, *Administrative Behaviour,* Free Press, New York, 1976, p. 154.
9. Herbert G. Hicks, *The Management of Organizations*, McGraw-Hill, New York, 1967.
10. John J. Corson, 'Management — Tongue-tied, Deaf and Blind ?' *Advanced Management,* Vol. 12, September, 1956.
11. E. Peterson & E.G. Plowman, *Business Organization & Management,* Richard D. Irwin, Homewood, 1948, p. 444.
12. Charles E. Redfield, *Communication in Management*, Chicago University Press, Chicago, 1958, p. 3.

13. Robert D. Berth, 'Human Relations & Communication are Twins', *Personnel Journal,* December, 1952, p. 529.
14. Peter F. Drucker, *The Practice of Management,* Harper & Row Publishers, New York, 1954, p. 346.
15. George R. Terry, *Principles of Management,* Richard D. Irwin, Homewood, 1970.
16. John M. Piffner & Frank P. Sherwood, *Administrative Organization,* Prentice Hall, Englewood Cliffs, N.J., 1960.
17. William H. Newman, Charles E. Summer Jr., & E. Kirby Warren, *The Process of Management: Concepts, Behaviour & Practice,* Prentice Hall, Englewood Cliffs, 1972.
18. A. Bavelas & D. Barrett, 'An Experimental Approach to Organizational Communication', *Personnel,* March 1951, p. 368.
19. William Scholz, *Communication in Business Organization,* Prentice Hall, New Jersey, 1963.
20. A.J. Ayer, 'What is Communication ?' in A.J. Ayer & Others (ed.) *Studies in Communication,* Martin Secker & Worburyg, London, 1955.
21. William Scholz, *Communication in Business Organization,* Prentice Hall, New Jersey, 1963.
22. Dale Yoder, *Personnel Management & Industrial Relations,* Prentice Hall, New Delhi, 1976.
23. Chester I. Bernard, *The Functions of the Executive,* Harvard University Press, Cambridge, 1947, p. 226.

❐ ❐ ❐

CHAPTER

15

COMMUNICATION — ITS PRINCIPLES

CONTENTS

QUOTABLE QUOTES

1. "People think with their heart and not with their mind."

   ➡ **DALE S. BEACH** (*on the 'Principle of Attention'*)

2. "Integrity without knowledge is weak and useless.
   Knowledge without integrity is dangerous and dreadful."

   ➡ **ABRAHAM LINCOLN**

3. "Little people with little minds and little imagination jog through life in little ruts, smugly resisting all changes which would jar their little worlds."

   ➡ **MARIE FRASER**

4. "Only 10 per cent or less of our meaning is transmitted by words in face-to-face communication, and another 30 to 40 percent by the way the words are used. All the rest — more than half of our meaning — is transmitted non-verbally. Our eyes, our body, our clothes — all that we are and do — express our meaning."

   ➡ **MARION M. WOOD**

LEARNING OBJECTIVES

After going through this chapter, you should be able to —

- Define the term 'principle';
- Identify various principles of communication;
- List out at least five principles you think more important than the rest and justify why you think so.

15. PRINCIPLE OF COMMUNICATION

A *'principle'* is defined as a generally accepted rule of action. In order to make communication effective, certain scientific principles are required to be followed. Suggested herewith a list enumerating broad principles to serve as a fundamental guide to effective communication:

15.1. PRINCIPLE OF INFORMATION

Communicating on the 'communication realism', **George R. Terry** says that the first principle of effective communication is to *"inform yourself fully."* It implies that, first of all, the sender must be clear in his mind what he wants to communicate. Better the understanding, more effective the communication would be.

15.2. PRINCIPLE OF CLARITY

The beginning of all communication is some message. The message must be clear and unambiguous. It must be kept in mind that *"words do not speak themselves but the speaker gives them meaning."* According to **Gibson, Ivancevich & Donnelly**, the message can be conveyed properly only if it is clearly formulated in the mind of the communicator. Clear communication is a clean ladder to success in any business. That's why, recently many schools of business have either started or expanded their communication programs.[1] The **Amos and Waters study** substantiated the fact that communication skills need to be incorporated into college curricula.[2]

BOX 15.1 : UNSKILLED COMMUNICATORS EXPRESS UNCLEAR COMMUNICATIONS

The parents of a Houston High School pupil received a message from the principal about a special meeting on a proposed educational program. It read :

> *"Our school's cross-graded, multi-ethnic, individualized learning program is designed to enhance the concept of an open-ended learning program with emphasis on a continuum of multi-ethnic academically enriched learning using the identified intellectually gifted child as the agent or director of his own learning. Major emphasis is on cross-graded, multi-ethnic learning with the main*

objective being to learn respect for the uniqueness of a person."

The parent wrote to the principal :

"I have a college degree, speak two foreign languages and four Indian dialects, have been to a member of county fairs and three goat ropings, but I haven't the faintest idea as to what the hell you are talking about ? Do you?"

Source : *Johnson City Press Chronicle*, January 26, 1977, reported by Associated Press, cited by **Dale A. Level, Jr. & William P. Galle, Jr.**, *Managerial Communications*, Business Publications, Inc., Plano, Texas, 1988, pp. 7-8.

15.3. PRINCIPLE OF OBJECTIVE

The communicator must know clearly the objective of communication before actually transmitting the message. The objective may be to receive information or send information or initiate an action or change another person's attitude and so on. Once the purpose of communication is clear, it would be easier to choose an appropriate mode of communication.

15.4. PRINCIPLE OF ATTENTION

Dale S. Beach once remarked *"people think with their heart and not with their mind."* Hence, to make the communication effective, the receiver's attention should be drawn to the message communicated. One should, therefore, pay undivided attention to all incoming and outgoing messages. He cannot, therefore, afford to be negligent nor lethargic. The principle of *'actions speak louder than words'* should be borne in mind in this respect.

BOX 15.2 : THE CHINESE LOOKING GLASS

An elderly British Gentleman who was from quite a wealthy and distinguished family was invited to a royal public dinner in London. He was disconcerted to find himself seated next to a silent Chinese. Wanting to be courteous, however, he leaned toward him and asked, tentatively, ***"Likee soupee?"*** *The Chinese looked at him briefly, nodded, but said nothing, and conversation lapsed.*

However, it appeared that the Chinese was a foreign guest of some note, for as coffee was served he was called upon to say a few words. He rose, *bowed, and made a fifteen-minute speech in impeccable English about the sociological significance of the European Common Market. Amid polite applause, he then sat down, turned to his abashed English neighbour, and after the briefest of pauses, asked softly : **"Likee speechee?"***

***Source*: Dannis Bloodworth,** *The Chinese Looking Glass*, Farrar, Straus & Giroux, New York, 1967, p. 6.

15.5. PRINCIPLE OF CONSISTENCY

The messages to be communicated should not be mutually conflicting, rather they should be consistent with the overall objectives, plans, policies, programs and procedures of the organization. Self-contradictory or inconsistent messages always create chaos and confusion in the organization and ultimately cause cancerous effect on organization's health.

15.6. PRINCIPLE OF UNDERSTANDING THE RECEIVER

The communication sent must create a proper understanding in the receiver. In the words of **Ray A. Killian**[3], communicate with an awareness of the total physical and human setting in which the information will be received. Picture the place of work; determine the receptivity and understanding levels of the receivers; be aware of social climate and customs; question the information's timeliness. Ask what, when, and in what manner you would like to be communicated with if you were in the similar environment and position.

15.7. PRINCIPLE OF ADEQUACY & COMPLETENESS

The information should be adequate and complete in all respects. Incomplete and inadequate information delays action, spoils understanding and good relations as also affects efficiency of both the sender and the receiver of the communication. In order to ensure adequacy and completeness of message, it is necessary to check for the **Five "W" questions** viz. *Why, What, Who, Where, When*. For example, if you announce a meeting, specify ***why*** the meeting is being held, ***what*** is to discussed in the meeting, ***who*** is to attend the meeting, ***where*** and ***when*** the meeting is to be held.

15.8. PRINCIPLE OF TIMELINESS

The message must be conveyed at the appropriate time, otherwise it may fail to evoke the desired response and lose its importance and become itself merely a historical document on account of delay.

15.9. PRINCIPLE OF INTEGRATION

Communication is a means to an end, and not an end in itself. It is a means to attain the objectives of the organization through integrated efforts of all personnel in the organization. As **Koontz & O'Donnell**[4] remarked that the purpose of managerial communication is to support understanding by individuals as they achieve and maintain the co-operation needed to meet enterprise goals. All communications should be framed and transmitted in such a way as to support the integrity of the formal organization.

15.10. PRINCIPLE OF CREDIBILITY

Every communication transmitted should bear an element of source-credibility for whom it is meant. If there is no congruence between what is practised and what is said, it is difficult to make communication effective. An autocratic manager ordering subordinate supervisors to practise participative management will create a credibility gap that will be difficult to overcome.[5]

BOX 15.3 : THE 'DOCTOR FOX' EFFECT — VITALITY OF PRESENTATION

The effects of personal dynamism or vitality on source credibility were shown in the famous "Dr. Fox" studies. In these studies, an actor, Michael Fox was hired to present lectures to students. The context and the delivery style of the lectures varied. In some, factual information was presented in a very dry manner; in others, the lecturer presented non-sense material to the students but in a very energetic or interesting manner. When the lecturer presented material in a dynamic and entertaining manner, he was rated quite high by the students, even though the actual content of his lecture was nonsense. In addition, a person arguing for a position that appears to be opposite to his or her own best interests is seen as more credible than when arguing for his or her own actual interests.

Source **: J. Ware,** "Seduction in the Classroom : The Dr. Fox Effect", *Proceedings of Midwest Divisioỵ of Academy of Management Conference*, 1975.

15.11. PRINCIPLE OF INFORMALITY

When formal communications prove ineffective in evoking the needed response from the subordinates, managers should adopt the strategy of making use of grapevine i.e. informal channels of communication. According to **Koontz & O'Donnel**, the most effective communication results when managers utilise the informal organization to supplement the communication channels of the formal organization.

LAUGH A LITTLE
THINK A LITTLE

PRINCIPLE OF LIFE

A beautiful, young woman walked up to a little old man rocking in a chair on his porch. "I couldn't help noticing how happy you look", she said. "What's your secret for a long happy life?"

The little old man said, "I smoke three packs of cigarettes a day; I also drink a case of whisky a week, eat oily, fatty foods, and never exercise."

"That's amazing", The woman said, "How old are you?"

"Twenty-six only," The little old man said.

Source : Anon

15.12. PRINCIPLE OF TWO-WAY COMMUNICATION

To be effective and purposeful, communication should have information flow in both directions viz. *downward* and *upward*. The office boss may make his subordinates listen, but there's no way to make them understand. The communication is not truly successful until that which is received is also understood. This is popularly known as ***"getting through"*** to a person. The sender must get through the receiver. A much-desired condition of two way communication is that the boss (=sender) should not only speak, instruct and order but should also be prepared to listen, understand and consider the reactions (i.e. *suggestion and criticism*) of the subordinates (=*receivers*) who are there at the bottom of the ladder to carry out his insructions. **William V. Haney**[6] talks of an interesting experiment suggesting thereby utility of two-way communication. In the words of **Haney**, one experiment with eighteen groups reported that 90 percent of their members felt frustrated with one-way (*unilateral*) communication. They lacked confidence in their accuracy of performance, and their actual accuracy was low. With two-way (*bilateral*) communication, accuracy was much higher, and confidence in accuracy was over twice as great.

15.13. PRINCIPLE OF STRATEGIC USE OF MEDIA

Any message whether conveyed orally or in writing should be transmitted most quickly and clearly. The sender while transmitting the message should select the medium — either oral or written — keeping in view the category of the receiver (e.g. *his educational, socio-cultural, occupational status,* etc.) and the type of the message to be conveyed (e.g. *formal, informal, legal, technical, confidential* etc.) as also the purpose behind conveying such message.

15.14. PRINCIPLE OF STRATEGIC SELECTION OF COMMUNICATION NETWORK

Communication network refers to the route or channel through which communication travels to its destination. i.e. the person for whom it is meant. A number of such networks may exist in the organization at a particular point of time. But management should figure out, in a given situation, only such networks which will contribute a lot in boosting the morale of individual members working in the organization.

15.15. PRINCIPLE OF FEEDBACK

Feedback is a reversal process in which the receiver acknowledges receipt of message and expresses his reaction to the sender of message. In the words of **Hicks & Gullett,**[7] feedback enables the source to know whether or not the message has been received and interpreted correctly. Feedback can cause the original source to modify future communication according to the way in which the source perceives the reaction of the receiver. According to **Gray & Smeltzer,**[8] feedback binds the sender and the receiver together, so that they are truly communicating.

BOX 15.4 : READ BEYOND THE YAWNING OF AN INTERVIEWEE

In an interview, for instance, feedback is so immediate and so massive that participants may attach too much significance to unintentional non-verbal reactions. An interviewee may yawn, causing the interviewer to make numerous assumptions :

- *the interviewee is bored,*
- *stays up too late at night,*
- *has poor manners, and so on.*

The importance of feedback for management cannot, therefore, be overstated. Research has indicated that both employees and managers perform better when they receive and attend to feedback.

Source **: Gray & Smeltzer,** *Management—The Competitive Edge,* p. 551. Also see **Robert C. Leden & Terrence R. Mitchell,** "Reactions to Feedback : The Role of Attributions", *Academy of Management Journal,* Vol. 28, No. 2, 1985, pp. 291-308.

SUMMARY

"Brevity is the soul of wit."

➡ WILLIAM SHAKESPEARE

A principle is a generally accepted rule of action. In order to make communication effective, certain principles are required to be followed. They are, for example, principle of information, principle of clarity, principle of objective, principle of attention, principle of consistency, principle of adequacy and completeness, principle of timeliness, principle of credibility, principle of informality, principle of feedback etc. The sender must inform himself fully; his message should be clear, unambiguous, complete, adequate, purposeful, credible and timely. The sender must get through the receiver. He must pay undivided attention to all incoming and outgoing messages. Feedback enables the sender to know whether or not his message is received and interpreted correctly by the receiver.

KEY TERMS & CONCEPTS

"Most of the disputes in the world arise from words."

➡ WILLIAM MURRAY

- Communication realism
- Unambiguous
- Multi-ethnic
- Cross-graded
- Continuum
- Two-way communication
- Socio-cultural
- Self-contradictory message
- Cancerous effect
- Integrity of organization
- Participative management
- Source — Credibility
- Informal Channel of Communication
- Communication network
- Personal dynamism

REVIEW & DISCUSSION QUESTIONS

"Questions clarify the concepts."

➡ ANON

Group A : OBJECTIVE TYPE QUESTIONS :

1. Fill in the blanks :

(a) The communicator must know clearly the ________ of communication before actually transmitting the message.

(b) ________ speak louder than ________.

(c) Self-contradictory or ________ messages always create chaos and confusion in the organization and ultimately cause ________ effect on organization's ________.

(d) Communication is a ________ to an end and not an ________ in itself.

(e) An autocratic manager ordering subordinate supervisors to practise participative management will create a ________ ________ that will be difficult to overcome.

2. State whether the following statements are True (T) or False (F) and JUSTIFY your answer:

(i) If there is no congruence between what is practised and what is said, it is difficult to make communication effective.

(ii) When informal communications prove ineffective in evoking the needed response from the subordinates, managers should adopt the strategy of making use of grapevine.

(iii) A much-desired condition of two-way communication is that the boss should only speak, instruct, order, and the subordinates who are there at the bottom of the ladder are to carry out his instructions.

(iv) Communication network refers to the medium through which communication travels its destination.

(v) Feedback can cause the original source to modify future communication according to the way in which the source perceives the reaction of the receiver.

Group B : SHORT ANSWER TYPE QUESTIONS :

1. What do you mean by the term "principle." Explain the role of 'principle of clarity' to make communication effective. Give suitable examples.
2. What does 'principle of objective' signify? Why is it so important?
3. According to Dale S. Beach, people think with their heart and not with their mind. Elucidate the remark and suggest remedial measures.
4. "The messages to be communicated should not be mutually conflicting." Why?
5. Explain the significance of 'principle of understanding the receiver.' Cite appropriate examples in support of your views.

Group C : ESSAY TYPE QUESTIONS :

1. "In order to ensure adequacy and completeness of message, it is necessary to check for the five 'W' questions." What are those five 'W' questions? Apply those questions in a situation of your choice to justify the veracity of the statement.
2. "Communication is a means to an end and not an end in itself." Explain in detail.
3. Define the 'principle of credibility.' What is Doctor Fox effect? What are its implications?
4. Explain the 'principle of two-way communication.' What are the criteria for selection of communication networks?
5. What does it mean to say that feedback is a reversal process? "Feedback makes the communication effective." Substantiate with suitable examples.

REFERENCES & NOTES

1. Mary Munter, "Trends in Management Communication at Graduate Schools," *The Journal of Business Communication,* Vol. 20, No. 1, 1983, pp. 5-11.
2. Nancy N. Amos & Gail R. Waters, "A Nation at Risk : The Imperative for Effective Communication," *The Journal of Business Education,* Vol. 60, No. 5, 1985, pp. 184-187.
3. Ray A. Killian, "Managing by Design for Maximum Executive Effectiveness," *American Management Association,* New York, 1968, pp. 225-26.

4. Harold Koontz & Cyril O'Donnell, *Principles of Management,* McGraw-Hill, New York, 1979.
5. Harold Koontz & Heinz Weihrich, *Essentials of Management,* Tata McGraw-Hill, New Delhi, 2001, p. 380.
6. William V. Haney, "A Comparative Study of Unilateral & Bilateral Communication" in *Academy of Management Journal,* June 1964, pp. 128-136.
7. Herbert G. Hicks & C. Ray Gullett, *Management*, p. 513.
8. Edmund R. Gray & Larry R. Smeltzer, *Management — The Competitive Edge,* p. 549.

❐ ❐ ❐

CHAPTER

16

COMMUNICATION — ITS MYTHS & REALITIES, AND ALSO LIMITATIONS

CONTENTS

QUOTABLE QUOTES

1. "The ability to speak well is the short-cut to distinction."

   ➡ **DALE CARNEGIE**

2. "You never get a second chance to make a first impression."

   ➡ **DAVE ROBERTSON**

3. "Your attitude determines your altitude."

   ➡ **VINCE LOMBARDI**

4. "If you think you are beaten, you are.
   If you think you dare not, you don't.
   If you'd like to win, but you think you can't;
   It is almost certain you won't.

   If you think you'll lose, you're lost;
   For out of the world we find
   Success begins with a fellow's will.
   It's all in the state of mind.

   Life's battles don't always go
   To the stronger or faster man;
   But sooner or later the man
   Who wins, is the man who thinks he can."

   ➡ **ADAPTED**

LEARNING OBJECTIVES

After going through this chapter, you should be able to —

- Define myth or misconception;
- Differentiate reality from myth;
- List out important misconceptions about communication;
- Understand and diagnose the realities underneath those misconceptions.

16.1. MYTHS & REALITIES OF COMMUNICATION

In all the previous fifteen chapters we have discussed at length ***what communication is.*** And now in this concluding chapter, let us discuss ***what communication is not*** by refuting several communication myths or misconceptions.[1] **A myth is an unfounded belief or misconception.** A person may have seen some type of movies or may have heard friends, talk about certain occupations, leading him/her to accept without scrutiny certain things. Such baseless, blind acceptances may affect him/her adversely in near future. **These misconceptions arise mainly because we shy away from reality or are unware of underlying truths.** Recognizing such misconceptions is important, not only because they ought to be avoided by any one knowledgeable about the subject, but also because following them can get you into trouble.[2] The following table will illustrate the myths and realities of communication.[3]

TABLE 16.1 : MYTHS AND REALITIES OF COMMUNICATION

	MYTHS		REALITIES
1.	The **myth** is that we communicate only when we consciously and deliberately choose to communicate.	1.	The **reality** is that we frequently 'communicate' messages we are not consciously aware of communicating.
2.	The **myth** is that we communicate as if words themselves have the same meaning to our listener as they do to us.	2.	The **reality** is that words do not really have meanings; rather meanings are in terms of people's past experiences and perceptions.
3.	The **myth** is that we think we communicate primarily with words.	3.	The **reality** is that the majority of the messages we communicate are not based on words, but rather on non-verbal symbols.
4.	The **myth** is that communication is a one-way activity of telling people.	4.	The **reality** is that communicating is a two-way activity in which feedback from the other party is crucial.
5.	The **myth** is that the message we send is identical to the message received by the listener.	5.	The **reality** is that the message as it is finally received by the listener is never exactly the same as the message we originally sent.
6.	The **myth** is that you can never give someone too much information.	6.	The **reality** is that people can be given too much information. This overload can be just as much of a problem as not having enough information.

Adler & Rodman[4] have suggested another seven myths or misconceptions, which are discussed in the following table continued from the above :

	MYTHS		REALITIES
7.	The **myth** is that communication is always a good thing.	7.	The **reality** is that communication is neither good or bad in itself. Rather, its value comes from the way it is used. *In this sense, communication is similar to fire : Flames in the fireplace on a coldnight keep you warm and create a cozy atmosphere, but the same flames can kill if they spread into the room.* Communication can be a tool for expressing warm feelings and useful facts but under different circumstances the same words and actions can cause both physical and emotional pain.
8.	The **myth** is that any single thing we say or do causes an outcome.	8.	The **reality** is that *many factors play a role in how others wll react to your communication in a single situation.* Suppose, *for example*, that you lose your temper and say something to a friend that you regret as soon as the words escape your lips. Your friend's reaction will depend on a whole host of events besides your unjustified remark : *her frame of mind at the moment* (upright or mellow), *elements of her personality* (judgemental or forgiving), *your relational history* (supportive or hostile), and *her knowledge of any factors in your life* that might have contributed to your unfair remark.
9.	The **myth** is that communication solves all problems.	9.	The **reality** is that *this is sometimes true.* It's an exaggeration to say that communicating — even communicating clearly — is a guaranteed panacea.
10.	The **myth** is that meanings rest in words.	10.	The **reality** is that meanings *rest in people, not in words.* It is a mistake to think that just because you use a word in one way, others will do so, too.

	MYTHS		REALITIES
11.	The **myth** is that communication is simple. It is rather like breathing. People develop this aptitude without the need for training.	11.	The **reality** is that *communication skills are rather like athletic ability.* Even the most inept of us can learn to be more effective with training and practice, and those who are talented can always become better.
12.	The **myth** is that more communication is always better.	12.	The **reality** is that *this is partially true.* There are situations when too much communication is a mistake, even unproductive, or can actually aggravate a problem. As **McCroskey & Wheeless** put it, more and more negative communication merely leads to more and more negative results.[5]
13.	The **myth** is that communication always requires complete understanding.	13,	The **reality** is that though some understanding is necessary for us to comprehend one another's thoughts, *there are some types of communication in which understanding isn't the primary goal.* Consider, *for example,* social rituals. *"How's it going ?"* you ask. *"Great"*, the other person replies. The primary goal in exchanges like these is mutual acknowledgement. There's obviously no serious attempt to exchange information.
14.	The **myth** is that communication is free.	14.	The **reality** is that this is not true. According to **Eileen Scholes**, *communication is not without its costs,* and in some situations may not be worth the effort.[6]

BOX 16.1 : OPERATION HALLEY'S COMET — MESSAGE DISTORTION IN SERIAL TRANSMISSION — AN AMUSING ILLUSTRATION

Colonel to Executive Officer : *Tomorrow evening at approximately 2000 hours, Halley's Comet will be visible in this area, an event which occurs only once every 75 years. Have the men fall out in the battalion area in fatigues, and I will explain this rare phenomenon to them. In case of rain, we will not be able to see anything, so assemble the men in the theater and I will show them films on it.*

Executive Officer to Company Commander : *By order of the Colonel, tomorrow at 2000 hours, Halley's Comet will appear above the battalion area. If it rains, fall the men out in fatigues, then march to the theater where this rare phenomenon will take place, something which occurs only once every 75 years.*

Company Commander to Lieutenant : *By order of the Colonel, the phenomenal Halley's Comet will appear in the theater in fatigues at 2000 hours tomorrow evening. In case of rain in the battalion area, the Colonel will give another order, something which occurs once every 75 years.*

Lieutenant to Sergeant : *Tomorrow at 2000 hours, the Colonel will appear in the theater with the phenomenal Halley's Comet in fatigues, something which happens every 75 years. If it rains, the Colonel will order the comet into the battalion area.*

Sergeant to Squad : *When it rains tomorrow at 2000 hours, the phenomenal 75-year old General Halley, accompanied by the Colonel, will drive his Comet through the battalion area theater in fatigues.*

Comments among all the units :

Tomorrow, if it rains, General Halley will drive away the Colonel from the battalion area. It is a shame that this does not occur every day.

Source : **Adapted**

16.2. LIMITATIONS OF COMMUNICATION

Communication is limited broadly by the following three types of variables viz.,

16.2.1 **Organizational variables,**

16.2.2 **Personal variables,** and

16.2.3 **Psychological variables.**

They can be illustrated in a tabular form as follows:

TABLE 16.2 : LIMITATIONS OF COMMUNICATION

Types of Variables	Illustrations
(A) Organizational	1. An unfavourable corporate climate, 2. Absence of appropriate communication policy, 3. In-built complexities in organizational structure, 4. Information/communication overload, 5. Lack of proper supervision, 6. Fanning of unethical/illegal messages to promote and protect short-term interests, etc.
(B) Personal	1. Poor communication skills, 2. Faulty transmission of messages, 3. Filtering of messages due to difference in people's mental filters, 4. Time-pressures at both ends — sender's as also receiver's. 5. Wrong interpretation/Premature evaluation, 6. Source credibility etc.
(C) Psychological	1. Indifferent attitude and personality of top executives, 2. Inability to deal with the noises within, 3. Improper listening/Selective listening, 4. Perceptual differences/Selective perception, 5. Ineffective feedback, 6. Changing attitudes and beliefs of people etc.

DIAGRAM 16.1 : LIMITATIONS OF COMMUNICATION

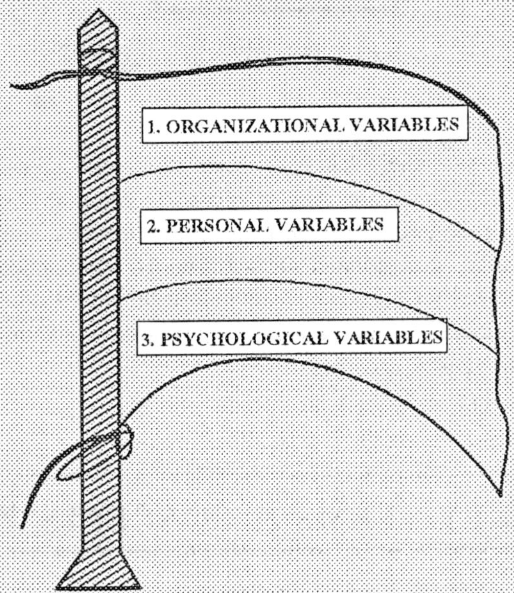

Source : Based on different communication theorists

Diagram : Exclusively designed by the Author (**Dr. Roy**).

LAUGH A LITTLE
THINK A LITTLE

LIMITATION : A DRUMMER VS. A MUSICAL DIRECTOR

A musical director was having a lot of trouble with one drummer. He talked and talked and talked with the drummer, but his performance simply did not improve. Finally, before the whole orchestra, he said : "When a musician can't handle his instrument and doesn't improve when given help, they take away the instrument, and give him two sticks and make him a drummer."

A stage whisper was heard from the percussion section : "And if he can't handle even that, they take away one of his sticks and make him a musical director."

Source : Adapted

SUMMARY

'Brevity is the soul of wit.'

➡ **WILLIAM SHAKESPEARE**

In this concluding chapter, an attempt has been made to identify certain myths or misconceptions of communication. Identifying those myths or misconceptions is important, not only because they ought to be avoided, but also because following them can get you into trouble. Some common misconceptions are : we communicate consciously, we communicate with words, communication is a one-way activity, message sent and message received are identical, communication solves all problems, meanings rest in words, communication is simple, more communication is always better, communication is free. We have also pointed out the underlying truth against each misconception.

Lastly, limitations of communication are dealt with through three types of variables viz. organizational variables, personal variables, and psychological variables.

KEY TERMS & CONCEPTS

"Most of the disputes in the world arise from words."

➡ **WILLIAM MURRAY**

- Myths/Misconceptions
- Realities
- Selective Perception
- Non-verbal symbols
- Information overload
- Emotional pain
- Personality
- Pancea
- Athletic ability
- Organizational Variables
- Filtering of messages
- Premature evaluation
- Short-term interest
- Selective listening
- Ineffective feedback

REVIEW & DISCUSSION QUESTIONS

'Questions clarify the concepts.'

➡ **ANON**

Group A : OBJECTIVE TYPE QUESTIONS :

1. Fill in the blanks :

(a) Misconceptions arise mainly because we shy away from ________ or are unaware of underlying ________.

(b) Majority of the messages we communicate are not based on ________, but rather on ________ symbols.

(c) Communication is neither ________ or bad in itself; its value comes from the ________ it is used.

(d) Meanings rest in ________, not in ________.

(e) More and more negative communications merely lead to more and more ________ results.

2. State whether the following statements are True (T) or False (F) and JUSTIFY your answer:

(i) Communication is always a good thing.
(ii) You can never give someone too much information.
(iii) The message we send is identical to the message received by the listener.
(iv) Communication solves all problems.
(v) Communication always requires complete understanding.

Group B : SHORT ANSWER TYPE QUESTIONS :

1. What is myth or misconception ? List out five common misconceptions of communication.
2. "Meanings rest in people, not in words." Do you agree with the view ? If yes, substantiate.
3. "More communication is always better." Give reasons for and against the view.
4. "Communication is a conscious, deliberate attempt." In the context of the above, offer your own view. Cite suitable examples in support of your view.
5. Prove that communication is neither good nor bad in itself.

Group C : ESSAY TYPE QUESTIONS :

1. "Communication is simple and free." Do you corroborate this view ? If yes, why ? If not, why not ?
2. "Majority of the messages we communicate are not based on words, but rather on non-verbal symbols". Elucidate with appropriate examples.
3. "To make communication effective, feedback from the receiver is crucial." Give at least two reasons. Cite examples in support of this view.
4. "Any single thing we say or do causes an outcome." Examine the veracity of this statement.
5. Write a short note on limitations of communication.

REFERENCES & NOTES

1. Adapted from J.C. McCroskey & L.K. Wheeless, *Introduction to Human Communication,* Allyn & Bacon, Boston, 1976, pp. 3-10.
2. Ronald B. Adler & George Rodman, *Understanding Human Communication,* Oxford University Press, 9th Edition, 2006, p. 24.
3. Richard C. Huseman, James M. Latiff & John D. Hatfield, *Business Communication*, Helt-Saundere Japan Ltd., Tokyo, 1981, pp. 21-25.
4. Ronald B. Adler & George Rodman, *Understanding Human Communication,* Oxford University Press, New York, 9th Edition, 2006, pp. 24-27.
5. McCroskey & Wheeless, op. cit., p. 5.
6. Eileen Scholes, *Handbook of Communication*, Infinity Books, New Delhi, 1st Indian Edition, 2003, p. 233.

❒ ❒ ❒

APPENDICES

SECTION 1 : QUESTION BANK

GROUP A :	SHORT ANSWER TYPE QUESTIONS
GROUP B :	ESSAY TYPE QUESTIONS

SECTION 2 : EXPERIENTIAL & CASE EXERCISES

GROUP A :		EXPERIENTIAL EXERCISES
	1.	ASSESSING YOUR COMMUNICATION SKILLS
	2.	COMMUNICATION INVENTORY
	3.	HANEY TEST OF UNCRITICAL INFERENCES
	4.	RUMOUR CLINIC
	5.	ROLE-PLAYIING EXERCISE
GROUP B :		CASE EXERCISES
	1.	DO YOU KNOW WHAT I LIKE ABOUT YOU?
	2.	DONNA AND HER TEAM-MATES
	3.	MICHAEL HILL
	4.	THE NATIONAL BANK OF GLENVILLE
	5.	COMMUNICATION TRAGEDY AT EGYPT AIR FLIGHT 990

SECTION-1 :

QUESTION BANK

GROUP A : SHORT ANSWER-TYPE QUESTIONS

1. How does an individual, according to Marion M. Wood, spend nearly 70% of his waking hours?
2. How do people communicate their ideas and feelings?
3. Is there any difference between a sign and a signal?
4. What is a symbol? How is it related to a sign?
5. Illustrate with examples how can faulty interpretation of the message convey wrong meaning to a communication.
6. Show the consequential change in meaning with shifting of emphasis on each word in a sentence.
7. Communication is involved in at least four main types of managerial activities. What are they?
8. Enumerate two reasons why communication is important for managers.
9. Define and elaborate etymological meaning of communication.
10. What are the basic ingredients of any communication situation?
11. Write short notes on:
    (*a*) Communication is Exception.
    (*b*) Communication is Perception.
    (*c*) Communication is Interactional and Transactional.
    (*d*) Communication is Intentional or Unintentional.
    (*e*) Communication is not a natural but an acquired quality.
    (*f*) Communication is both an art and a science.
    (*g*) Myths and Realities of Communication.
12. Compare and Contrast:
    (*a*) Communication and Communications
    (*b*) Communication and Information.
    (*c*) Interpersonal communication and Intrapersonal communication.

(*d*) Organizational communication and Management communication.

(e) Mass Communication and Group Communication.

(f) Participative level of communication and Confrontive level of Communication.

(g) Business Communication and Social Communication.

(h) Glass Ceiling Syndrome and Horns effect in Performance Appraisal.

13. Enumerate the reasons why people don't communicate well.
14. Why communication is at all needed? Enlist some of the important reasons in support of your answer.
15. List out ten objectives of each of superior-initiated and subordinate-initiated communication.
16. What are the functions communication serves, according to Stephen P. Robbins or Lee Thayer, in an organisation?
17. What are the purposes of:

(*a*) Internal communication

(*b*) External communication

(*c*) Interactive communication

(*d*) Persuasive communication

(*e*) Supportive communication.

(f) Cross-wire communication

(g) Ethical communication

(h) Web-based communication

18. Which, according to Michael A. Hitt et . al., or Keith Davis, or John Adair, are the purposes of communication?
19. Enumerate the factors responsible for growing importance of communication in business.
20. What are the types of variables that limit communications? Illustrate them suitably.

GROUP B : ESSAY-TYPE QUESTIONS

1. 'Communicating to people is our everyday activity.' Do you agree? Substantiate with examples.
2. What are the roles of sounds, signs and symbols in communication?
3. 'The differencc between the right word and the almost right word is the difference between 'lightning' and the 'lightning bug'. Examine critically.
4. What are the different types of meanings words can have? Illustrate with suitable examples.
5. What is meant by abstraction of words? What is conveyed by Prof. Hayakawa through his 'ladder of abstraction'?
6. 'Communication does play significant roles in our lives and in business organisations.' Discuss.
7. 'Communication can be described as the ears and eyes of management.' Critically examine.
8. According to Mintzberg, a manager has to perform three types of roles in the organisation, and communication plays a vital role in each. Comment.
9. Define the term 'communication' as defined by Keith Davis and also Louis. A. Allen, and comment on them.
10. Attempt a simple but concise definition of the term 'communication' as suggested by Dr. Roy. Bring out the essence of this definition.
11. List out the important characteristics of communication.

12. Discuss in details the key elements of communication.
13. What are the four fundamentals of communication? Write a brief note on each.
14. How would you classify communication into different categories? Write a note on each category of communication with suitable examples.
15. Mention some of the postulates or attributes of communication.
16. Describe the four levels of communication and bring out their salient features.
17. Do you agree with the view that communication is much varied and complex in nature. Give a reasoned answer for or against this view.
18. Scope of communication is very much wider. Explain and illustrate.
19. What are the major objectives of communication according to Scott & Mitchell?
20. Enlist the objectives of communication in any business organisation as suggested by William Scholz.
21. Critically examine the various functions of communication.
22. Elucidate in details the main purposes of communication as suggested by John G. Glover.
23. Describe, with the help of a diagram, the important purposes of organizational communication as prescribed by David D. Vanfleet.
24. Discuss in details the importance and significance of communication with reference to today's fast changing organizational scenario.
25. What do you mean by principles of communication? Explain at least twelve principles which serve as a fundamental guide to effective communication.

❒ ❒ ❒

SECTION-2 :

EXPERIENTIAL & CASE EXERCISES

GROUP A : EXPERIENTIAL EXERCISES

EXPERIENTIAL EXERCISE - 1

Name of the Exercise : ASSESSING YOUR COMMUNICATION SKILLS.

Objective of the Exercise : This execise is designed to —

(*i*) Evaluate how well you communicate by responding to some well-planned statements.

(*ii*) Identify your weakest areas that need to hone so as to bring overall improvement in your communication skills.

Procedure : There are in all 32 (thirty-two) statements. Each statement has four options. viz. 1,2,3,4. Mark the options that are closest to your experience. Be as honest as you can.

If your answer is "NEVER", mark option 1;

If your answer is "OCCASIONALLY", mark option 2;

If your answer is "FREQUENTLY", mark option 3;

If your answer is "ALWAYS", mark option 4.

Now, you write answers to all the 32 statements and thereafter, add your scores together and refer to the "ANALYSIS" to ascertain how skilled you are at communicating. Don't be complacent; remember that there is always room for improvement.

Analysis:

If your total score comes between	It indicates that
32-64	You are not communicating effectively or enough. Listen to feed-back, and try to learn from your mistakes.
65-95	Your communication performance is patchy. Plan to improve your weaknesses.
96-128	You communicate extremely well. But remember that you can never communicate too much.

Statements:

1.	I communicate the right message to the right person at the right time.	1	2	3	4
2.	I think carefully about a message before I decide how to communicate it.	1	2	3	4
3.	I project self-confidence and speak confidently.	1	2	3	4
4.	I welcome feedback about my communication.	1	2	3	4
5.	I listen intently and check I have understood before I reply.	1	2	3	4
6.	I try to exclude personal prejudices of all kinds when judging others.	1	2	3	4
7.	I am constructive and civil when I meet others.	1	2	3	4
8.	I take time to give people the information they need and want.	1	2	3	4
9.	I use one-to-one meetings for reviews of performance and coaching.	1	2	3	4
10.	I question people to find out what they think and how they are getting on.	1	2	3	4
11.	I hand out written briefs that give all pertinent information on a task.	1	2	3	4
12.	I use professional phone techniques to improve my communication.	1	2	3	4
13.	I communicate via all available electronic media.	1	2	3	4
14.	I apply the rules of good writing to external and internal communications.	1	2	3	4
15.	I use an effective system of note-taking for minutes, interviews and research.	1	2	3	4
16.	I test important letters and documents on reliable critics before finalizing.	1	2	3	4
17.	I use fast reading techniques to speed up my work rate.	1	2	3	4

18.	I prepare speeches carefully and deliver them well after rehearsal.	1	2	3	4
19.	I take an active and highly visible role in internal training.	1	2	3	4
20.	I plan important events, such as conferences, to high professional standards.	1	2	3	4
21.	I apply the rules of soft and hard selling to put across my points of view.	1	2	3	4
22.	I enter negotiations fully primed on issues and on the other side's needs.	1	2	3	4
23.	I make my reports accurate, concise, clear and well-structured.	2	3	4	
24.	I research thoroughly before putting forward a written proposal.	1	2	3	4
25.	I try to understand how all relevant audiences react to the organization.	1	2	3	4
26.	I consider how skilled advisers can help on public relations issues.	1	2	3	4
27.	I make useful contacts with journalists and other media people.	1	2	3	4
28.	I make sure specialist work such as design is done by qualified professionals.	1	2	3	4
29.	My briefs to advertising agencies are based on clearly defined business targets.	1	2	3	4
30.	I give priority to communicating regularly with employees.	1	2	3	4
31.	I receive and react positively to feedback from employees and others.	1	2	3	4
32.	I have a strategy for communications and check activities against this plan.	1	2	3	4
	Source: Adapted from *"Communicate Clearly"* by **Mr. Robert Heller,** London, 1998, pp. 66-69.				

EXPERIENTIAL EXERCISE - 2

Name of the Exercise : COMMUNICATION INVENTORY

Objective of the Exercise : This exercise will help you assess your interpersonal relationships and patterns of communication with people with whom you mingle and work daily.

Procedure :

1. Given below you will find a set of forty questions.
2. Be honest and frank in your answers.
3. Answer each question quickly and spontaneously.
4. Solve each question independently and according to your real feelings without consulting anybody.
5. Tick mark your answer in one of the three boxes on the right as "YES", "NO" "OCCASIONALLY."
6. From the score table attached at the end of questionnaire-set, check up how much you have scored. Enter your score next to the question. Find out the total.

Sl. No.	*Questions*	*Yes*	*No*	*Occasionally*
1.	Do you avoid saying something hurtful to others?	☐	☐	☐
2.	Do you take it for granted that the other person automatically understands what you are saying?	☐	☐	☐
3.	Do you always mean what you say while conversing?	☐	☐	☐
4.	Do you have difficulty conversing with others?	☐	☐	☐
5.	Do you feel upset if somebody does not agree with you?	☐	☐	☐
6.	Do you feel scared that someone might get angry if you don't agree with them?	☐	☐	☐
7.	Do you place yourself in the other person's position during conversation?	☐	☐	☐
8.	Do you understand the effect of the tone of your voice?	☐	☐	☐
9.	Do you hurt somebody's feelings and apologise later?	☐	☐	☐
10.	Do you ask somebody to explain the meaning when they ask you a question?	☐	☐	☐
11.	Do you try to elicit the opinion of the other person about any point that you make?	☐	☐	☐
12.	Do other persons prompt you when you are explaining something?	☐	☐	☐

Sl. No.	*Questions*	*Yes*	*No*	*Occasionally*
13.	Do you get angry when there is a disagreement between you and the other person?	☐	☐	☐
14.	Do you try to talk more than the other person during the conversation?	☐	☐	☐
15.	When others differ from you, do you find it difficult to carry on the conversation?	☐	☐	☐
16.	If you are annoyed by someone, is it difficult for you to think clearly?	☐	☐	☐
17.	While talking to somebody, do you discuss things which are of common interest?	☐	☐	☐
18.	Are you ready to permit criticism of the constructive kind from others?	☐	☐	☐
19.	Do you try to discuss the matter with someone if your feelings have been hurt?	☐	☐	☐
20.	Do you find it difficult to confide in others?	☐	☐	☐
21.	While somebody is conversing with you, does your mind wander?	☐	☐	☐
22.	When someone is speaking, do you try to listen for meaning?	☐	☐	☐
23.	Do you trust other people?	☐	☐	☐
24.	Is it difficult for you to praise others?	☐	☐	☐
25.	Do you help others to understand the way you believe, think or feel?	☐	☐	☐
26.	When your feelings are being discussed, do you feel like changing the topic?	☐	☐	☐
27	Do you feel that the other person wishes you were different?	☐	☐	☐
28.	Are your feelings understood by other people?	☐	☐	☐
29.	When you are not listening, do you pretend that you are listening?	☐	☐	☐
30.	When you are wrong about something, are you willing to admit it?	☐	☐	☐
31.	Are you conscious of the reaction on others to what you are saying?	☐	☐	☐
32.	Can you make out the difference between what the other person is saying and what he is feeling?	☐	☐	☐

Sl. No.	*Questions*	*Yes*	*No*	*Occasionally*
33.	Do you find it difficult while discussing to understand the other person's point of view?	☐	☐	☐
34.	Do others pass remarks that you always think you are right?	☐	☐	☐
35.	Do you settle your differences with others satisfactorily?	☐	☐	☐
36.	Do you sulk if somebody doesn't agree or upsets you?	☐	☐	☐
37.	If somebody praises you, do you feel uneasy?	☐	☐	☐
38.	Do you allow, while conversing, to let the other person finish talking before you react?	☐	☐	☐
39.	When you are talking, do you also seem to be listening?	☐	☐	☐
40.	Do you get annoyed when children make noise at home?	☐	☐	☐

SCORE TABLE

Sl. No.	*Yes*	*No*	*Occasionally*	*Sl. No.*	*Yes*	*No*	*Occasionally*
1.	3	0	2	21.	0	3	1
2.	0	3	1	22.	3	0	2
3.	3	0	2	23.	3	0	2
4.	0	3	1	24.	0	3	1
5.	0	3	1	25.	0	3	1
6.	0	3	1	26.	0	3	1
7.	3	0	2	27.	0	3	1
8.	3	0	2	28.	3	0	2
9.	3	0	2	29.	0	3	1
10.	3	0	2	30.	3	0	2
11.	3	0	2	31.	3	0	2
12.	0	3	1	32.	3	0	2
13.	3	0	2	33.	0	3	1
14.	0	3	1	34.	0	3	1
15.	0	3	1	35.	3	0	2
16.	0	3	1	36.	0	3	1
17.	3	0	2	37.	0	3	1
18.	0	3	1	38.	3	0	2
19.	3	0	2	39.	3	0	2
20.	0	3	1	40.	0	3	1

ANALYSIS

If your total score comes between	It indicates that
0-40	You require development in your interpersonal skills; you have low sense of self-awareness.
41-59	You will find difficulty in some areas of interpersonnel relationships; your self awareness is fairly low; you have to find in which areas you have difficulty in communication and try to improve them.
60-79	There are few areas of communication which require improvement. Your interpersonnel skills are having a fare self-concept.
80 plus	You understand quite well how to interact with others and your communicating skills are effective. Try to improve on them.
Source: Unknown.	

EXPERIENTIAL EXERCISE - 3

Name of the Exercise : HANEY TEST OF UNCRITICAL INFERENCES

Objective of the Exercise : To measure your power of comprehension and analysis of each statement of the story, given below, before drawing an inference.

Procedure : Read the story presented below, and indicate whether you believe the statements that follow the story are **true** (T), **false** (F), or **unknown** (?). Then, get together with a group designated by your instructor, and determine as a group whether each statement is true, false, or unknown.

The Story : A businessman had just turned off the lights in the store when a man appeared and demanded money. The owner opened a cash register. The contents of the cash register were scooped up, and the man sped away. A member of the police force was notified promptly.

Statements about the Story :

1. A man appeared after the owner had turned off his store lights.	T	F	?
2. The robber was a man.	T	F	?
3. The man who appeared didn't demand money.	T	F	?
4. The man who opened the cash register was the owner.	T	F	?
5. The store owner scooped up the contents of the cash register and ran away.	T	F	?
6. Someone opened a cash register.	T	F	?

7.	After the man who demanded the money scooped up the contents of the cash register, he ran away.	T	F	?
8.	While the cash register contained money, the story doesn't state how much.	T	F	?
9.	The robber demanded money of the owner.	T	F	?
10.	A businessman had just turned off the lights when a man appeared in the store.	T	F	?
11.	It was broad daylight when the man appeared.	T	F	?
12.	The man who appeared opened the cash register.	T	F	?
13.	No one demanded money.	T	F	?
14.	The story concerns a series of events in which only three persons are referred to : the owner of the store, a man who demanded money, and a member of the police force.	T	F	?
15.	The following events occurred : someone demanded money; a cash register was opened; its contents were scooped up; and a man dashed out of the store.	T	F	?

Source : **William V. Haney** (ed.), *Communication & Interpersonal Relations,* Irwin, Homewood, Illinois, 5th Edition, 1986, pp. 214-222; Quoted by Kathryn M. Bartol & David C. Martin, McGraw-Hill, New York, 2nd Edition, 1994, p. 463.

EXPERIENTIAL EXERCISE - 4

Name of the Exercise : RUMOUR CLINIC EXERCISE

Objective of the Exercise : To illustrate distortions which may occur in transmission of information from an original source through several individuals to a final destination.

Group Size : Unlimited. There should be a minimum of eight participants.

Time Required : Thirty minutes.

Materials :

1. Copies of the 'Rumour Clinic Observation Form' for **'Process Observers'.**
2. Flipchart paper and a felt-tipped marker.

Physical Setting:

1. A **'Meeting Room'**. All observers are seated facing an area where the Rumour Clinic is staged.
2. A separate room termed as **'Isolation Room'** in which volunteers can be isolated.

PROCEDURE :

Stage 1

The facilitator asks for six volunteers (the rest of the group remains to act as 'Process Observers').

Stage 2

Five of the six volunteers are asked to go into the 'Isolation Room'. One remains in the Meeting Room with the facilitator and the observers.

Stage 3

The facilitator distributes 'Rumour Clinic Observation Forms' to the observers, who are to take notes on the proceedings.

Stage 4

The facilitator then reads the **'Accident Report'** on the Observation Form to the single volunteer who is with the observers in the meeting room. The volunteer may not take notes on the report.

Stage 5

The facilitator asks a volunteer in the 'Isolation Room' to return. The first volunteer repeats the 'Accident Report' to the volunteer from the 'Isolation Room'. **It is important that the volunteers transmit the message in their own way, without help.** After passing the message, the volunteer can be given an observation sheet and sits in with the observers to watch the remaining volunteers passing the message.

Stage 6

Another volunteer returns from the 'Isolation Room', and the second repeats the 'Accident Report'. **It important that the volunteers transmit the message in their own way, without help.**

Stage 7

The process is repeated until all the volunteers but the last have had the message transmitted to them.

Stage 8

Then the last volunteer returns to the room. **This volunteer is told to assume the role of a police-officer.** The fifth participant repeats the 'Accident Report' to the police-officer. Afterwards, the police-officer writes the message on flipchart paper so that the group can read it.

Stage 9

The facilitator then posts the original message (previously prepared on flipchart paper), so that it can be compared with the police-officer's version.

Stage 10

Observers are asked to report their notes. Volunteers then discuss their experience. The facilitator leads a discussion with the entire group on implications of the Rumour Clinic.

Variations:

I. The succession of messages can be recorded (either audio or video) for replay during the processing.

II. The message can be rewritten to be more pertinent to the particular group.

III. The entire group can be used as conveyers of messages (no observers are used). Groups of six are formed, and five persons from each group are sent to the 'Isolation Room'. The facilitator reads the message to the remaining participants. One member from each group is brought back into the meeting room at the same time to receive the message. The final members simultaneously write the message for all to see.

Rumour Clinic Observation Form

Accident Report

"I cannot wait to report this accident to the police. I must get to the hospital as soon as possible.

The delivery truck, heading south, was turning right at the junction when the sports car, heading north, was attempting to turn left. When they saw that they were turning into the same lane, they both honked their horns but continued to turn without slowing down. In fact, the sports car seemed to be accelerating just before the crash."

Volunteer	*Additions*	*Deletions*	*Distortions*
No. 1. Mr. A			
No. 2 Mr. B			
No. 3 Mr. C			
No. 4 Mr. D			
No. 5 Mr. E			
No. 6 Police Officer			

Source: Reading Materials from ***Thames Valley University,*** London.

EXPERIENTIAL EXERCISE - 5

Name of the Exercise : ROLE-PLAYING EXERCISE

Objective of the Exercise : This exercise aims at identifying your reasoning ability so that others get ultimately convinced to support your views.

Time required : Half-an-hour.

No. of Volunteers required: Two.

Situation : It is the time for MBA examination of a reputed university in India. You are working as Head in the examination department of the University that takes care of every details of conducting the examination. You have been working all around the clock for the past two weeks. You do not seem to be nearing the end, what with developments almost on hourly basis.

You are dependent upon two of your junior colleagues viz. Ram and Rahim in this rush period. Ram has applied to you long time back for leave during this period for his sister's marriage. He is supposed to go on leave from the next day. In your estimate, the work will require another week to complete. You have indicated this to your another colleague Rahim that Ram's leave period may be curtailed.

Having somehow learnt this, Ram gets terribly upset. He has requested for a meeting with you. The meeting will now take place.

Questions : You are now required to converse with Ram as per the directions serially numbered in the following four quadrant:

(1) What are the situational issues to remember?	(2) What will you definitely speak about?
(3) What will you definitely not speak about?	(4) What is the objective of the communication?

(***Source :*** Unknown)

GROUP B : CASE EXERCISES

CASE EXERCISE 1 : DO YOU KNOW WHAT I LIKE ABOUT YOU ?

Jim McCabe, only 33, is a successful bloodstock agent in the highly volatile and competitive thoroughbred horse industry. He locates thoroughbred buyers and sellers for his clients, as well as breeding rights for stallions and mares. It is a complicated and risky business. His knowledge of thoroughbred horses and their bloodlines, along with much hard work, has enabled him to achieve success.

Educated in the physical sciences (master's degree), McCabe chose the thoroughbred industry because of his love of horses. His firm, which he began alone five years ago, now employs five other agents, three researchers whose task it is to research thoroughbred bloodlines, three secretaries, an office manager, and myself. My title, when I was hired four months ago, was assistant office manager, but no one ever told me what I was supposed to do. For a part-time job while in college, the pay is good, and I'm learning a great deal about a business I knew nothing about previously. In addition, there is always some kind of excitement around the office.

One day I stood by the door of McCabe's office. He was on the phone, and before I could knock, he motioned for me to come in and sit down. Every inch of his desk was covered by reports, memos, horse-sale catalogs, telephone messages, and racing results. Other reminders on bits of paper were taped to the wall, and a "to do" list with at least 10 entries on it was taped to the base of the telephone. Evidently these were things that he had to do immediately. While talking on the phone, he added another item to this list.

As he continued the phone conversation, he was shaking his head and signing letters at the same time. Finally, he put his hand over the phone and said to me "This is Robinson in Florida on that two-year-old filly deal. All the tests on her leg are not in yet, but he insists on giving me every detail on the entire test procedure. The guy is going to drive me nuts."

Turning his attention back to the phone he removed his hand and resumed talking. "Right, Robbie, OK... Great... OK... Sure... Call me back on that....... Terrific...' Bye."

He hung up the phone with a sigh of relief and looked at me. "Do you know what I like about you, Tinsley?" I didn't have time to answer, nor did he, because the phone rang again. "Yeah... Fine... Terrific... Count me in...' Bye."

At this point, his secretary looked in and said, "John Towne of Winthrop Farms is on hold. It sounds urgent."

McCabe shook his head again and went back to the telephone. After a few minutes of conversation, he put his hand over the receiver and called to his secretary. "Get Johnson and Burke in here, fast." Johnson was the office manager, and Burke was an agent. They arrived as he hung up the phone.

"Burke," he said, "you know that deal you put together for the syndication of that three-year-old, Ol' Blue? Well, they don't like it. Put this information into it and tell me what effect the changes will have on us. When you get it finished, bring it to me so I can call Towne back." Burke left.

"Johnson, I want all of the training fees, jockey expenses, and all other expenses on that horse. Don't give them to me by the month like you did last time. I need totals in all categories; and for crying out loud, this time break out the 'other' category a little better. I looked real good last week when Towne asked me what the $6,300 in 'other expenses' was for. I want all the information at my fingertips in case we've got to go to war with these people." Johnson left.

"Now, Tinsley, what did you need me for?"

"Just sign this bill of sale," I said. "No reason to spend a lot of time on it. It's for the sale of that yearling you asked me to take care of."

"That's what I like about you, Tinsley," he said as he leaned back in his chair and signed the bill of sale, "When I give you a job, you listen. Then you do it right the first time and tell me when it's done. You don't tell me how you did it, the problems you're having doing it, who you met while doing it, and every other Mickey Mouse detail. If the rest of the people around here had that ability, I might be able to get some work done. I think I got more work done five years ago when I had nobody working for me."

As I left his office, I didn't have time to thank him, because the phone began ringing.

QUESTIONS FOR ANALYSIS

1. What is your impression of McCabe?
2. What is your opinion of his communications to the other employees of the firm?
3. What might be the reasons for his demands on employees?
4. Could this influence the effectiveness of the organisation? In what ways?

Source: Based on **Donnelly, Gibson & Ivancevich,** *'Fundamentals of Management'* (9th Edition), 1995, pp. 438-39.

CASE EXERCISE 2 : DONNA & HER TEAM-MATES: COMMUNICATION CHALLENGES

Donna, 29, is from Mountain View in Silicon Valley, California. She is a new hire to this $2 billion global manufacturing firm located in the Midwest. She is an E-business specialist, who has five years of experience in a consulting firm that automates business processes through intranets and extranets. She has assisted Fortune 500 firms in developing Web-based systems to streamline operations and connect suppliers, customers, and vendors. She is an extrovert, "Get-it-done-now" person who has a B.S. in computer science and marketing. She loves moving from project to project, eliminating unnecessary paper-heavy tasks. Her former employer noted that "she likes flattening organizations and authority structures." Her responsibility is to examine each of the major functions of the firm's headquarters by forming a core team "to help move operations into the New Economy" and to present a change plan for automating operations in one month. She will have to work with the following three people as a start.

Andrea, 25, is from Greece. She has a B.S. from a U.S. university. An information specialist, she is quiet and soft spoken, and very detail and results oriented. She works best alone and with small groups in which she can feel comfortable. She does not like change. She is excellent at her work, and her skills are very marketable. Hans, 43, is German and has been with the company as a finance professional for 10 years. He is an extrovert, also detail oriented but likes to know the "big picture" as well. He is a "by-the-book," rules-based person. He is also very logical and systematic in his work. His motto is 'The best predictor of the future is past performance." He has built a loyal following in the company and enjoys being a leader and mentor. George is 58, has been with the company 15 years, is very energetic, does not like to think about retiring, and has difficulty using computers. He believes in change as long as it doesn't affect him. He also has difficulty working with some of the "newcomers" since, he has said, "some of them know more about technology than I do, but I know more about our business."

QUESTIONS FOR ANALYSIS

1. List out the major issues and opportunities you observe in the above-stated case-scenario.
2. Identify the communication and "people" challenges Donna faces in forming the team to carry out her task.
3. Write to Donna a brief memo offering your informed observations and advice regarding some ideas and insights she can expect to encounter with her three new team members.
4. What should Donna do to proceed? List your observations and advice.

Source: Adapted from *"Organisational Behavior & Change"* (2nd Edn.) (2001) by **Joseph W. Weiss,** p. 191.

CASE EXERCISE 3 : MICHAEL HILL

Michael Hill has been administrative assistant for two years to a senior department head in a state government agency. He has always performed his job well and is liked and respected by his fellow employees. His boss has come to depend upon him quite heavily for assistance in the management of the department.

For the last month, Michael has often been late for work and has been snappy with the office staff, sloppy in some aspects of his work, and uncommunicative with the department head. While the situation is not critical, the department head is greatly concerned about his assistant's recent behavior.

Two months ago, Michael was an unsuccessful candidate for the position of section chief reporting to the department head. Until recently, there was no reason to suspect that failure to get the job might have upset Michael. At the time the appointment of the new section chief was made, the department head had fully explained that Michael had nowhere near the qualifications of the person selected for the position. Furthermore, the department head indicated to Michael that, despite being passed over, a bright future awaited him either in the department or somewhere else in government.

QUESTIONS FOR ANALYSIS

1. If something at work is upsetting Michael, what are some possible reasons why he has not chosen to tell the department head?
2. Should the department head ask Michael directly if the failure to be promoted is upsetting him? Why or why not?
3. What other approach might the department head take to get to the root of the problem? How should be proceed?
4. If the two men do sit down to discuss the problem, what obstacles to communication are most likely to get in the way of a mutual understanding?
5. If the department head decides to meet with Michael to tell him that his behavior is upsetting the office, what steps should he take to ensure that the meeting has the effect of helping Michael to change his behavior?

Source: **Samuel D. Deep,** *Human Relations in Management,* Glencoe Publishing Co., California, 1978, pp. 116-117.

CASE EXERCISE 4: THE NATIONAL BANK OF GLENVILLE

The National Bank of Glenville is the oldest and largest bank in that city. The bank has enjoyed a reputation as one of the most progressive banks in the state. Although the bank has been profitable, the president recently requested all officers to look for methods to cut costs.

Just prior to the president's request, Hal Roberts, the operations officer, had implemented a study to look for areas where costs could be cut. A systems analyst working on the project recommended that the customer service department be moved from the first floor to the sixth floor.

Roberts found this to be a sound idea and wasted no time in making the change. Within two weeks it was discovered that the department staff could be reduced by 50 per cent since fewer customers "dropped by" to check their balances or to obtain other account information.

A few weeks later Roy Atkins, the director of public relations, stormed into Hal Robert's office in a rage. "What do you think you are doing," he asked. "I spend years trying to create an image of being concerned about the customer and you come around creating problems. I want the customer service department moved back to the first floor, or I'm taking this matter to the president."

QUESTIONS FOR ANALYSIS

1. What is the real problem?
2. Do you think that Roy Atkins has a legitimate complaint?
3. Should Hal Roberts have handled the situation any differently?

Source: Adapted from **Rue & Bayers,** *Management Theory & Application* (1977) p. 299.

CASE EXERCISE 5 : COMMUNICATION TRAGEDY AT EGYPT AIR FLIGHT 990

On October 31, 1999, a terrible human tragedy took place: Egypt Air Flight 990 plunged into the ocean off the island of Nantucket, Massachusetts, killing more than 200 people. Within a few days, it became apparent that this was not only a human tragedy, but also a tragedy of communication. American investigators interpreted statements made by the Egyptian copilot in a potentially incriminating way; members of the Egypt Air organization, as well as Egyptian citizens and journalists, interpreted the statements differently and accused Americans of jumping to conclusions based on stereotypes of Middle Eastern culture and religion. Thus, the U.S. National Transportation Safety Board, the FBI, Egypt air, and various Egyptian government officials became embroiled in disagreements that were only intensified by the media on both sides.

Using the news listings on your search engine, such as Reuters, AP, ZDNet News, or the like, look for a story about an unfortunate event that involves more than one culture and the complications of communication in the situation. When you find a relevant story, consider the following questions.

QUESTIONS FOR ANALYSIS

1. Try to determine how the situation might have been avoided or improved if communication had been more effective.
2. Which communication channels might have been the best choice?
3. Imagine that you are a journalist covering the event or situation. Write an editorial on the subject referring to communication as one of the factors either in the cause or the outcome of the situation.

Source : Farnaz Fassihi, "Egypt Recoils from Suicide Speculation," *The Providence Journal,* accessed on Yahoo! News, November 18, 1999; "Suicide Theory Takes Center Stage in Egypt Air Probe," (AFP), The Yahoo! Singapore-News, November 17, 1999, Quoted by Dr. Richard L. Daft & Prof. Raymond A. Noe, *Organizational Behaviour,* Harcourt College Publishers, Orlando, USA, 2001, p. 333.

SECTION-3 :

SUGGESTED READINGS

[A] BOOKS

- **Albert Mehrabian,** *Silent Messages : Implicit Communication of Emotions and Attitudes,* Wadsworth, Belmont CA, 2nd Edition, 1981.
- **Andrew Ellis & Geoffrey Beatie,** *The Psychology of Language and Communication,* The Guilford Press, New York, 1986.
- **Abraham H. Maslow,** *Toward A Psychology of Being,* D.Van Nostrand, New York, 2nd Edition, 1968.
- **B. Aubrey Fisher,** *Perspectives on Human Communication,* Macmillan, New York, 1978.
- **Brent C. Oberg,** *Interpersonal Communication : An Introduction to Human Interaction,* Jaico Publishing House, Mumbai, 2006.
- **Carroll C. Arnold & John Waite Bowers,** *Handbook of Rhetorical & Communication Theory,* Allyn & Bacon, Boston, 1984.
- **Charles E. Redfield,** *Communication in Management,* Chicago University Press, Chicago, 1958.
- **Cheryl Hamilton& Cordell Parker,** *Communicating for Results,* Wadsworth, Belmont, California, 2nd Edition, 1987.
- **Chester I. Barnard,** *The Functions of the Executive,* Harvard University Press, Cambridge, 1947.

- **Courtland L. Bovee& John V. Thill,** *Business Communication Today,* Dorling Kindersley (India) Pvt. Ltd., New Delhi, 8th Edition, 2008.
- **Dalmer Fisher,** *Communication in Organizations,* Jaico Publishing House, Mumbai, 2nd Edition, 2007.
- **David K. Berlo,** *The Process of Communication :An Introduction to Theory & Practice,* Holt, Rinehart & Winston, New York, 1960.
- **David W. Johnson,** *Reaching Out : Interpersonal Effectiveness & Self-Actualization,* Prentice Hall, Inc., Englewood Cliffs, New Jersey, 1986.
- **Don Hellriegel & John W. Slocum,Jr.,** *Management,* Addison-Wesley Publishing Co.,1982.
- **--------------------,** *Organizational Behaviour,* Thomson Asia Pvt. Ltd., Singapore, 10th Edition, 2005.
- **Donald P. Cushman & Dudley D. Cahn, Jr.,** *Communication in Interpersonal Relationships,* State University of New York Press, Albany, NY, 1985.
- **Eileen Scholes,** *Handbook of Communication,* Infinity Books, New Delhi, 1st Indian Edition, 2003.
- **Frank E.X. Dance & Carl E. Larson,** *The Functions of Human Communication: A Theoretical Approach,* Holt, Rinehart & Winston, New York, 1976.
- **Fred Luthans,** *Organizational Behaviour,* McGraw Hill International Book Company, 1981.
- **Gerald M. Goldhaber,** *Organizational Communication,* Wm. C. Brown, Dubuque, 1974.
- **Gerald I. Nierenberg & Harry Calero,** *Meta – Talk,* Simon & Schuster, New York, 1973.
- **Glenn C. Pearce, Ross F. Figgins, & Steven P. Golen,** *Business Communication : Principles and Applications,* John Wiley& Sons, Inc., USA, 2nd Edition, 1988.
- **H.G. Hicks & C. R. Gullett,** *Management,* McGraw Hill International, 1981.
- **Harold Koontz & Cyril O'Donnell,** *Principles of Management,* McGraw Hill, New York, 1979.
- **Harold Koontz & Heinz Weihrich,** *Essentials of Management,* Tata McGraw Hill, New Delhi, 2001.
- **Ian Thomson & Alistair MacDonald,** *Corporate Communication : Standards, Practice, and Issues – Access to Information:A Key to Building Trust,* International Institute for Environment and Development, Vancouver, Canada, 2001.
- **Irene C. Kassorola,** *Go For It! How to Win at Love, Work & Play,* Dell Publishing, New York, 1984.
- **James J. Kilpatrick,** *The Writer's Art,* Andrews, McMeel & Parker, New York, 1984.

- **John Adair**, *The Effective Communicator*, Jaico Publishing House, Mumbai, 2002.
- **John Adair,** *Training for Communication,* Macdonald & Co., London, 1973.
- **John C. Condon, Jr.,** *Semantics & Communication,* Macmillan, New York, 3rd Edition, 1985.
- **John E. Baird, Jr.,** *The Dynamics of Organizational Communication,* Harper & Row Publishers Inc., New York, 1977.
- **John Penrose, Robert Rasberry& Bob Myers,** *Advanced Business Communication,* Thomson Asia Pvt. Ltd., Singapore, 4th Edition, 2001.
- **Judy Cornelia Pearson,** *Gender & Communication,* Wm. C. Brown, Dubuque, IA, 1985.
- **Julia T. Wood,** *Human Communication : A Symbolic Interactionist Perspective,* Holt, Rinehart & Winston, New York, 1982.
- **K. H. Roberts,** *Communicating in Organizations,* Science Research Associates, Chicago, 1984.
- **Keith Davis,** *Human Behaviour At Work,* Tata McGraw Hill, New Delhi, 1979.
- **Lee O. Thayer,** *Administrative Communication,* Richard D. Irwin, Homewood, III, 1961.
- **Leland Brown,** *Communicating Facts & Ideas in Business,* Prentice Hall, Inc., Englewood Cliffs, New Jersey, 1982.
- **Lyman K. Steil, Larry L. Barker & Kittie W. Watson**, *Effective Listening : Key to Your Success,* Random House, New York, 1988.
- **M. T. Myers & G. E. Myers,** *Managing by Communication: An Organizational Approach,* McGraw Hill International Book Company, 1982.
- **Mary Allen Guffey,** *Business Communication: Process and Product,* Thomson Asia Pvt. Ltd., Singapore, 2002.
- ———, *Essentials of Business Communication,* South-Western Publishing Co.,Ohio, 6th Edition, 2002.
- **Neil Postman,** *Crazy Talk, Stupid Talk,* Delta, New York, 1977.
- **Owen Hargie, David Dickson & Dennis Tourish,** *Communication in Management,* Gower Publishing House, Hampshire, 1999.
- **Pamela E. Butler,** *Talking to Yourself : Learning the Language of Self-Support,* Harper & Row, San Francisco, 1981.
- **Patricia Andrews & Herschel,** *Organizational Communication,* Houghton Mifflin Co., Boston, 1997.
- **Paul V. Anderson,** *Technical Communication,* Thomson Asia Pvt. Ltd., Singapore, 2003.

- **Peter F. Drucker,** *People and Performance,* Harper College Press, New York, 1977.
- ——————, *The Practice of Management,* Harper & Row Publishers, New York, 1954.
- **Philip G. Clampitt,** *Communication for Managerial Effectiveness,* Sage Publication, California, 2005.
- **Phillip V. Lewis,** *Organizational Communications : The Essence of Effective Management,* Grid, Inc., Ohio, USA, 9th Printing, 1975.
- **'Raymond V. Lesikar & Marie E. Flatley,** *Basic Business Communication,* Tata McGraw Hill, New Delhi, 10th Edition, 2005.
- **Richard C. Huseman, James M. Lahiff& John D. Hatfield,** *Business Communication,* Holt-Saunders Japan Ltd., Tokyo, 1981.
- **Ron Ludlow & Fergus Panton,** *The Essence of Effective Communication,* Prentice Hall of India, New Delhi, 1999.
- **Ronald B. Adler & George Rodman,** *Understanding Human Communication,* Oxford University Press, New York, 9th Edition, 2006.
- **S. I. Hayakawa,** *Language in Thought & Action,* Harcourt Brace, Jovanovich, New York, 4th Edition, 1978.
- **Samuel D. Deep,** *Human Relations in Management,* Glencoe Publishing Co., Inc., California, 1978.
- **Sarah Trenholm,** *Human Communication Theory,* Prentice Hall, Inc., Englewood Cliffs, NJ, 1986.
- **Scot Ober,** *Contemporary Business Communication,* Biztantra, New Delhi, 5th Edition, 2004.
- **Stephen W. LittleJohn,** *Theories of Human Communication,* Wadsworth, Belmont CA, 2nd Edition, 1983.
- **Stephens P. Robbins** et. al., *Organizational Behaviour,* Prentice Hall of India, New Delhi, 13th Edition, 2009.
- **Stewart L. Tubbs & Sylvia Moss,** *Human Communication-Principles and Contexts,* McGraw Hill, New York, 9th Edition, 2003.
- **Susan R. Glaser & Anna Eblen,** *Toward Communication Competency : Developing Interpersonal Skills,* Holt, Rinehart & Winston, New York, 1986.
- **Tony Alessandra & Phil Hunsaker,** *Communicating At Work,* Embassy Books, Mumbai, 2007.
- **William Scholz,** *Communication in Business Organization,* Prentice Hall, Inc., New Jersey, 1963.
- **William D. Brooks & Philip Emmert,** *Interpersonal Communication,* Wm. C. Brown, Dubuque, Iowa, 1976.

[B] JOURNALS & BULLETINS

- Journal of Communication
- Journal of Business Communication
- Personality & Social Psychology Bulletin
- Management Communication Quarterly
- IBA Bulletin
- Readers Digest
- IJTD Journal
- Advanced Management Journal
- Academy of Management Journal
- Academy of Management Executive
- Harvard Business Review
- NIPM Journal
- Human Communication Research
- Communication World.